Clipper:
A Programmer's Guide

GARY BEAM

This book is dedicated to Mr. Les Willis, who tried to convince me many years ago that computers were fun . . . he was right.

TRADEMARKS

Clipper	is a registered trademark of Nantucket Corporation
dBASE, dBASE III, and dBASE III PLUS	are registered trademarks of Ashton-Tate Corporation
MS-DOS and Paintbrush	are registered trademarks of Microsoft Corporation
PLINK86 and PLINK86Plus	are registered trademarks of Phoenix Software Associates
TLINK	is a registered trademark of Borland International
PC Paintbrush	is a registered trademark of ZSoft

SilverComm, SilverPaint, and **PowerTools** are copyrighted by SilverWare Incorporated
The Silver Bullet is copyrighted by Larry Stewart and John Halovanic
The Breeze is copyrighted by Logitek Corporation
Professional Clipper is copyrighted by Jason Matthews
InstaHlp is copyrighted by Richard A. Murphy and XEC Development, Incorporated
Steve Straley's Toolkit is copyrighted by Stephen J. Straley and Four Seasons Publishing Company, Incorporated

FIRST EDITION
FIRST PRINTING

Library of Congress Cataloging in Publication Data

Beam, Gary.
    Clipper : a programmer's guide / by Gary Beam.
        p.   cm.
    Includes index.
    ISBN 0-8306-3207-7 (pbk.)
    1. Clipper (Computer program language)   I. Title.
QA76.73.C56B43   1989
005.13'3—dc19   88-32299
                                                                      CIP

TAB BOOKS Inc. offers software for sale. For information and a catalog, please contact TAB Software Department, Blue Ridge Summit, PA 17294-0850.

Questions regarding the content of this book should be addressed to:

    Reader Inquiry Branch
    TAB BOOKS Inc.
    Blue Ridge Summit, PA 17294-0214

Edited by David M. Harter

Contents

List of Illustrations

Acknowledgments

My personal thanks to many fine Clipper programmers whose ideas, works, and enthusiasm are a continual encouragement to me to do better . . . John Halovanic, Larry Stewart, Steve Straley, and David Witenstein.

A special thanks to Bob Ostrander, Ray Collins, Ron Powers, and the staff at TAB Books for having patience with me on this one, and for their splendid efforts to publish books that only we Clipper folks could focus on.

Finally, to Brian Russell, Barry ReBell, Ray Love, David Morgan, and the entire Nantucket staff—thanks not only for giving us such a fine dBASE development tool as Clipper, but also for continuing to enhance what has now become the Language of Clipper.

Introduction

In the Spring of 1987, Nantucket Corporation announced plans to release its enhanced version of the dBASE language Clipper compiler, dubbed the Summer '87 version. Development problems were encountered by Nantucket, primarily because of their conversion from Lattice C to Microsoft C 5.0. Delays by Microsoft in releasing 5.0 resulted in subsequent delays in the new Clipper; fortunately for Clipper programmers, Nantucket spent the extra time adding a wealth of new commands and functions. Developers anxiously awaited the new Clipper.

In December 1987, Nantucket began shipping the delayed Summer '87 compiler. Despite a few bugs, which were quickly documented by Nantucket and subsequently eliminated with an updated library, the new Clipper has proven itself as a powerful database programming tool.

This book is designed to be an applications guide for Summer '87 Clipper. Nantucket has provided many, many new commands and functions in Summer '87; it is these new features that this book will discuss and illustrate.

As in my previous books on Clipper, a real-world database application serves as a programming example by which commands and functions are discussed and evaluated. The Cost Management (CM) programming example is an application designed to track and report expenses and income for any small business. The programming techniques utilize many of the new features that Summer '87 provides.

Chapter 1 is an overview of the primary enhancements of Clipper Summer '87, including speed increases for both compilation and the runtime environment. Also discussed are new features that may be used to reduce memory overhead, and thus speed up applications even more. Different tables are presented that briefly describe the many new and revised Clipper commands and functions.

Chapter 2 begins the discussion of our programming example called Cost Management. CM is designed using a modular programming structure. The database and index structures are also presented.

Chapter 3 examines the CM initialization and main menu program modules. Many features are included in CM, and new Clipper Summer '87 commands and functions abound. Array functions are used, for example, to determine the existence of database and index files.

Chapter 4 discusses the expense and receipt program modules of Cost Management. Various MEMO function techniques are presented for maintaining expense information.

Chapter 5 examines the maintenance activities of Cost Management, including how one set of maintenance program files can accommodate several different database files.

Chapter 6 shows how an application can be developed so that the user has control over display colors, printer configuration, audio error tones, and business name.

Chapter 7 discusses the various reports that can be generated by CM.

Chapter 8 discusses data backup and recall, database indexing, and data summary activities.

Chapter 9 discusses the CM help facility, a comprehensive system that utilizes Clipper's enhanced DBEDIT( ) function.

Chapter 10 takes a closer look at the custom user-defined functions that have been created for CM to satisfy particular programming needs. These may be easily converted for use in any program.

Chapter 11 discusses the new Clipper error-handling system.

Chapter 12 demonstrates compiling and linking with Summer '87, including overlay linking and use of the new Clipper MAKE facility.

Chapter 13 discusses the DBU utility that can be a useful tool during program development.

Chapter 14 shows how telecommunications capability can be added to any Clipper application through the use of a communications library called *SilverComm*. Source code for a communications terminal procedure called CMX is included.

Chapter 15 describes a color graphics and sound library for Clipper called *SilverPaint*. Source code for a graphics and sound opening logo for the CM application is included.

Chapter 16 discusses other function libraries that can be used with Clipper applications.

Chapter 17 describes several low-cost Clipper development tools that can greatly reduce program development time.

Appendix A includes the complete source code for the Cost Management (CM) application example. Appendix B is a summary of all Clipper commands. Appendix C is a summary of all Clipper functions.

Summer '87 Overview

The Summer '87 release of Nantucket's Clipper compiler offers a slew of enhancements over previous versions. There are dozens of new commands and functions, as well as numerous improvements to existing commands and functions. Additionally, there are various other features that can make programming with Clipper all the more enjoyable.

Probably the most noticable change when first using Summer '87 Clipper is the tremendous speed increase during program compilation. In previous versions, each program line number was displayed on the screen as a program was compiled. In Clipper Summer '87, only each one-hundredth program line number is displayed on the screen. The reason is two-fold. For one, reporting only each one-hundredth line helps speed up the compiling process. Secondly, the new compiler operates too fast for one to be able to read the individual program line numbers anyway.

The second noticable speed increase with Summer '87 is during execution of the application program itself. The video display interface has been greatly improved, and the screen reaction time is noticably faster.

Most database activities are also much faster in Summer '87 versus Autumn '86, including indexing (over 4 times faster), appending (over 3 times faster), and sorting (over 17 times faster).

Clipper Summer '87 now allows the use of parenthetical expressions that can make the programmer's job a bit easier, as well as reduce application memory usage and speed up program execution. Basically, Summer '87 now allows a parameter to be defined and then used as an expression contained within a set of parentheses. In previous versions of Clipper, the macro substitution was needed to perform equivalent tasks. The parentheses technique will also work with file and index names, and thus can enhance the readability of a program's source code. However, this technique may not be used in conjunction with the Clipper SET FILTER TO command.

```
  BEGIN SEQUENCE..END
  COMMIT
* SET CURSOR ON/off
* SET SOFTSEEK on/OFF                Fig. 1-1. New commands.
  SET TYPEAHEAD TO
* SET WRAP on/OFF
```

A new expression in Summer '87 is REST. It can be used in a DO..WHILE or FOR..NEXT loop to, for example, DELETE REST.

Summer '87 SET..ON/OFF commands can be replaced with logical expressions such as SET CURSOR (.F.) in lieu of SET CURSOR OFF.

The term END can be used in Clipper '87 to replace the ENDCASE, ENDIF, and ENDDO term required by earlier versions.

Clipper applications can now be made to utilize dBASE compatible index (.NDX) files by linking NDX.OBJ with the other object code files.

All Clipper-supplied programming extensions are included in a single (EXTEND.LIB) library in Clipper Summer '87. This replaces the EX-TENDA, EXTENDC, and EXTENDDB files that were in previous versions.

The Clipper DEBUG utility has been totally rewritten for Clipper Summer '87 and adds a lot more debugging options. The DBU direct database utility has also been vastly improved.

A new option to be used with the SET CLIPPER DOS command sets the maximum number of files that may be opened by a Clipper application program. The SET CLIPPER = Fxxx configures the environment to a maximum of xxx open files.

Another new option, to be used with the SET CLIPPER DOS command, eliminates "snow" caused by some graphics video cards during display writes. The SET CLIPPER = S1 helps to eliminate the video problem if it occurs; the default value is S0.

Clipper Summer '87 includes several new commands that may be used in your applications programming. These are listed in *Fig. 1-1*. Further-

```
* CLEAR
  CLOSE ALL
* COPY FILE
  DIR
* FOR..[EXIT]..NEXT
* PARAMETERS                         Fig. 1-2. Revised commands.
* PRIVATE
* PUBLIC
  SET COLOR TO
* SET MESSAGE TO..[CENTER]
  SET RELATION [ADDITIVE] TO
```

```
           *  ACHOICE()
              ACOPY()
           *  AFIELDS()
              ALTD()
           *  ASORT()
              BIN2I()
              BIN2L()
              BIN2W()
              BROWSE()
              DBFILTER()
              DBRELATION()
              DBRSELECT()
              DESCEND()
              DOSERROR()
              ERRORLEVEL()
              FCLOSE()
              FCREATE()
              FERROR()
              FOPEN()
              FREAD()
              FREADSTR()
              FSEEK()
              FWRITE()
              INDEXEXT()
              INDEXKEY()
              INDEXORD()
           *  MLCOUNT()
           *  MEMOLINE()
              NEXTKEY()
              PROCFILE()
              RAT()
              READEXIT()
           *  READINSERT()
              READVAR()
              RESTSCREEN()
              SAVESCREEN()
           *  SCROLL()
              SETCANCEL()
           *  SETCOLOR()
              STRTRAN()
           *  TONE()
              USED()
```

Fig. 1-3. New functions.

more, those new commands that are marked with an asterisk are used in the Cost Management application example included in this book.

Clipper Summer '87 also includes some revised commands, as listed in *Fig. 1-2*. Furthermore, those revised commands that are marked with an asterisk are used in the Cost Management application example included in this book.

```
* ADIR( )
* CHR( )
* DBEDIT( )
* FILE( )
* MEMOEDIT( )
* SELECT( )
* SUBSTR( )
* TYPE( )
```

Fig. 1-4. Revised functions.

Clipper Summer '87 includes quite a number of new functions. These are listed in *Fig. 1-3*. Furthermore, the new functions that are marked with an asterisk are used in the Cost Management application example included in this book.

Clipper Summer '87 also includes several revised functions, as listed in *Fig. 1-4*. Furthermore, those revised functions that are marked with an asterisk are used in the Cost Management application example included in this book.

2

CM Application

The example application program for this book, *Cost Management,* is a system designed to track business expenses and receipts. CM is a fairly basic system. However, it does make use of the many new commands and functions of Clipper Summer '87. Various enhancements and programming alternatives for CM will be included in the program discussion.

DESCRIPTION
Cost Management is centered around two main database files named EXPENSES and RECEIPTS. The expenses database contains information fields relative to each individual expense including: expense date, amount, description, expense type code, supplier code, invoice number, check number, and paid date. The receipts database contains fields including receipt date, amount, description, client code, and check number.

Maintenance codes are used for expense type, supplier, and client. Use of these codes makes it easier to perform data entry because only the abbreviated code needs to be entered in lieu of the complete expense type, supplier, or client description. Additionally, these codes can be easily maintained, and entered codes can be easily validated.

A single-record data file is used to contain the initialization information for Cost Management, including: business name, display color configuration, printer configuration, and system password.

FEATURES
Cost Management includes several features that allow it to be custom configured per end-user requirements.

The CM application includes a variety of audio warning signals and messages. However, the user is given the option of enabling or disabling these generated tones. The CM defaults to the error tones ON setting.

```
File Name    Field Name    Type    Wid    Dec         Description
---------    ----------    ----    ---    ---    --------------------------
CM_SETUP     BUS_NAME      Char     20     0     Business Name
             COL_CODE      Num       1     0     Color Configuration Code
             ERR_TONE      Log       1     0     Audio Error Tones Toggle
             PRN_EXPA      Num       2     0     Expanded Print Code
             PRN_RELE      Num       2     0     Expanded Print Release
             PRN_CPRS      Num       2     0     Compressed Print Code
             PRN_RELC      Num       2     0     Compressed Print Release
             PRN_FEED      Num       2     0     Form Feed Print Code

EXPENSES     EXPNNUMB      Char      4     0     Expense Number
             EXPNDATE      Date      8     0     Expense Date
             EXPNDESC      Char     20     0     Expense Description
             EXPNAMNT      Num       8     2     Expense Amount
             TYPECODE      Char      3     0     Expense Type Code
             SUPPCODE      Char      3     0     Supplier Code
             INVCNUMB      Char     10     0     Invoice Number
             PAIDDATE      Date      8     0     Paid Date
             CHEKNUMB      Char     10     0     Check Number
             EXPNMEMO      Log       1     0     Expense Memo

RECEIPTS     RCPTNUMB      Char      4     0     Receipt Number
             RCPTDATE      Date      8     0     Receipt Date
             RCPTDESC      Char     20     0     Receipt Description
             RCPTAMNT      Num       8     2     Receipt Amount
             CLNTCODE      Char      3     0     Client Code
             CHEKNUMB      Char     10     0     Check Number

CLNTCODE     CLNTCODE      Char      3     0     Client Code
             CLNTNAME      Char     20     0     Client Name

SUPPCODE     SUPPCODE      Char      3     0     Supplier Code
             SUPPNAME      Char      3     0     Supplier Name

TYPECODE     TYPECODE      Char      3     0     Expense Type Code
             TYPENAME      Char     20     0     Expense Type Name
```

Fig. 2-1. CM database structure.

```
File Name    Index Name    Key Field
---------    ----------    ---------
EXPENSES     EXPENSES      EXPNNUMB

RECEIPTS     RECEIPTS      RCPTNUMB

CLNTCODE     CLNTCODE      CLNTCODE

SUPPCODE     SUPPCODE      SUPPCODE

TYPECODE     TYPECODE      TYPECODE
```

Fig. 2-2. CM index structure.

```
Program Module Name                    Description
-------------------        --------------------------------------------
CM.PRG                     Initialization and Logo
  D_INST.PRG               Database Installation
  M_MAIN.PRG               Main Menu
    M_EXPN.PRG             Expenses Menu
      E_EXPN.PRG           Enter a New Expense
      C_EXPN.PRG           Change or Delete an Expense
      V_EXPN.PRG           View or Search Expenses
      S_EXPN.PRG           List Expenses Submenu
        L_EXPN.PRG         List or Print Expenses
      E_MEMO.PRG           Text Edit an Expense Memo
    M_RCPT.PRG             Receipts Menu
      E_RCPT.PRG           Enter a New Receipt
      C_RCPT.PRG           Change or Delete a Receipt
      V_RCPT.PRG           View or Search Receipts
      S_RCPT.PRG           List Receipts Submenu
        L_RCPT.PRG         List or Print Receipts
    M_RPRT.PRG             Analysis Reports Menu
      R_CLNT.PRG           Analysis Report per Client
      R_SUPP.PRG           Analysis Report per Supplier
      R_TYPE.PRG           Analysis Report per Expense Type
      R_FULL.PRG           Full Business Analysis Report
    M_MNTE.PRG             Maintenance Menu
      E_MNTE.PRG           Enter a New Code
      C_MNTE.PRG           Change or Delete a Code
      V_MNTE.PRG           View or Search Codes
      L_MNTE.PRG           List or Print Codes
    M_OPER.PRG             Operations Menu
      C_TONE.PRG           Toggle Error Tones (on/off)
      C_COLS.PRG           Change Display Colors
      C_PRTR.PRG           Change Printer Configuration
      C_NAME.PRG           Change CM Business Name
    M_FILE.PRG             Files Menu
      D_BACK.PRG           Data Backup
      D_RCLL.PRG           Data Recall
      D_INDX.PRG           Data Reindex
      D_SUMM.PRG           Data Summary

HELP.PRG                   CM Help Facility

FUNC.PRG                   CM Functions

ERRORSYS.PRG               CM Error Handling
```

Fig. 2-3. CM program structure.

Cost Management also gives the user control over the screen display colors. Different color combinations may be selected for text, lines and boxes, help screens, memo screens, and background. CM has separate default combinations for color and monochrome video displays.

Because printer setup codes can differ from one printer to another, CM also allows the user to change the printer configuration codes. These codes default to the standard IBM printer setup.

CM has provisions to change the business name which is both displayed on the screen and printed on output reports. A single password for CM access may also be changed.

DATABASE STRUCTURE

CM utilizes six different database files to maintain the cost tracking information. The database file structure for CM is shown in *Fig. 2-1*.

Additionally, a memo file may exist for each record in the expenses database, because the user is given the option for entering an extended description of each expense. These files are created only as needed, and are named with a "CM" prefix followed by the assigned expense number and the ".TXT" identifier. For example, the memo generated for expense number 109 would have a CM109.TXT name.

INDEX STRUCTURE

The index structure for the CM databases is shown in *Fig. 2-2*. Note that only one index file is maintained per database file, except for the single-record CM initialization file (CM__SETUP.DBF) that does not require an index file.

PROGRAM STRUCTURE

The Cost Management application consists of 39 program modules used in a highly-structured programming approach. A consistent naming method is used to identify the different module types, as shown in the program structure diagram of *Fig. 2-3*.

The functions program file (FUNC.PRG) contains UDF's that are used throughout the CM application. Additional UDF's, specific to a particular activity, are included in many program modules.

The help program file (HELP.PRG) contains all of the generic and specific user-help for CM.

ENHANCEMENTS

Throughout the remainder of this book, various enhancements to the Cost Management application will also be discussed, including such items as a graphics opening logo and data communications capability. Such options normally involve the use of an additional Clipper function library.

3

CM Initialization

The Cost Management application program for this book uses many of the Clipper Summer '87 new commands and functions. Code techniques that utilize the new Clipper features will be emphasized. Remember that Clipper is a very creative language. The methods and techniques used in CM are tried and tested, but do not interpret them as the only solution to a programming problem. The complete source code for CM appears in Appendix A.

INITIALIZATION COMMANDS

The initialization (CM.PRG) module for Cost Management accomplishes five primary tasks. First, the Clipper environment is established through a series of PUBLIC and SET commands. Second, the database files are installed and indexed if they do not already exist. Third, the CM setup information is retrieved from the initialization (CM_SETUP.DBF) file. Fourth, the CM logo and copyright notice are displayed to the user. Finally, the password entry screen is displayed.

The Clipper SET commands utilize the logical true-false option (see *Fig. 3-1*) that has been made available with Summer '87. For example, instead of SET DELETED ON, CM uses the SET DELETED(.T.) syntax. Either is acceptable.

The SET BELL(.F.) command turns off the computer beep that is normally sounded at the end of a GET. The **? CHR(7)** command can still be used to sound the bell, but CM uses various tones to generate most error messages.

The SET WRAP(.T.) command turns on the menu-wrapping feature that is new to Clipper Summer '87.

SET DELETED(.F.) causes database records that are marked for deletion to be ignored in most database activities. This way, it is not necessary to PACK a file in order to ignore deleted entries.

```
* Program Name ......... CM.PRG
* Revised Date ......... 07/01/88
*
CLEAR                                 && clears screen
SET BELL(.F.)                         && sets computer bell off
SET WRAP(.T.)                         && sets menu wrap on
SET DELETED(.T.)                      && ignores deleted records
SET CONFIRM(.T.)                      && requires [Enter] to confirm
SET SCOREBOARD(.T.)                   && enable line 0 messages
SET SAFETY OFF                        && disable warning messages
SET MESSAGE TO 24 CENTER              && sets menu message line
sdate = CMONTH(DATE())+" "+STR(DAY(DATE()),2)+ ;
        ", "+STR(YEAR(DATE()),4)
hcode = 0
*
PUBLIC pexpa,pcprs,pfeed,prele,prelc
PUBLIC ccode,cnorm,cinve,cline,chelp,cmemo,cmess,clogo
PUBLIC atone,bname,scode,hcode
*
* cm.prg continues ...
```

Fig. 3-1. CM initialization source code (A).

SET CONFIRM(.T.) requires that the user press the Return key to complete each GET.

SET SCOREBOARD(.T.) is left ON in order to notify the user when the Insert key has been toggled during a READ or MEMOEDIT( ). Using SET SCOREBOARD(.F.) eliminates these line zero messages.

The SET SAFETY OFF command causes the built-in Clipper warning messages to be suppressed. Note that the logical option SET SAFETY(.F.) may not be used with this command.

```
* cm.prg continued ...
*
PRIVATE dbffile[6]                    && array of CM databases
dbffile[1] = "EXPENSES"
dbffile[2] = "RECEIPTS"
dbffile[3] = "CLNTCODE"
dbffile[4] = "SUPPCODE"
dbffile[5] = "TYPECODE"
dbffile[6] = "CM_SETUP"
FOR n = 1 TO 6
   IF ! FILE(dbffile[n]+".DBF")       && database file does not exist
      DO d_inst WITH n                && install the missing database
   ENDIF
NEXT
*
* cm.prg continues ...
```

Fig. 3-2. CM initialization source code (B).

```
* d_inst.prg (partial)
*
PARAMETERS n                        && passed from cm.prg
*
SETCOLOR("W+*")
  @ 10,00 SAY M_CNTR("Installation")
SETCOLOR("W")
SET CURSOR(.F.)
*
DO CASE
  CASE n = 1                        && create EXPENSES.DBF
    CREATE dummy
    STORE "EXPNNUMB  C4  "  TO field1
    STORE "EXPNDATE  D8  "  TO field2
    STORE "EXPNDESC  C20 "  TO field3
    STORE "EXPNAMNT  N8 2"  TO field4
    STORE "TYPECODE  C3  "  TO field5
    STORE "SUPPCODE  C3  "  TO field6
    STORE "INVCNUMB  C10 "  TO field7
    STORE "PAIDDATE  D8  "  TO field8
    STORE "CHEKNUMB  C10 "  TO field9
    STORE "EXPNMEMO  L1  "  TO field10
    FOR f = 1 TO 10
      fnumber = IIF(f<10,str(f,1),str(f,2))
      APPEND BLANK
      STORE "field" + fnumber TO fn
      REPLACE field_name WITH SUBSTR(&fn,1,10);
              field_type WITH SUBSTR(&fn,11,1);
              field_len  WITH VAL(SUBSTR(&fn,12,2));
              field_dec  WITH VAL(SUBSTR(&fn,14,1))
    NEXT
    CREATE expenses FROM dummy
    CLOSE DATABASES
    ERASE dummy.dbf
*
* end of d_inst.prg (partial)
```

Fig. 3-3. Database installation source code.

SET MESSAGE TO 24 CENTER causes all menu messages to be centered on line 24. The centering option is new to Clipper Summer '87.

Various memory variables are declared as public using the Clipper PUBLIC command. These variables include the printer, color, business name, error tone status, and system password codes. Any of these codes may later be changed by the user during operations activities.

CM checks for the existence of the database files by using an array filled with the six database file names, as shown in *Fig. 3-2*. Note that the new Clipper PRIVATE command is used to declare the array.

A FOR . . . NEXT loop is then used, along with the FILE( ) function to determine whether each data file already exists. If a named file does

```
* cm.prg continued ...
*
USE cm_setup                    && contains CM setup parameters
STORE bus_name TO bname         && business name
STORE prn_expa TO pexpa         && expanded print code
STORE prn_cprs TO pcprs         && compressed print code
STORE prn_rele TO prele         && expanded release code
STORE prn_relc TO prelc         && compressed release code
STORE prn_feed TO pfeed         && form feed code
STORE col_code TO ccode         && numeric color code
STORE err_tone TO atone         && logical error tones code
STORE sys_code TO scode         && system password code
CLOSE DATABASES
*
DO COLOR WITH ccode             && color setup procedure
*
SETCOLOR(cnorm)                 && normal color
CLEAR
SETCOLOR(clogo)                 && logo color
   @ 02,25 SAY "                              "
   @ 03,25 SAY "                              "
   @ 04,25 SAY "                              "
   @ 05,25 SAY "                              "
   @ 06,25 SAY "                              "
   @ 07,25 SAY "                              "
   @ 08,25 SAY "                              "
   @ 09,25 SAY "                              "
   @ 11,00 SAY "                              "
   @ 12,00 SAY "                              "
   @ 13,00 SAY "                              "
   @ 14,00 SAY "                              "
   @ 15,00 SAY "                              "
   @ 16,00 SAY "                              "
   @ 11,41 SAY "                              "
   @ 12,41 SAY "                              "
   @ 13,41 SAY "                              "
   @ 14,41 SAY "                              "
   @ 15,41 SAY "                              "
   @ 16,41 SAY "                              "
SETCOLOR(cline)                         && line color
   @ 19,23 SAY "   Cost Management version 1.20   "
   @ 20,23 SAY "Copyright (c) 1988 by GLB SOFTWARE"
   @ 21,23 SAY "        All Rights Reserved       "
SETCOLOR(cmess)
   @ 24,23 SAY "        Press any key ...         "
SETCOLOR(cnorm)
*
SET CURSOR(.F.)                 && turns cursor off
INKEY(60)                       && delay for 60 sec or keypress
SET CURSOR(.T.)                 && turns cursor on
*
* cm.prg continues ...
```

Fig. 3-4. CM initialization source code (C).

```
* part of cm.prg
*
PROCEDURE color                                 && set colors procedure
PARAMETERS ccode                                && passed color code
DO CASE
  CASE ccode = 1
    cnorm = "GR+/B,W/R,B,,R/W"                  && normal
    cinve = "R/W"                               && inverse
    cline = "W+/B"                              && lines
    chelp = "BG+/B"                             && help
    cmemo = "G+/B"                              && memos
    cmess = "G+/B"                              && messages
    clogo = "R+/B"                              && logo and business name
  CASE ccode = 2
    cnorm = "G/N,W/R,N,,R/W"
    cinve = "R/W"
    cline = "W/N"
    chelp = "BG+/N"
    cmemo = "BG+/N"
    cmess = "G+/N"
    clogo = "R+/N"
  CASE ccode = 3
    cnorm = "GR+/N,N/GR,N,,GR/N"
    cinve = "GR/N"
    cline = "W/N"
    chelp = "N/W"
    cmemo = "N/W"
    cmess = "G+/N"
    clogo = "R+/N"
  CASE ccode = 4
    cnorm = "W/N,N/W,N,,N/W"
    cinve = "N/W"
    cline = "W+/N"
    chelp = "N/W"
    cmemo = "W+/N"
    cmess = "W+/N"
    clogo = "W+/N"
ENDCASE
RETURN
```

Fig. 3-5. COLOR procedure source code.

not exist, then program control branches off to the installation (D__INST.PRG) module, and the named database is then installed, as shown in the source code of *Fig. 3-3*.

Once the file-checking process has been completed, various setup codes are retrieved from the CM__SETUP.DBF file and stored to public memory variables, as shown in the top of *Fig. 3-4*. These include: the business name (bname); printer configuration codes (pexpa, pcprs, prele, prelc, pfeed); single-digit color code (ccode); logical error tones toggle (atone); and system password (scode).

```
* cm.prg continued ...
*
CLEAR
SETCOLOR(clogo)                      && logo color for business name
  @ 00,00 SAY M_CNTR(TRIM(bname))
SETCOLOR(cmess)                      && message color for date
  @ 02,78-LEN(sdate) SAY sdate
SETCOLOR(cline)                      && line color for separator lines
  @ 01,00 SAY REPLICATE("-",80)
  @ 03,00 SAY REPLICATE("-",80)
  @ 23,00 SAY REPLICATE("-",80)
SETCOLOR(cnorm)                      && normal color
*
PRIVATE ntxfile[5]                   && array of CM indexes
ntxfile[1] = "EXPENSES"
ntxfile[2] = "RECEIPTS"
ntxfile[3] = "CLNTCODE"
ntxfile[4] = "SUPPCODE"
ntxfile[5] = "TYPECODE"
FOR n = 1 TO 5
  IF ! FILE(ntxfile[n]+".NTX")       && index file does not exist
    DO d_indx                        && reindex 'em all
    EXIT
  ENDIF
NEXT
*
DO WHILE .T.
  SAYHEADER("Password Entry")        && header display UDF
  HELPKEY()                          && help key UDF
  STORE SPACE(10) TO mpassword
  SETCOLOR(cline+",x")               && invisible data entry
    @ 12,23 SAY "Enter your password ...." ;
            GET mpassword PICTURE "@!"
  READ
  SETCOLOR(cnorm)
  IF LASTKEY() = 27                  && escape terminates CM
    SET CURSOR(.T.)                  && remember to reset the cursor
    SETCOLOR("W/N")                  && and reset the colors
    CLEAR                            && and clear the screen
    QUIT                             && before quitting
  ENDIF
  IF mpassword == scode              && valid password
    DO m_main                        && sends you to the main menu
  ELSE                               && invalid password
    M_ERROR()                        && displays error message
    LOOP                             && but lets you try again
  ENDIF
ENDDO
RETURN
*
* end of cm.prg
```

Fig. 3-6. CM initialization source code (D).

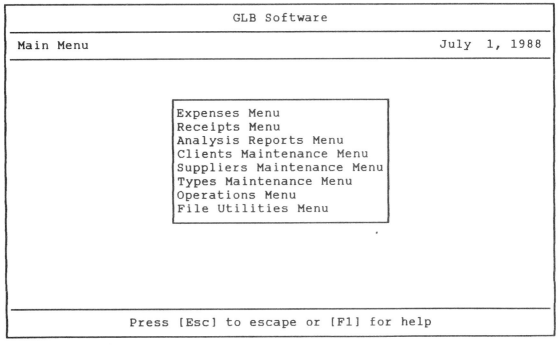

```
                          GLB Software
─────────────────────────────────────────────────────────────
Main Menu                                        July  1, 1988
─────────────────────────────────────────────────────────────



                ┌──────────────────────────────┐
                │ Expenses Menu                │
                │ Receipts Menu                │
                │ Analysis Reports Menu        │
                │ Clients Maintenance Menu     │
                │ Suppliers Maintenance Menu   │
                │ Types Maintenance Menu       │
                │ Operations Menu              │
                │ File Utilities Menu          │
                └──────────────────────────────┘




─────────────────────────────────────────────────────────────
            Press [Esc] to escape or [F1] for help
```

Fig. 3-7. CM main menu screen.

The color code value (ccode) is passed to a procedure called COLOR, which also exists in the initialization module as shown in *Fig. 3-5.* One of five different color combinations may be user-selected in CM. The most recently selected code is maintained in the setup (CM_SETUP.DBF) file. The COLOR procedure is used to establish the display colors for text (cnorm), inverse (cinve), lines (cline), help (chelp), memos (cmemo), messages (cmess), and logo (clogo).

Once the screen display colors are established, the Cost Management logo and copyright information are displayed.

The CM screen header, which remains constant throughout the Cost Management application, is created as shown in the remainder of the initialization source code shown in *Fig. 3-6.*

The index files are also checked for their existence using Clipper arrays. However, if just one of the five required index files is found to be missing, then all of the index files are re-created. The actual indexing module (D_INDX.PRG) source code will be discussed in a later chapter.

PASSWORD ENTRY

Password entry into CM consists of entering a password (**mpassword memvar)** that must exactly match the system password memvar (**scode).** If an

```
* Program Name ......... m_main.prg
* Revised Date ......... 07/01/88
*
DO WHILE .T.
  SAYHEADER("Main Menu")              && displays activity name
  HELPKEY()                           && help available message
  MENUBOX(07,26,16,53)                && box function for menus
    @ 08,27 PROMPT "Expenses Menu              "
    @ 09,27 PROMPT "Receipts Menu              "
    @ 10,27 PROMPT "Analysis Reports Menu      "
    @ 11,27 PROMPT "Clients Maintenance Menu   "
    @ 12,27 PROMPT "Suppliers Maintenance Menu"
    @ 13,27 PROMPT "Types Maintenance Menu     "
    @ 14,27 PROMPT "Operations Menu            "
    @ 15,27 PROMPT "File Utilities Menu        "
  CLEAR TYPEAHEAD                     && clears keyboard buffer
  MENU TO m_main
  DO CASE
    CASE LASTKEY() = 27               && escape key
      EXIT
    CASE m_main = 1
      DO m_expn                       && expenses
    CASE m_main = 2
      DO m_rcpt                       && receipts
    CASE m_main = 3
      DO m_rprt                       && analysis reports
    CASE m_main = 4
      DO m_mnte WITH m_main           && client code maintenance
    CASE m_main = 5
      DO m_mnte WITH m_main           && supplier code maintenance
    CASE m_main = 6
      DO m_mnte WITH m_main           && expense type code maintenance
    CASE m_main = 7
      DO m_oper                       && CM operations setup
    CASE m_main = 8
      DO m_file                       && file utilities
  ENDCASE
ENDDO
RETURN
*
* end of m_main.prg
```

Fig. 3-8. Main menu source code.

unacceptable password is entered, an error tone is sounded. Pressing the Escape key at the password entry terminates CM and returns the user to the DOS prompt.

MAIN MENU

The Cost Management main menu screen is shown in *Fig. 3-7*, and the main menu source code is shown in *Fig. 3-8*. A function called SAYHEADER(   )

strategically clears the screen, displays the activity name, and sounds an audible tone if the user has the error tones toggle (atone) turned on. The HELPKEY( ) function displays a key description message on line 24, and the MENUBOX( ) function creates a box outline for the listed menu items. These functions will be discussed in more detail in a later chapter of this book.

The expenses menu selection from the CM main menu allows entry, change/delete, view/search, list/print, and memo text editing of expense information.

The receipts menu selection allows entry, change/delete, view/search, and list/print of receipt information.

The analysis reports menu selection allows generation of various CM reports, including client analysis, supplier analysis, expense type analysis, and full business report.

The clients, suppliers, and expense types menus allow entry, change/delete, view/search, and list/print of the respective maintenance codes.

The operations menu allows a change of: business name, screen display color, printer codes, and audio error tones.

The files menu provides for data backup, recall, indexing, and summary. Pressing the Escape key while at the main menu returns the user to the password entry screen.

## 4

CM Expenses and Receipts

The Cost Management application includes five different activities for handling user expenses, and four different activities for handling user receipts. The primary activities, called from each respective menu, include: entry, change or delete, view or search, and list or print. The expenses menu also includes an option to directly edit an expense memo. Only the code for expenses will be discussed in this chapter; the code for receipts, because of it's similarity, will not be discussed.

EXPENSES MENU

The **Expenses** menu screen for Cost Management is shown in *Fig. 4-1*. Selection of **Enter, Change/Delete,** or **View/Search** eads the user directly to the named activity. Selection of **List/Print** results in thc display of a submenu from which the user may select how the expense information is to be listed and subsequently printed.

EXPENSE ENTRY

The expense entry screen is shown in *Fig. 4-2*. The expense number is a sequential number assigned automatically by CM and may not be changed by the user. The expense date defaults to the current date, but may be changed during expense entry.

The source code for the expense entry (E__EXPN.PRG) begins in *Fig. 4-3,* which shows how the data prompts are displayed, and how the data memory variables are initialized. The expense number is determined by first going to the last (bottom) record in the indexed expenses (EXPENSES.DBF) database and then adding one (1) to the value of the last record's expense number. The expense number is then displayed on the screen.

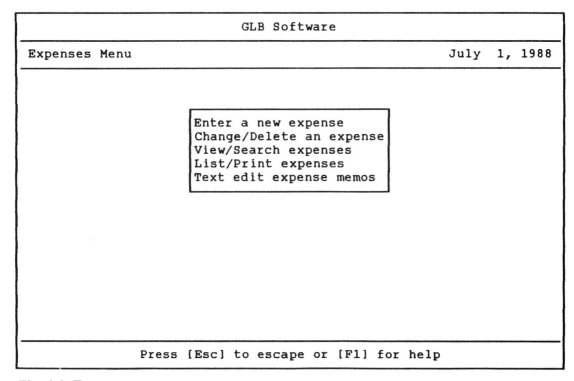

```
                          GLB Software
─────────────────────────────────────────────────────────────
Expenses Menu                                  July  1, 1988
─────────────────────────────────────────────────────────────



                 ┌──────────────────────────┐
                 │Enter a new expense        │
                 │Change/Delete an expense   │
                 │View/Search expenses       │
                 │List/Print expenses        │
                 │Text edit expense memos    │
                 └──────────────────────────┘






─────────────────────────────────────────────────────────────
          Press [Esc] to escape or [Fl] for help
```

Fig. 4-1. Expenses menu screen.

A data-entry loop then allows the user to enter the expense information as shown in *Fig. 4-4*. Note that the Clipper PICTURE command is used to format the entered data. For example, the PICTURE "@D" command is used to ensure that dates are entered in a "mm/dd/yy" format, while the PICTURE "Y" command is used to accept only a "Y" or "N" data input for logical-type fields.

Both the expense type code and the supplier code must be valid codes as maintained in the TYPECODE.DBF and SUPPCODE.DBF databases. Once the user has entered the respective code, the Clipper VALID( ) function is used to test its validity. The user-defined function (UDF) that performs this test is called VE__EXPN1 for expense type codes and VE__EXPN2 for supplier codes. The source code for each is quite similar, and the code function is contained in the expense entry module (shown in *Fig. 4-5*) for expense type validation.

For both functions, the entered code must be passed to the validation UDF. The respective database file is then opened, and the entered code is searched for. If the code is not found, an error tone is sounded and an error message is displayed on display line 24. The user is then allowed to re-enter

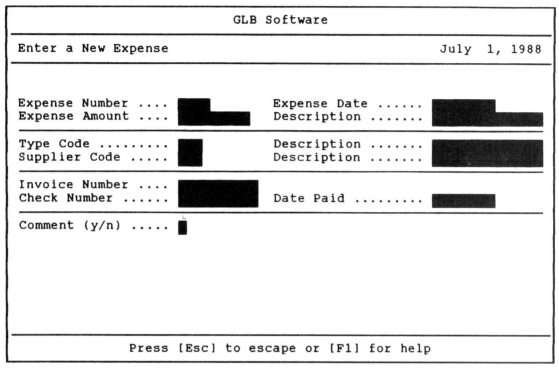

```
┌──────────────────────────────────────────────────────────────────┐
│                          GLB Software                              │
├──────────────────────────────────────────────────────────────────┤
│ Enter a New Expense                              July  1, 1988     │
│                                                                    │
│                                                                    │
│    Expense Number ....  ████▋     Expense Date ......  █████▊      │
│    Expense Amount ....  ████▋     Description .......  █████████   │
│   ─────────────────────────────────────────────────────────────   │
│    Type Code ........   ██▊       Description .......  █████████   │
│    Supplier Code .....  ██▊       Description .......  ██████████  │
│   ─────────────────────────────────────────────────────────────   │
│    Invoice Number ....  ██████                                     │
│    Check Number ......  ██████    Date Paid ........   █████▊      │
│   ─────────────────────────────────────────────────────────────   │
│    Comment (y/n) .....  ▋                                          │
│                                                                    │
│                                                                    │
│                                                                    │
│                                                                    │
├──────────────────────────────────────────────────────────────────┤
│          Press [Esc] to escape or [F1] for help                    │
└──────────────────────────────────────────────────────────────────┘
```

Fig. 4-2. Expense entry screen.

the code. If the entered code is valid, the description is displayed by the validation UDF, and entry of expenses is allowed to continue.

The expense entry source code is continued in *Fig. 4-6*. The entry menu prompts are displayed which allow the user to accept the entered data, make additional changes, or abort entry by returning to the expenses menu.

If the user chooses to append the displayed expense information, a blank record in the expenses (EXPENSES.DBF) database is searched for first. If not found, a new blank record is appended to the file. The database fields are then replaced with the entered memvar equivalents.

If the user has responded with a "Y" to the expense memo field (mEXPNMEMO) entry, then the user is allowed to enter an additional text memo or comment. Various Clipper MEMOEDIT( ) functions are used for this text entry, with the memo then stored to a text file whose name consists of "CM" plus the expense number and ".TXT" as the extension. For example, an expense memo for expense number 17 would have CM17.TXT as its name.

A function called MEMOBOX1( ) is used to create the memo editing box outline as shown in the memo editing screen of *Fig. 4-7*. The source code for this function, which also sets the memo writing colors, is included in

```
* Program Name ......... e_expn.prg
* Revised Date ......... 07/01/88
*
SAYHEADER("Enter a New Expense")        && activity name UDF
  @ 07,00 SAY "Expense Number ...."      && display GET prompts
  @ 07,40 SAY "Expense Date ......"
  @ 08,00 SAY "Expense Amount ...."
  @ 08,40 SAY "Description ......."
  @ 10,00 SAY "Type Code ........."
  @ 10,40 SAY "Description ......."
  @ 11,00 SAY "Supplier Code ....."
  @ 11,40 SAY "Description ......."
  @ 13,00 SAY "Invoice Number ...."
  @ 14,00 SAY "Check Number ......"
  @ 14,40 SAY "Date Paid ........."
  @ 16,00 SAY "Comment (y/n) ....."
SETCOLOR(cline)
  @ 09,00 SAY REPL("—",80)              && field separators
  @ 12,00 SAY REPL("—",80)
  @ 15,00 SAY REPL("—",80)
SETCOLOR(cnorm)
*
STORE SPACE(03)        TO mtypecode, msuppcode
STORE SPACE(04)        TO mexpnnumb
STORE SPACE(10)        TO minvcnumb, mcheknumb
STORE SPACE(20)        TO mexpndesc
STORE DATE()           TO mexpndate    && current date
STORE CTOD("  /  /  ") TO mpaiddate    && empty date
STORE 0                TO mexpnamnt
STORE .F.              TO mexpnmemo     && logical false
*
USE expenses INDEX expenses
GO BOTTOM                              && to last record in file
STORE STR(VAL(expnnumb)+1,4) TO mexpnnumb
CLOSE DATABASES
*
SETCOLOR(cinve)                        && inverse color
  @ 07,20 SAY mexpnnumb                && auto-assigned expense #
SETCOLOR(cnorm)                        && normal color
*
* e_expn.prg continues
```

Fig. 4-3. Expense entry source code (A).

the functions (FUNC.PRG) procedure file, which normally contains functions that may be used throughout the CM application.

The memo is initially defined as SPACE(1) and, because the entered memo is to be stored to disk under the already established text name, the MEMOWRIT( ) function is used in conjunction with MEMOEDIT( ) to write the edited memo.

```
* e_expn.prg continued
*
entering = .T.                              && the expense entry loop
DO WHILE entering
  HELPKEY()                                 && help key UDF
    @ 07,60 GET mexpndate PICTURE "@D"
    @ 08,20 GET mexpnamnt PICTURE "##,###.##"
    @ 08,60 GET mexpndesc
    @ 10,20 GET mtypecode PICTURE "@!" VALID ve_expn1(mtypecode)
    @ 11,20 GET msuppcode PICTURE "@!" VALID ve_expn2(msuppcode)
    @ 13,20 GET minvcnumb PICTURE "@!"
    @ 14,20 GET mcheknumb PICTURE "@!"
    @ 14,60 GET mpaiddate PICTURE "@D"
    @ 16,20 GET mexpnmemo PICTURE "Y"
  READ
  M_CLEAR()                                 && clears message area
  IF LASTKEY() = 27                         && escape key
    RETURN
  ENDIF
  entering = .F.
*
* e_expn.prg continues
```

Fig. 4-4. Expense entry source code (B).

The MEMOEDIT( ) function is specified with: the memo name (memo); upper-left and lower-right row and column parameters; the logical element which determines if editing is allowed; and the name of the UDF (dbm) which analyzes the MEMOEDIT( ) keystrokes. The MEMO-EDIT( ) UDF will be discussed in more detail later in this book.

```
* part of e_expn.prg
*
FUNCTION ve_expn1                && expense type code validation
PARAMETERS mtypecode             && passed parameter
USE typecode INDEX typecode
SEEK mtypecode
IF ! FOUND()                     && invalid entry
  ok = .F.                       && validation is false
  M_ERROR()                      && error message UDF
ELSE                             && valid entry
  ok = .T.                       && validation is true
  SETCOLOR(cinve)                && inverse color
    @ 10,60 SAY typename         && display the name/description
  SETCOLOR(cnorm)                && normal color
ENDIF
CLOSE DATABASES
RETURN(ok)                       && return the validation
```

Fig. 4-5. Expense type validation source code.

```
* e_expn.prg continued
*
  mchoice = 1                            && menu memvar
  @ 22,31 PROMPT "Append" MESSAGE "  Add this expense to the file"
  @ 22,38 PROMPT "Change" MESSAGE "  Change this expense"
  @ 22,45 PROMPT "Quit"   MESSAGE "  Quit and abort"
  CLEAR TYPEAHEAD                        && clears keyboard buffer
  MENU TO mchoice                        && menu command
  M_CLEAR()
  DO CASE
    CASE mchoice = 1                     && append the entry
      M_WAIT()                           && wait message UDF
      USE expenses INDEX expenses
      SET DELETED OFF                    && include deleted records
      SEEK "    "                        && SEEK an empty record
      IF ! FOUND()                       && no blanks in file
        APPEND BLANK                     && so add a blank record
      ELSE                               && blank record found
        RECALL                           && so re-use it
      ENDIF
      REPLACE expnnumb WITH mexpnnumb, expndate WITH mexpndate,;
              expndesc WITH mexpndesc, expnamnt WITH mexpnamnt,;
              typecode WITH mtypecode, suppcode WITH msuppcode
      REPLACE invcnumb WITH minvcnumb, paiddate WITH mpaiddate,;
              cheknumb WITH mcheknumb, expnmemo WITH mexpnmemo
      SET DELETED ON                     && ignore deleted records
      CLOSE DATABASES
      M_CLEAR()
      IF mexpnmemo                       && for memo text
        memobox1()                       && memo box UDF
        STORE SPACE(1) TO memo           && initialize a memo
        STORE "CM"+LTRIM(mexpnnumb)+".TXT" TO mfilename
        SETCOLOR(cmemo)                  && memo color
        MEMOWRIT(mfilename,MEMOEDIT(memo,05,04,18,75,.T.,"dbm"))
        SETCOLOR(cnorm)                  && normal color
      ENDIF
      EXIT
    CASE mchoice = 2                     && change displayed entry
      entering = .T.
      LOOP
    CASE mchoice = 3 .OR. LASTKEY() = 27
      EXIT
  ENDCASE
ENDDO
RETURN
*
* end of e_expn.prg
```

Fig. 4-6. Expense Entry source code (C).

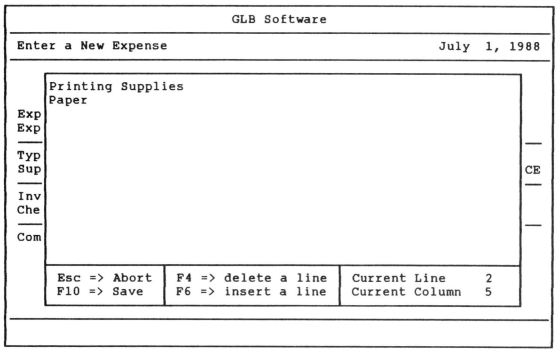

Fig. 4-7. Expense memo editing screen.

```
* part of c_expn.prg
*
  CASE mchoice = 2                  && delete an expense
    DELETETONE()                    && warning tone
    STORE "N" TO msure              && initialize delete memvar
      @ 24,31 SAY "Are you sure (y/n)?" GET msure PICTURE "Y"
    READ
    M_CLEAR()                       && clear message area UDF
    IF LASTKEY() = 27               && escape key
      RETURN
    ENDIF
    IF msure = "Y"                  && continue to delete
      M_WAIT()                      && wait message UDF
      USE expenses INDEX expenses
      SEEK mexpnnumb
      REPLACE expnnumb WITH "     "
      DELETE                        && marked for deletion
      CLOSE DATABASES
      STORE "CM"+LTRIM(mexpnnumb)+".TXT" TO mfilename
      IF FILE(mfilename)
        ERASE(mfilename)            && erase any expense memo
      ENDIF
      M_CLEAR()                     && clear message area UDF
    ENDIF
    RETURN
```

Fig. 4-8. Expense Change/Delete source code (A).

```
* part of c_expn.prg
*
      STORE "CM"+LTRIM(mexpnnumb)+".TXT" TO mfilename
      IF mexpnmemo                  && from the expenses file
        MEMOBOX1()                  && memo box UDF
        SETCOLOR(cmemo)             && memo color
        IF FILE(mfilename)          && if the expense memo exists
          MEMOWRIT(mfilename,MEMOEDIT(MEMOREAD(mfilename),;
                   05,04,18,75,.T.,"dbm"))
        ELSE
          STORE SPACE(1) TO memo    && otherwise create it
          MEMOWRIT(mfilename,MEMOEDIT(memo,05,04,18,75,.T.,"dbm"))
        ENDIF
        SETCOLOR(cnorm)             && normal color
      ELSE
        IF FILE(mfilename)          && if it exists but shouldn't!
          ERASE mfilename           && erase it
        ENDIF
      ENDIF
      EXIT
```

Fig. 4-9. Expense Change/Delete source code (B).

```
┌────────────────────────────────────────────────────────────────┐
│                         GLB Software                             │
├────────────────────────────────────────────────────────────────┤
│ View/Search Expenses                             July  1, 1988   │
├────────────────────────────────────────────────────────────────┤
│                                                                  │
│                                                                  │
│ Expense Number ....    1      Expense Date ...... 04/01/88       │
│ Expense Amount ....    449.25 Description ....... POSTAGE        │
├────────────────────────────────────────────────────────────────┤
│ Type Code ........ ADV        Description ....... ADVERTISING    │
│ Supplier Code ..... USP       Description ....... US POST OFFICE │
├────────────────────────────────────────────────────────────────┤
│ Invoice Number ....                                              │
│ Check Number ...... 1002      Date Paid ........ 04/01/88        │
├────────────────────────────────────────────────────────────────┤
│ Comment (y/n) ..... Y                                            │
│                                                                  │
│                                                                  │
│                                                                  │
│                                                                  │
│       Next Last Forward Backward Top End Search Memo Quit        │
├────────────────────────────────────────────────────────────────┤
│                   View the next expense                          │
└────────────────────────────────────────────────────────────────┘
```

Fig. 4-10. Expenses View/Search screen.

```
* Program Name ......... v_expn.prg
* Revised Date ......... 07/01/88
*
SAYHEADER("View/Search Expenses")        && activity name UDF
  @ 07,00 SAY "Expense Number ...."
  @ 07,40 SAY "Expense Date ......"
  @ 08,00 SAY "Expense Amount ...."
  @ 08,40 SAY "Description ......."
  @ 10,00 SAY "Type Code ........."
  @ 10,40 SAY "Description ......."
  @ 11,00 SAY "Supplier Code ....."
  @ 11,40 SAY "Description ......."
  @ 13,00 SAY "Invoice Number ...."
  @ 14,00 SAY "Check Number ......"
  @ 14,40 SAY "Date Paid ........."
  @ 16,00 SAY "Comment (y/n) ....."
SETCOLOR(cline)                          && line color
  @ 09,00 SAY REPL("—",80)               && field separators
  @ 12,00 SAY REPL("—",80)
  @ 15,00 SAY REPL("—",80)
SETCOLOR(cnorm)                          && normal color
*
DO WHILE .T.
  M_BLANK()                              && blank-entry message UDF
  HELPKEY()                              && help key UDF
  STORE 0 TO mexpnnr                     && initialize as numeric
    @ 07,20 GET mexpnnr PICTURE "####" VALID vv_expn1(mexpnnr)
  READ
  M_CLEAR()                              && clear message area UDF
  IF LASTKEY() = 27                      && escape key
    EXIT
  ENDIF
  STORE STR(mexpnnr,4) TO mexpnnumb      && convert numeric entry
  SELECT 3
  USE suppcode INDEX suppcode
  SELECT 2
  USE typecode INDEX typecode
  SELECT 1
  USE expenses INDEX expenses
  SET RELATION TO suppcode INTO c, TO typecode INTO b
  SET SOFTSEEK(.T.)                      && allow non-exact seeking
  SEEK mexpnnumb
  SET SOFTSEEK(.F.)
*
* v_expn.prg continues
```

Fig. 4-11. Expenses View/Search source code (A).

EXPENSE CHANGE/DELETE

The expense **Change/Delete** activity allows the user to change any expense information (including expense memo), or to delete an expense altogether. Only two specific features of the expense change (C_EXPN.PRG) program

```
* part of v_expn.prg
*
FUNCTION vv_expn1                  && expense number validation
PARAMETERS mexpnnr                 && passed parameter
STORE STR(mexpnnr,4) TO mexpnnumb  && numeric to string conversion
USE expenses INDEX expenses
SET SOFTSEEK(.T.)
SEEK mexpnnumb
SET SOFTSEEK(.F.)
IF FOUND()                         && valid entry
  ok = .T.
ELSE
  IF ! EOF()                       && valid entry with soft seek
    ok = .T.
  ELSE                             && invalid entry
    ok = .F.
    M_ERROR()
  ENDIF
ENDIF
CLOSE DATABASES
RETURN(ok)
```
Fig. 4-12. Expense Number Validation source code.

module will be discussed here, because the change procedure is so similar to expense entry. In CM, when information is changed, the same expense entry UDF's that were defined in the entry module are used for data validation.

If an expense is deleted, the database record in EXPENSES.DBF is marked for deletion, the expense number (EXPNNUMB) field is replace with SPACE(4), and the expense memo (if it exists) is erased. The partial module code for this deletion process is shown in *Fig. 4-8.*

If an expense is changed, then the expense memo (if it exists) may also be changed as shown in *Fig. 4-9.* In this instance, the memo is first read with MEMOREAD( ), then edited with MEMOEDIT( ), and then stored to disk with MEMOWRIT( ). All three functions are included in the same line of program code. Note that if the memo did not previously exist—which is possible in this expense change scenario—then a new expense memo is created.

EXPENSES VIEW/SEARCH

The view expenses activity allows the user to view expense records one at a time, as shown in *Fig. 4-10.* A specific expense number to be searched may also be entered.

The **View Expenses** module is somewhat unique in that the new Clipper SET SOFTSEEK command is used during expense number search validation, as shown in the expenses **View/Search** (V__EXPN.PRG) source code of *Fig. 4-11,* and the validation source code of *Fig. 4-12.* Assume, for

```
* v_expn.prg continued
*
  DO WHILE .T.
    SETCOLOR(cinve)                     && inverse color
      @ 07,20 SAY expnnumb               && display the fields
      @ 07,60 SAY expndate
      @ 08,20 SAY TRAN(expnamnt,"##,###.##")
      @ 08,60 SAY expndesc
      @ 10,20 SAY typecode
      @ 10,60 SAY typecode->typename
      @ 11,20 SAY suppcode
      @ 11,60 SAY suppcode->suppname
      @ 13,20 SAY invcnumb
      @ 14,20 SAY cheknumb
      @ 14,60 SAY paiddate
      @ 16,20 SAY IIF(expnmemo,"Y","N")
    SETCOLOR(cnorm)                      && normal color
      @ 22,15 PROMPT "Next"     MESSAGE ;
          " View the next entry"
      @ 22,20 PROMPT "Last"     MESSAGE ;
          " View the last (previous) entry"
      @ 22,25 PROMPT "Forward"  MESSAGE ;
          " Skip forward 20 entries and view"
      @ 22,33 PROMPT "Backward" MESSAGE ;
          " Skip backward 20 entries and view"
      @ 22,42 PROMPT "Top"      MESSAGE ;
          " View at the beginning of the file"
      @ 22,46 PROMPT "End"      MESSAGE ;
          " View at the end of the file"
      @ 22,50 PROMPT "Search"   MESSAGE ;
          " Enter an expense number to search for"
      @ 22,57 PROMPT "Memo"     MESSAGE ;
          " View the expense memo"
      @ 22,62 PROMPT "Quit"     MESSAGE ;
          " Quit and abort"
    CLEAR TYPEAHEAD                      && clear keyboard buffer
    MENU TO mchoice                      && menu command
    M_CLEAR()                            && clear message area UDF
*
* v_expn.prg continues
```

Fig. 4-13. Expenses View/Search source code (B).

example, that the expenses file (EXPENSES.DBF) contains 50 entries and that expense number (EXPNNUMB) 25 has been deleted. With SET SOFT-SEEK OFF, entering expense number 25 to SEEK would return a !FOUND( ) and EOF( ) true condition, normally processed as an error message to the user. However, with SET SOFTSEEK ON, Clipper would still return a NOT FOUND( ), but EOF( ) would not be true because Clipper found another record after expense number 25, and before it reached EOF( ). In the expenses **View** situation, entering expense number 25 to

```
* v_expn.prg continued
*
    DO CASE
       CASE mchoice = 1                          && next
          SKIP 1
          IF EOF()                               && end of file
             SKIP -1
             FILETONE()                          && file marker beep
          ENDIF
       CASE mchoice = 2                          && last
          SKIP -1
          IF BOF()                               && beginning of file
             FILETONE()
          ENDIF
       CASE mchoice = 3                          && forward
          SKIP
          IF EOF()
             SKIP -1
             FILETONE()
          ELSE
             SKIP 20
          ENDIF
       CASE mchoice = 4                          && backward
          SKIP -1
          IF BOF()
             FILETONE()
          ELSE
             SKIP -20
          ENDIF
       CASE mchoice = 5                          && top
          SKIP -1
          IF BOF()
             FILETONE()
          ELSE
             GO TOP
          ENDIF
       CASE mchoice = 6                          && end
          SKIP
          IF EOF()
             SKIP -1
             FILETONE()
          ELSE
             GO BOTTOM
          ENDIF
       CASE mchoice = 7                          && search
          EXIT
*
* v_expn.prg continues
```

Fig. 4-14. Expenses View/Search source code (C).

search for would result in the display of the information for the next expense number (26).

Three different databases are opened simultaneously for **Expenses View.** A relationship (SET RELATION) is defined between the expenses (EXPENSES.DBF) file and the expense type codes (TYPECODE.DBF) and supplier codes (SUPPCODE.DBF) files. The expense information is then displayed, followed by the **View/Search** menu as shown in *Fig. 4-13.*

A DO..CASE command evaluates the user choice after an expense is viewed. Error tones are included to warn the user if file markers have been reached. For example, if the user is currently viewing the last expense in the file and selects the **Forward** option to view the next expense, and error tone is sounded as indicated in the *Fig. 4-14* code.

If an expense memo exists for any record, the user may view the memo, as shown in *Fig. 4-15,* by selecting **Memo** from the menu choices. However, the user cannot edit the expense memo during expenses **View.** Expense memo view is shown in the conclusion of the expense view/source code of *Fig. 4-16.*

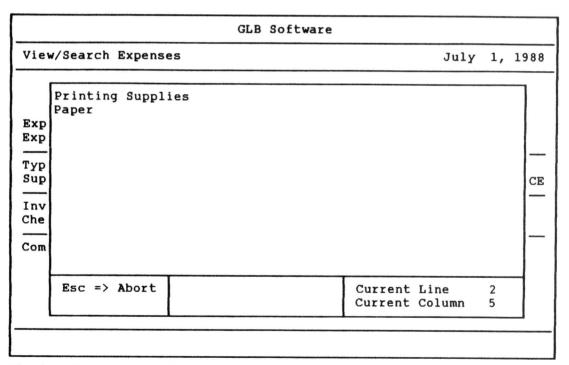

Fig. 4-15. *Expense Memo View screen.*

```
* v_expn.prg continued
*
      CASE mchoice = 8                       && memo
        STORE "CM"+LTRIM(expnnumb)+".TXT" TO mfilename
        IF FILE(mfilename)                  && see if memo text exists
          SAVE SCREEN                       && save current screen
          MEMOBOX2()                        && display memo box
          MEMOEDIT(MEMOREAD(mfilename),05,04,18,75,.F.,"dbm")
          SETCOLOR(cnorm)
          RESTORE SCREEN                    && recall saved screen
        ENDIF
      CASE mchoice = 9 .OR. LASTKEY() = 27
        CLOSE DATABASES
        RETURN
    ENDCASE
  ENDDO
  CLOSE DATABASES
    @ 07,20 SAY SPACE(04)
    @ 07,60 SAY SPACE(08)
    @ 08,20 SAY SPACE(10)
    @ 08,60 SAY SPACE(20)
    @ 10,20 SAY SPACE(03)
    @ 10,60 SAY SPACE(20)
    @ 11,20 SAY SPACE(03)
    @ 11,60 SAY SPACE(20)
    @ 13,20 SAY SPACE(10)
    @ 14,20 SAY SPACE(10)
    @ 14,60 SAY SPACE(08)
    @ 16,20 SAY SPACE(01)
  LOOP
ENDDO
RETURN
*
* end of v_expn.prg
```

Fig. 4-16. Expenses View/Search source code (D).

EXPENSES LIST SUB-MENU

If the user selects the **List/Print** option from the expenses menu, then a sub-menu will be displayed. This menu gives the user a selection of listing criteria, as shown in the sub-menu screen of *Fig. 4-17*. Selection of one of the listing options results in the passing of the actual menu memvar value to the listing (L_EXPN.PRG) procedure.

EXPENSES LIST/PRINT

The **List Expenses** activity allows the user to list expense records ten expenses at a time, as shown in *Fig. 4-18*. The user may also select the print option from the list menu to print the expenses.

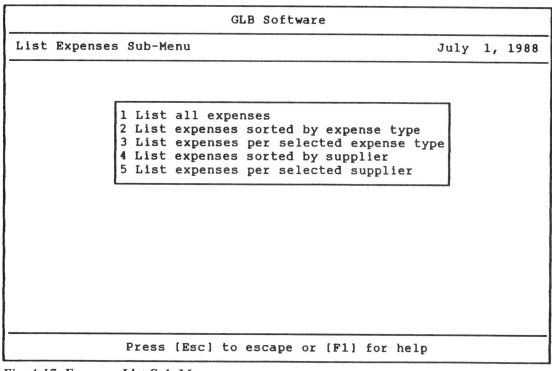

```
                          GLB Software

List Expenses Sub-Menu                          July  1, 1988


              ┌─────────────────────────────────────┐
              │1 List all expenses                  │
              │2 List expenses sorted by expense type│
              │3 List expenses per selected expense type│
              │4 List expenses sorted by supplier   │
              │5 List expenses per selected supplier│
              └─────────────────────────────────────┘




              Press [Esc] to escape or [F1] for help
```

Fig. 4-17. Expenses List Sub-Menu screen.

Expenses may be listed as per criteria selected by the user from the **Expenses** sub-menu. The user may choose to list all expenses, expenses sorted by expense type code, expenses per an entered type code, etc. as shown in *Fig. 4-19.* In situations where expenses must be listed per selected criteria, the expenses data (EXPENSES.DBF) is copied to a temporary database per the entered criteria. This is normally much faster than using the SET FILTER command, and also makes printing the list easier to handle. Also, for selected criteria, the entered expense type code or supplier code is validated, as shown in *Fig. 4-20,* for type code select.

List Expenses source code is continued in *Fig. 4-21.* Note that if the expenses file (or resultant temporary file) contains no data records, then the listing activity is automatically terminated and the user is returned to the **List Expenses** sub-menu.

As in expenses **View/Search,** three databases are opened and a relation is set for listing of expenses as shown in *Fig. 4-22.*

Expenses are displayed ten at a time as indicated in the *Fig. 4-23* code. Note that the screen is cleared prior to listing each group of ten by using the SCROLL( ) function. This method is not only faster than the CLEAR command, but also tends to appear cleaner. SCROLL( ) is used by specify-

```
┌──────────────────────────────────────────────────────────────────────────┐
│                            GLB Software                                    │
├──────────────────────────────────────────────────────────────────────────┤
│ List/Print All Expenses                                   July  1, 1988    │
├──────────────────────────────────────────────────────────────────────────┤
│                                                                            │
│  Exp#   Date    Exp Description  Type  Supp   Amount    Invoice   Check     │
│  ───── ──────── ──────────────── ───── ─────  ──────── ────────  ───────   │
│                                                                            │
│     1 03/01/88 Office Supplies  SUP   KEN     12.50               412       │
│     2 03/01/88 Postage          ADV   USP      4.40                         │
│     3 03/02/88 Stationary       SUP   KEN     59.75 K-20112 456             │
│     4 03/05/88 Postage          ADV   USP     16.40                         │
│     5 03/10/88 Office Supplies  SUP   KEN      4.29                         │
│     6 03/12/88 Office Supplies  SUP   KEN      2.21                         │
│     7 03/21/88 Book             PUB   TAB     18.61               453       │
│     8 03/21/88 Computer Repair  REP   A1      65.00 32001   454             │
│     9 03/22/88 Gas              TRA   OTH     12.00                         │
│    10 03/29/88 Office Rent      OFF   C21    600.00               458       │
│                                                                            │
│                                                                            │
│                                                                            │
│            Forward Backward Top End Print Quit                             │
├──────────────────────────────────────────────────────────────────────────┤
│                  List the next 10 expenses                                 │
└──────────────────────────────────────────────────────────────────────────┘
```

Fig. 4-18. Expenses List/Print screen.

ing the boundaries to be scrolled, as well as the scroll parameter — which is zero (0) for screen clearing.

A DO..CASE command evaluates the user choice after a group of expenses is listed. Again, error tones are used to notify the user that the end-of-file or the beginning-of-file has been reached, as shown in the *Fig. 4-24* code.

Cost Management contains its own printed report capability. *Fig. 4-25* shows the printer initialization procedure, and *Fig. 4-26* shows the actual list-printing code. The printer configuration codes — contained in the setup (CM_SETUP.DBF) file and stored to public memvars in the top-level initialization (CM.PRG) module — are used throughout the print procedure.

The user is allowed to terminate printing at any time by pressing the Escape key. This technique, however, is not effective when used in conjunction with print spooler software.

Compressed and expanded print are used in the generation of most CM printouts. The heading consists of the date and page number in compressed (132 character) print, the business name in a combination compressed/expanded (66 character) print, and the column headings in compressed print.

```
* Program Name .......... l_expn.prg
* Revised Date .......... 07/01/88
*
PARAMETERS s_expn                          && passed parameter
*
DO CASE
  CASE s_expn = 1
    header = "All Expenses"
  CASE s_expn = 2
    header = "Expenses Sorted by Expense Type"
  CASE s_expn = 3
    header = "Expenses per Selected Expense Type"
  CASE s_expn = 4
    header = "Expenses Sorted by Supplier"
  CASE s_expn = 5
    header = "Expenses per Selected Supplier"
ENDCASE
*
SAYHEADER("List/Print "+header)           && activity name UDF
HELPKEY()                                 && help key UDF
DO CASE
  CASE s_expn = 1                         && all expenses
    USE expenses INDEX expenses
  CASE s_expn = 2                         && expense type sort
    M_WAIT()                              && wait message
    USE expenses
    INDEX ON typecode TO tempfile
  CASE s_expn = 3                         && expense type select
    STORE SPACE(03) TO mtypecode
       @ 07,20 SAY "Type Code ........."
       @ 08,20 SAY "Description ......."
       @ 07,40 GET mtypecode PICTURE "@!" VALID vl_expn1(mtypecode)
    READ
    IF LASTKEY() = 27                     && escape key
      RETURN
    ENDIF
    M_WAIT()                              && wait message
    USE expenses INDEX expenses
    COPY TO tempfile FOR typecode == mtypecode
    CLOSE DATABASES
    IF FILE("TEMPFILE.DBF")
      USE tempfile
    ELSE
      RETURN
    ENDIF
*
* l_expn.prg continues
```

Fig. 4-19. Expenses List/Print source code (A).

```
* part of l_expn.prg
*
FUNCTION vl_expn1                       && type code validation
PARAMETERS mtypecode                    && passed parameter
USE typecode INDEX typecode
SEEK mtypecode
IF FOUND()                              && valid entry
  ok = .T.
  SETCOLOR(cinve)                       && inverse color
    @ 08,40 SAY typename
  SETCOLOR(cnorm)                       && normal color
ELSE
  ok = .F.
  M_ERROR()                             && error message UDF
ENDIF
CLOSE DATABASES
RETURN(ok)
```

Fig. 4-20. Expenses List/Print validation source code.

```
* l_expn.prg continued
*
  CASE s_expn = 4                       && supplier sort
    USE expenses
    M_WAIT()                            && wait message
    INDEX ON suppcode TO tempfile
  CASE s_expn = 5                       && supplier select
    STORE SPACE(03) TO msuppcode
      @ 07,20 SAY "Supplier Code ....."
      @ 08,20 SAY "Description ......."
      @ 07,40 GET msuppcode PICTURE "@!" VALID vl_expn2(msuppcode)
    READ
    IF LASTKEY() = 27                   && escape key
      RETURN
    ENDIF
    M_WAIT()                            && wait message
    USE expenses INDEX expenses
    COPY TO tempfile FOR suppcode == msuppcode
    CLOSE DATABASES
    IF FILE("TEMPFILE.DBF")
      USE tempfile
    ELSE
      RETURN
    ENDIF
ENDCASE
M_CLEAR()                               && clear message area
*
IF RECCOUNT() = 0                       && empty database file
  CLOSE DATABASES
  ERASE tempfile.dbf                    && erase database file
  ERASE tempfile.ntx                    && erase index file
  RELEASE ALL
  RETURN
ENDIF
*
* l_expn.prg continues
```

Fig. 4-21. Expenses List/Print source code (B).

```
            * l_expn.prg continued
            *
            SELECT 3
            USE suppcode INDEX suppcode
            SELECT 2
            USE typecode INDEX typecode
            SELECT 1
            SET RELATION TO typecode INTO b, TO suppcode INTO c
            GO TOP
            *
            * l_expn.prg continues
```

Fig. 4-22. Expenses List/Print source code (C).

```
* l_expn.prg continued
*
CLS()                                    && clear screen UDF
SETCOLOR(cline)                          && line color
  @ 05,01 SAY "Exp#   Date    Expense Description   Type "+;
            "Supp  Amount   Invoice #   Check #   "
  @ 06,01 SAY "_____ _____ _____ ____ "+;
            "_____ _____ _____ _____"
SETCOLOR(cnorm)                          && normal color
ESCKEY()                                 && escape key UDF
DO WHILE .T.
  SCROLL(07,00,22,79,00)                 && clear screen area
  @ 07,00                                && cursor reference
  DISPLAY OFF NEXT 10 SPACE(00)+expnnumb,expndate,expndesc,;
    typecode+" ",suppcode+" ",TRAN(expnamnt,"##,###.##"),;
    invcnumb,cheknumb
  mchoice = IIF(EOF(),3,1)               && initialize menu memvar
    @ 22,23 PROMPT "Forward"  MESSAGE ;
      " List the next 10 entries"
    @ 22,31 PROMPT "Backward" MESSAGE ;
      " List the last (previous) 10 entries"
    @ 22,40 PROMPT "Top"      MESSAGE ;
      " List at the top of the file"
    @ 22,44 PROMPT "End"      MESSAGE ;
      " List at the end of the file"
    @ 22,48 PROMPT "Print"    MESSAGE ;
      " Print the listing"
    @ 22,54 PROMPT "Quit"     MESSAGE ;
      " Quit and abort"
  CLEAR TYPEAHEAD                        && clear keyboard buffer
  MENU TO mchoice                        && menu command
  M_CLEAR()                              && clear message area
*
* l_expn.prg continues
```

Fig. 4-23. Expenses List/Print source code (D).

```
* l_expn.prg continued
*
  DO CASE
    CASE mchoice = 1                    && forward
      SKIP 1
      IF EOF()                          && end of file
        FILETONE()                      && file marker beep
      ENDIF
      SKIP -1
    CASE mchoice = 2                    && backward
      SKIP -18
      IF BOF()                          && beginning of file
        FILETONE()                      && file marker beep
      ENDIF
    CASE mchoice = 3                    && top
      SKIP -18
      IF BOF()
        FILETONE()
      ENDIF
      GO TOP
    CASE mchoice = 4                    && bottom
      SKIP 1
      IF EOF()
        FILETONE()
      ENDIF
      GO BOTTOM
    CASE mchoice = 5 .OR. mchoice = 6 .OR. LASTKEY() = 27
      EXIT
  ENDCASE
ENDDO
*
* l_expn.prg continues
```

Fig. 4-24. Expenses List/Print source code (E).

```
* l_expn.prg continued
*
IF mchoice = 5                          && print listing
  IF ! M_PRTR()                         && printer check UDF
    CLOSE DATABASES
    ERASE tempfile.dbf                  && erase database file
    ERASE tempfile.ntx                  && erase index file
    RETURN
  ENDIF
  M_PRINT()                             && print message UDF
  STORE 50 TO mline                     && initialize line counter
  STORE  0 TO mpage                     && initialize page counter
  SET CONSOLE OFF                       && disable screen display
  SET PRINT ON                          && enable printer
  GO TOP                                && go to top of file
  SUM expnamnt TO mtotal                && and sum the expenses
  GO TOP                                && go back to the top
  ?? CHR(pcprs)                         && set compressed print mode
*
* l_expn.prg continues
```

Fig. 4-25. Expenses List/Print source code (F).

```
* l_expn.prg continued
*
  DO WHILE ! EOF() .AND. INKEY() <> 27 && escape key stops printing
    IF mline > 40                           && page-break marker
      IF mpage > 0                          && unless it's page 1
        ? CHR(pfeed)                        && form feed
      ENDIF
      STORE 1 TO mline                      && reset line counter
      STORE mpage+1 TO mpage                && increment page counter
      ?   SPACE(122)+"Page "+STR(mpage,2)         && page number
      ?   SPACE(122)+DTOC(DATE())                 && current date
      ?
      ?   CHR(pexpa)+H_CNTR(ALLTRIM(bname),66)  && business name
      ?? CHR(prele)                             && expanded release
      ?? CHR(pcprs)                             && compressed print
      ?
      ?
      ?   H_CNTR(header,132)                && report title
      ?
      ?
      ?   SPACE(07)+"Exp#    Date     Expense Description   "+;
          "    Expense Type          Supplier Name       Amount    "+;
          "Invoice #   Check #     Paid   "
      ?   SPACE(07)+"==== ======== ==================== "+;
          "==================== ==================== ========= "+;
          "========== ========== ======="
    ENDIF
    ? SPACE(07)+expnnumb,expndate,expndesc,typecode->typename,;
      suppcode->suppname,TRAN(expnamnt,"##,###.##"),invcnumb,;
      cheknumb,paiddate
    STORE mline+1 TO mline                   && increment line counter
    SKIP                                     && skip a record
  ENDDO
  ?   SPACE(84)+"---------"                  && print expenses total
  ?   SPACE(84)+TRAN(mtotal,"##,###.##")
  ?? CHR(prelc)                              && release compressed print
  ?   CHR(pfeed)                             && form feed
  SET PRINT OFF                              && disable printer
  SET CONSOLE ON                             && enable console
ENDIF
CLOSE DATABASES
ERASE tempfile.dbf                           && erase database file
ERASE tempfile.ntx                           && erase index file
RETURN
*
* end of l_expn.prg
```

Fig. 4-26. Expenses List/Print source code (G).

```
* Program Name .......... e_memo.prg
* Revised Date .......... 07/01/88
*
SAYHEADER("Review/Edit an Expense Memo")
*
HELPKEY()
M_BLANK()                               && blank is allowed
STORE 0 TO mexpnnr
  @ 07,25 SAY "Expense Number ...."
  @ 09,25 SAY "Memo Name ........."
  @ 07,45 GET mexpnnr PICTURE "####" VALID ve_memo1(mexpnnr)
READ
IF LASTKEY() = 27
  RETURN
ENDIF
STORE "CM"+LTRIM(STR(mexpnnr,4))+".TXT" TO mmemo   && filename
*
IF mexpnnr = 0
  M_CLEAR()
  HELPKEY()
  STORE SPACE(10) to mmemo
    @ 09,45 GET mmemo PICTURE "@!" VALID ve_memo2(mmemo)
  READ
  IF LASTKEY() = 27
    RETURN
  ENDIF
ENDIF
*
SAYHEADER("Editing Expense Memo "+mmemo)
MEMOBOX1()                              && memo box outline
SETCOLOR(cmemo)
MEMOWRIT(mmemo,MEMOEDIT(MEMOREAD(mmemo),05,04,18,75,.T.,"dbm"))
SETCOLOR(cnorm)
RETURN
```

Fig. 4-27. Expense Memo Text Editing source code.

EXPENSE MEMO TEXT EDIT

The direct editing of expense memo text allows the user to bypass the expense information change procedure, and go directly into a memo edit procedure. The user may select the memo to edit by entering either the expense number or the actual memo file name. The memo text edit (E_MEMO.PRG) module source code is shown in *Fig. 4-27.*

## 5

CM Maintenance

Cost Management application includes maintenance files and activities for client, expense type, and supplier codes. The database structure for each of these files is similar; therefore, only one of each of the maintenance module types (menu, enter, change/delete, view/search, list/print) is needed to acco-modate activities for all three maintenance files.

MAINTENANCE CODES MENU

The maintenance menu for client codes is shown in *Fig. 5-1.* The same program module is used to display the maintenance menu for clients, ex-pense types, and suppliers. The parameter (m__main) passed from the main menu determines which codes are to be maintained, as shown in the mainte-nance menu (M__MNTE.PRG) source code of *Fig. 5-2.*

MAINTENANCE CODE ENTRY

The maintenance code entry screen for clients is shown in *Fig. 5-3,* and the maintenance code entry program (E__MNTE.PRG) module begins in *Fig. 5-4.*

Memory variables are initialized for data entry prompts, data entry memvar names, database field names, database name, and index name. Note that, due to the similarity in the CM naming convention, this number of variables could be reduced significantly if you so desire, and may even be contained in the menu module and then passed to each of the activity modules for additional code reduction.

The remainder of the maintenance code entry module is shown in *Fig. 5-5.* All of the previously defined memvars are used to display the entry prompt, GET the data memvar, and validate the GET.

A new maintenance code is appended by using these same memvars.

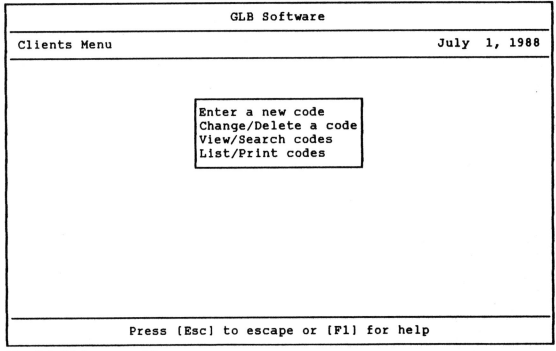

```
┌─────────────────────────────────────────────────────────────────────┐
│                            GLB Software                               │
├─────────────────────────────────────────────────────────────────────┤
│ Clients Menu                                          July  1, 1988   │
├─────────────────────────────────────────────────────────────────────┤
│                                                                       │
│                                                                       │
│                   ┌─────────────────────────┐                         │
│                   │ Enter a new code        │                         │
│                   │ Change/Delete a code    │                         │
│                   │ View/Search codes       │                         │
│                   │ List/Print codes        │                         │
│                   └─────────────────────────┘                         │
│                                                                       │
│                                                                       │
│                                                                       │
│                                                                       │
│                                                                       │
│                                                                       │
├─────────────────────────────────────────────────────────────────────┤
│            Press [Esc] to escape or [F1] for help                     │
└─────────────────────────────────────────────────────────────────────┘
```

Fig. 5-1. Maintenance Menu screen.

Note that macros are avoided by using Clipper Summer '87's parenthetical expressions, such as USE (dbfname) INDEX (dbfname).

Fig. 5-6 shows the data entry validation UDF for maintenance code entry. The entry memvar name, database name, and index names (all as previously defined variables) are passed to the UDF, which then checks to make sure the entered code does not already exist.

The validation for code name (description) is handled by the more general **V_STRING( )** UDF which is contained in the FUNC.PRG file. This UDF simply returns an error if the entered memvar information is blank.

MAINTENANCE CODE CHANGE/DELETE
The maintenance code change and delete (C_MNTE.PRG) source code example for clients begins in *Fig. 5-7.* Memory variables are initialized the same way as in the entry module for data entry prompts, data entry memvar names, database field names, database name, and index name.

Fig. 5-8 shows the validation UDF for maintenance code change. The memvar name, database name, and index names (all as previously defined variables) are passed to the UDF which then checks to make sure the entered code exists in the selected maintenance database.

```
* Program Name ......... m_mnte.prg
* Revised Date .......... 07/01/88
*
PARAMETERS m_main                           && passed from main menu
*
DO WHILE .T.
  DO CASE
    CASE m_main = 4
      SAYHEADER("Clients Menu")
      hcode = 4
    CASE m_main = 5
      SAYHEADER("Suppliers Menu")
      hcode = 5
    CASE m_main = 6
      SAYHEADER("Expense Types Menu")
      hcode = 6
  ENDCASE
  HELPKEY()
  MENUBOX(07,29,12,50)
    @ 08,30 PROMPT "Enter a new code     "
    @ 09,30 PROMPT "Change/Delete a code"
    @ 10,30 PROMPT "View/Search codes    "
    @ 11,30 PROMPT "List/Print codes     "
  CLEAR TYPEAHEAD
  MENU TO m_mnte
  DO CASE
    CASE LASTKEY() = 27                     && escape key
      EXIT
    CASE m_mnte = 1                         && enter
      DO e_mnte WITH m_main
    CASE m_mnte = 2                         && change/delete
      DO c_mnte WITH m_main
    CASE m_mnte = 3                         && view/search
      DO v_mnte WITH m_main
    CASE m_mnte = 4                         && list/print
      DO l_mnte WITH m_main
  ENDCASE
ENDDO
RETURN
*
* end of m_mnte.prg
```

Fig. 5-2. Maintenance Menu source code.

The maintenance code change module continues in *Fig. 5-9* and *Fig. 5-10*. For delete and update, again note that macros are not needed when using parenthetical expressions.

MAINTENANCE CODES VIEW/SEARCH

The maintenance codes view (V__MNTE.PRG) source code begins in *Fig. 5-11*. Memory variables are initialized the same way as in the previous modules.

```
┌─────────────────────────────────────────────────────────────┐
│                      GLB Software                             │
├─────────────────────────────────────────────────────────────┤
│  Enter a new Client Code                       July  1, 1988  │
│                                                               │
│                                                               │
│           Client Code .......  ██▌────────────                │
│           Client Name .......  ██▌──────────────────────      │
│                                                               │
│                                                               │
│                                                               │
│                                                               │
│                                                               │
│                                                               │
│                                                               │
│                                                               │
│                                                               │
│                                                               │
│                                                               │
├─────────────────────────────────────────────────────────────┤
│           Press [Esc] to escape or [F1] for help             │
└─────────────────────────────────────────────────────────────┘
```

Fig. 5-3. Maintenance Code Entry screen.

Fig. 5-12 includes the search GET code as well as the view/search menu code. As in all CM view/search modules, SET SOFTSEEK is used to allow relative (not exact) searching of a database's key field. The validation for the entered maintenance code to be searched is shown in *Fig. 5-13*.

The remainder of maintenance view/search source code is the same as in other view/search modules, and will not be discussed.

MAINTENANCE CODES LIST/PRINT

The maintenance codes list screen for clients is shown in *Fig. 5-14,* and the source code (L__MNTE.PRG) begins in *Fig. 5-15*. Memory variables are initialized the same way as in the previous modules.

Listing is accomplished by using the pre-defined database field mem-vars "dbfvar1" and "dbfvar2" for the pre-defined database "dbfname" and index "ntxname."

```
* Program Name .......... e_mnte.prg
* Revised Date .......... 07/01/88
*
PARAMETERS m_main                           && passed from maintenance
*                                           && and main menus
DO CASE
  CASE m_main = 4
    SAYHEADER("Enter a new Client Code")
    prompt1 = "Client Code ......."     && entry prompt
    prompt2 = "Client Name ......."     && entry prompt
    memvar1 = "mCLNTCODE"               && entry memvar name
    memvar2 = "mCLNTNAME"               && entry memvar name
    dbfvar1 = "CLNTCODE"                && database field name
    dbfvar2 = "CLNTNAME"                && database field name
    dbfname = "CLNTCODE"                && database file name
    ntxname = "CLNTCODE"                && index file name
  CASE m_main = 5
    SAYHEADER("Enter a new Supplier Code")
    prompt1 = "Supplier Code ....."
    prompt2 = "Supplier Name......"
    memvar1 = "mSUPPCODE"
    memvar2 = "mSUPPNAME"
    dbfvar1 = "SUPPCODE"
    dbfvar2 = "SUPPNAME"
    dbfname = "SUPPCODE"
    ntxname = "SUPPCODE"
  CASE m_main = 6
    SAYHEADER("Enter a new Expense Type Code")
    prompt1 = "Type Code ........."
    prompt2 = "Type Name ........."
    memvar1 = "mTYPECODE"
    memvar2 = "mTYPENAME"
    dbfvar1 = "TYPECODE"
    dbfvar2 = "TYPENAME"
    dbfname = "TYPECODE"
    ntxname = "TYPECODE"
ENDCASE
*
STORE SPACE(03) TO memvar1                   && initialize entry memvars
STORE SPACE(20) TO memvar2
*
* e_mnte.prg continues
```

Fig. 5-4. Maintenance Code Entry source code (A).

```
* e_mnte.prg continued
*
entering = .T.
DO WHILE entering
  HELPKEY()
    @ 07,20 SAY prompt1 GET memvar1 PICTURE "@!" ;
            VALID ve_mnte(memvar1,dbfname,ntxname)
    @ 08,20 SAY prompt2 GET memvar2 VALID v_string(memvar2)
  READ
  M_CLEAR()
  IF LASTKEY() = 27
    EXIT
  ENDIF
  entering = .F.
  mchoice = 1
    @ 22,31 PROMPT "Append" MESSAGE "  Add this code to the file"
    @ 22,38 PROMPT "Change" MESSAGE "  Change this code"
    @ 22,45 PROMPT "Quit"   MESSAGE "  Quit and abort"
  CLEAR TYPEAHEAD
  MENU TO mchoice
  M_CLEAR()
  DO CASE
    CASE mchoice = 1
      M_WAIT()
      USE (dbfname) INDEX (ntxname)    && note the lack of macros!
      SET DELETED OFF                  && include deleted records
      SEEK "   "                       && seek a blank record
      IF FOUND()
        RECALL                         && and recall it if found
      ELSE
        APPEND BLANK                   && otherwise append a blank
      ENDIF
      REPLACE &dbfvar1 WITH memvar1, &dbfvar2 WITH memvar2
      SET DELETED ON                   && exclude deleted records
      CLOSE DATABASES
      M_CLEAR()
    CASE mchoice = 2
      entering = .T.
      LOOP
    CASE mchoice = 3 .OR. LASTKEY() = 27
      EXIT
  ENDCASE
ENDDO
RETURN
*
* end of e_mnte.prg
```

Fig. 5-5. Maintenance Code Entry source code (B).

```
* part of e_mnte.prg
*
FUNCTION ve_mnte                        && code validation
PARAMETERS memvar1,dbfname,ntxname      && passed parameters
IF EMPTY(memvar1)                       && no blanks allowed
  ok = .F.
  M_ERROR()                             && error message UDF
ELSE
  USE (dbfname) INDEX (ntxname)         && note the parentheses
  SEEK memvar1
  IF FOUND()
    ok = .F.
    M_INFILE()                          && dupe entry message UDF
  ELSE
    ok = .T.
  ENDIF
  CLOSE DATABASES
ENDIF
RETURN(ok)
```

Fig. 5-6. Code Entry Validation UDF source code.

```
* Program Name .......... c_mnte.prg
* Revised Date .......... 07/01/88
*
PARAMETERS m_main                        && passed by maintenance
*                                        && and main menus
DO CASE
  CASE m_main = 4
    SAYHEADER("Change/Delete a Client Code")
    prompt1 = "Client Code ......."     && entry prompt
    prompt2 = "Client Name ......."     && entry prompt
    memvar1 = "mCLNTCODE"               && entry memvar name
    memvar2 = "mCLNTNAME"               && entry memvar name
    dbfvar1 = "CLNTCODE"                && database field name
    dbfvar2 = "CLNTNAME"                && database field name
    dbfname = "CLNTCODE"                && database file name
    ntxname = "CLNTCODE"                && index file name
  CASE m_main = 5
    SAYHEADER("Change/Delete a Supplier Code")
    prompt1 = "Supplier Code ....."
    prompt2 = "Supplier Name......"
    memvar1 = "mSUPPCODE"
    memvar2 = "mSUPPNAME"
    dbfvar1 = "SUPPCODE"
    dbfvar2 = "SUPPNAME"
    dbfname = "SUPPCODE"
    ntxname = "SUPPCODE"
  CASE m_main = 6
    SAYHEADER("Change/Delete an Expense Type Code")
    prompt1 = "Type Code ........."
    prompt2 = "Type Name ........."
    memvar1 = "mTYPECODE"
    memvar2 = "mTYPENAME"
    dbfvar1 = "TYPECODE"
    dbfvar2 = "TYPENAME"
    dbfname = "TYPECODE"
    ntxname = "TYPECODE"
ENDCASE
*
STORE SPACE(03) TO memvar1               && initialize entry memvar
HELPKEY()
  @ 07,20 SAY prompt1 GET memvar1 PICTURE "@!" ;
          VALID vc_mnte(memvar1,dbfname,ntxname)
  @ 08,20 SAY prompt2
READ
M_CLEAR()
IF LASTKEY() = 27
  RETURN
ENDIF
*
* c_mnte.prg continues
```

Fig. 5-7. Maintenance Code Change source code (A).

```
* part of c_mnte.prg
*
FUNCTION vc_mnte                      && code validation
PARAMETERS memvar1,dbfname,ntxname    && passed parameters
USE (dbfname) INDEX (ntxname)         && database and index
SEEK memvar1                          && seek the key field
IF FOUND()
   ok = .T.                           && valid
ELSE
   ok = .F.                           && invalid
   M_ERROR()                          && error message UDF
ENDIF
CLOSE DATABASES
RETURN(ok)
```

Fig. 5-8. Code Change Validation UDF source code.

```
* c_mnte.prg continued
*
USE (dbfname) INDEX (ntxname)
SEEK memvar1
STORE &dbfvar2 TO memvar2              && store the field contents
CLOSE DATABASES                       && to the memory variable
*
SETCOLOR(cinve)
  @ 08,40 SAY memvar2                 && display the memvar
SETCOLOR(cnorm)
*
mchoice = 1
  @ 22,31 PROMPT "Change" MESSAGE "  Change this code"
  @ 22,38 PROMPT "Delete" MESSAGE "  Delete this code"
  @ 22,45 PROMPT "Quit"   MESSAGE "  Quit and abort"
CLEAR TYPEAHEAD
MENU TO mchoice
M_CLEAR()
DO CASE
  CASE mchoice = 2                    && delete the code
    DELETETONE()                      && delete warning tone
    STORE "N" TO msure
      @ 24,31 SAY "Are you sure (y/n)?" GET msure PICTURE "Y"
    READ
    IF LASTKEY() = 27
      RETURN
    ENDIF
    IF msure = "Y"                    && gonna delete it
      M_WAIT()
      USE (dbfname) INDEX (ntxname)   && more parentheticals
      SEEK memvar1                    && seek the key field
      REPLACE &dbfvar1 WITH "   "     && blank out the key field
      DELETE                          && and mark for deletion
      CLOSE DATABASES
      M_CLEAR()
    ENDIF
    RETURN
  CASE mchoice = 3 .OR. LASTKEY() = 27 && escape/quit
    RETURN
ENDCASE
*
* c_mnte.prg continues
```

Fig. 5-9. Maintenance Code Change source code (B).

```
* c_mnte.prg continued
*
changing = .T.                              && change loop
DO WHILE changing
  HELPKEY()
    @ 08,40 GET memvar2 VALID v_string(memvar2)
  READ
  M_CLEAR()
  IF LASTKEY() = 27
    EXIT
  ENDIF
  changing = .F.
  mchoice = 1
  ESCKEY()
    @ 22,31 PROMPT "Update" MESSAGE "  Update file with changes"
    @ 22,38 PROMPT "Change" MESSAGE "  Change this code"
    @ 22,45 PROMPT "Quit"   MESSAGE "  Quit and abort"
  CLEAR TYPEAHEAD
  MENU TO mchoice
  M_CLEAR()
  DO CASE
    CASE mchoice = 1 .AND. UPDATED()    && data was actually changed
      M_WAIT()
      USE (dbfname) INDEX (ntxname)     && database and index
      SEEK memvar1                      && seek the key field
      REPLACE &dbfvar2 WITH memvar2     && update the data fields
      M_CLEAR()
      EXIT
    CASE mchoice = 2                     && continue changes
      changing = .T.
      LOOP
    CASE mchoice = 3 .OR. LASTKEY() = 27
      EXIT
  ENDCASE
ENDDO
RETURN
*
* end of c_mnte.prg
```

Fig. 5-10. Maintenance Code Change source code (C).

```
* Program Name .......... v_mnte.prg
* Revised Date .......... 07/01/88
*
PARAMETERS m_main                        && passed by maintenance
*                                        && and main menus
DO CASE
  CASE m_main = 4
    SAYHEADER("View/Search Client Codes")
    prompt1 = "Client Code ......."     && entry prompt
    prompt2 = "Client Name ......."     && entry prompt
    memvar1 = "mCLNTCODE"               && entry memvar name
    memvar2 = "mCLNTNAME"               && entry memvar name
    dbfvar1 = "CLNTCODE"                && database field name
    dbfvar2 = "CLNTNAME"                && database field name
    dbfname = "CLNTCODE"                && database file name
    ntxname = "CLNTCODE"                && index file name
  CASE m_main = 5
    SAYHEADER("View/Search Supplier Codes")
    prompt1 = "Supplier Code ....."
    prompt2 = "Supplier Name......"
    memvar1 = "mSUPPCODE"
    memvar2 = "mSUPPNAME"
    dbfvar1 = "SUPPCODE"
    dbfvar2 = "SUPPNAME"
    dbfname = "SUPPCODE"
    ntxname = "SUPPCODE"
  CASE m_main = 6
    SAYHEADER("View/Search Expense Type Codes")
    prompt1 = "Type Code ........."
    prompt2 = "Type Name ........."
    memvar1 = "mTYPECODE"
    memvar2 = "mTYPENAME"
    dbfvar1 = "TYPECODE"
    dbfvar2 = "TYPENAME"
    dbfname = "TYPECODE"
    ntxname = "TYPECODE"
ENDCASE
*
* v_mnte.prg continues
```

Fig. 5-11. Maintenance Code View source code (A).

```
* v_mnte.prg continued
*
DO WHILE .T.
  M_BLANK()                              && blanks allowed message
  HELPKEY()
  STORE SPACE(03) TO memvarl             && initialize memvar
    @ 07,20 SAY promptl GET memvarl PICTURE "@!" ;
          VALID vv_mnte(memvarl,dbfname,ntxname)
    @ 08,20 SAY prompt2
  READ
  M_CLEAR()
  IF LASTKEY() = 27
    EXIT
  ENDIF
  USE (dbfname) INDEX (ntxname)          && database and index
  SET SOFTSEEK(.T.)                      && softly seeking
  SEEK memvarl
  SET SOFTSEEK(.F.)                      && hardly seeking
  DO WHILE .T.
    SETCOLOR(cinve)
      @ 07,40 SAY &dbfvarl
      @ 08,40 SAY &dbfvar2
    SETCOLOR(cnorm)
      @ 22,17 PROMPT "Next"     MESSAGE ;
            " View the next code"
      @ 22,22 PROMPT "Last"     MESSAGE ;
            " View the last (previous) code"
      @ 22,27 PROMPT "Forward"  MESSAGE ;
            " Skip forward 20 codes and view"
      @ 22,35 PROMPT "Backward" MESSAGE ;
            " Skip backward 20 codes and view"
      @ 22,44 PROMPT "Top"      MESSAGE ;
            " View at the beginning of the file"
      @ 22,48 PROMPT "End"      MESSAGE ;
            " View at the end of the file"
      @ 22,52 PROMPT "Search"   MESSAGE ;
            " Enter a code to search for"
      @ 22,59 PROMPT "Quit"     MESSAGE ;
            " Quit and abort"
    CLEAR TYPEAHEAD
    MENU TO mchoice
    M_CLEAR()
*
* end of partial v_mnte.prg
```

Fig. 5-12. Maintenance Codes View source code (B).

```
* part of v_mnte.prg
*
FUNCTION vv_mnte                        && code validation
PARAMETERS memvarl,dbfname,ntxname      && passed parameters
USE (dbfname) INDEX (ntxname)           && database and index
SET SOFTSEEK(.T.)                       && enable relative seeking
SEEK memvarl
SET SOFTSEEK(.F.)                       && disable relative seeking
IF FOUND()
  ok = .T.                              && valid
ELSE
  IF ! EOF()
    ok = .T.                            && valid (relative match)
  ELSE
    ok = .F.                            && invalid (no match)
    M_ERROR()
  ENDIF
ENDIF
CLOSE DATABASES
RETURN(ok)
```

Fig. 5-13. Code View Validation UDF source code.

```
┌───────────────────────────────────────────────────────────────┐
│                        GLB Software                             │
├───────────────────────────────────────────────────────────────┤
│  List/Print Client Codes                       July  1, 1988    │
├───────────────────────────────────────────────────────────────┤
│                                                                 │
│                Code        Name                                 │
│                ────        ──────────────────                   │
│                ABC     ABC Rentals                              │
│                FNB     First National Bank                      │
│                                                                 │
│                                                                 │
│                                                                 │
│                                                                 │
│                                                                 │
│                                                                 │
│                                                                 │
│                                                                 │
│                                                                 │
│          Forward Backward Top End Print Quit                    │
├───────────────────────────────────────────────────────────────┤
│                 List at the top of the file                     │
└───────────────────────────────────────────────────────────────┘
```

Fig. 5-14. Maintenance Codes List screen.

```
* Program Name ......... l_mnte.prg
* Revised Date ......... 07/01/88
*
PARAMETERS m_main                        && passed by maintenance
*                                        && and main menus
DO CASE
  CASE m_main = 4
    header  = "Client Codes"             && header name
    dbfvar1 = "CLNTCODE"                 && database field name
    dbfvar2 = "CLNTNAME"                 && database field name
    dbfname = "CLNTCODE"                 && database file name
    ntxname = "CLNTCODE"                 && index file name
  CASE m_main = 5
    header  = "Supplier Codes"
    dbfvar1 = "SUPPCODE"
    dbfvar2 = "SUPPNAME"
    dbfname = "SUPPCODE"
    ntxname = "SUPPCODE"
  CASE m_main = 6
    header  = "Expense Type Codes"
    dbfvar1 = "TYPECODE"
    dbfvar2 = "TYPENAME"
    dbfname = "TYPECODE"
    ntxname = "TYPECODE"
ENDCASE
*
SAYHEADER("List/Print "+header)          && display the header name
*
USE (dbfname) INDEX (ntxname)            && database and index
IF RECCOUNT() = 0                        && check for zero records
  CLOSE DATABASES
  RETURN
ENDIF
*
SETCOLOR(cline)
  @ 05,27 SAY "Code          Name          "
  @ 06,27 SAY "_____   _____"
SETCOLOR(cnorm)
DO WHILE .T.
  SCROLL(07,27,18,53,00)                 && clear display area
  @ 07,00                                && park the cursor
  DISPLAY OFF NEXT 10 SPACE(26)+&dbfvar1+"   "+&dbfvar2
*
* end of partial l_mnte.prg
```

Fig. 5-15. Maintenance Codes List source code (A).

6

CM Operations

The Cost Management application includes several operational options that allow the user to change audio error tones, screen display color, printer configuration codes, and business name. These are available from the operations menu as shown in *Fig. 6-1*.

AUDIO ERROR TONES

Throughout the Cost Management application, audio tones are sounded normally whenever an error or warning condition exists. For example, if the user tries to change a non-existent client code, an error message is displayed and an audio error tone is sounded. If the user tries to print a client listing, and the printer is not ready, another error message is generated along with an error tone.

The audio error tones may be toggled on and off by the user. If the error tones are turned off, then error messages are still displayed but no error tone is sounded. The **Error Tones** option menu is shown in *Fig. 6-2*.

The actual module (C__TONE.PRG) code simply consists of a yes/no menu. Once a selection has been made from the **Error Tones** option menu, the choice is stored in the CM__SETUP.DBF database as shown in the source code of *Fig. 6-3*.

DISPLAY COLOR

This option gives the user four different screen color combinations to choose from. The user is instructed to press the Insert key to change from one color combination to the next, and to press the Enter key to save the current combination. The color change screen is shown in *Fig. 6-4*.

The color change program (C__COLS.PRG) module utilizes the Clipper Summer '87 new SETCOLOR( ) function, as shown in the *Fig. 6-5*

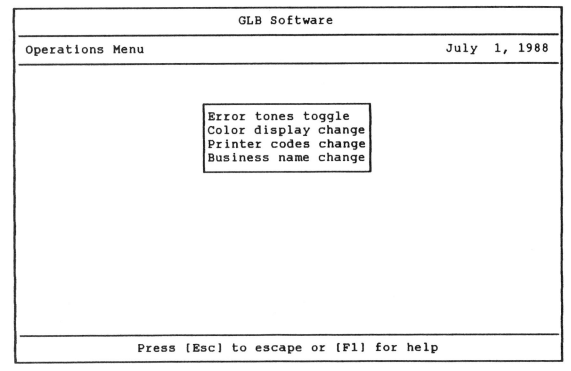

Fig. 6-1. Operations Menu screen.

source code. This module also utilizes the COLOR procedure that is contained in the CM initialization (CM.PRG module) to set the screen colors per the public color code "ccode" variable. A procedure within the color change module called SCREEN is used to repaint the display screen as color combinations are presented. Once a color combination has been selected, it is stored in the CM__SETUP.DBF file.

PRINTER CODES

This option allows the user to change printer configuration codes, as shown in *Fig. 6-6*. These codes include compressed print, compressed print release, expanded print, expanded print release, and form feed. Their values may be found in most printer manuals.

The code for the printer change (C__PRTR.PRG) module is shown in *Fig. 6-7*. The five printer code variables were declared public in the CM initialization module. Once the codes have been changed, the setup database file (CM__SETUP.DBF) is updated to retain the selected configuration.

```
┌─────────────────────────────────────────────────────────────┐
│                        GLB Software                           │
├─────────────────────────────────────────────────────────────┤
│  Error Tones Toggle                              July  1, 1988│
├─────────────────────────────────────────────────────────────┤
│                                                               │
│                 ┌───────────────────────────────┐             │
│                 │Yes, turn audio error tones ON  │             │
│                 │No, turn audio error tones OFF  │             │
│                 └───────────────────────────────┘             │
│                                                               │
│                                                               │
│                                                               │
│                                                               │
│                                                               │
│                                                               │
│                                                               │
│                                                               │
│                                                               │
├─────────────────────────────────────────────────────────────┤
│          Press [Esc] to escape or [F1] for help              │
└─────────────────────────────────────────────────────────────┘
```

Fig. 6-2. Error Tones Toggle screen.

```
* Program Name .......... c_tone.prg
* Revised Date .......... 07/01/88
*
DO WHILE .T.
  SAYHEADER("Error Tones Toggle")
  HELPKEY()
  MENUBOX(07,24,10,55)
    @ 08,25 PROMPT "Yes, turn audio error tones ON"
    @ 09,25 PROMPT "No, turn audio error tones OFF"
  tones = IIF(atone,1,2)                && initialize menu choice
  CLEAR TYPEAHEAD
  MENU TO tones
  IF LASTKEY() = 27
    EXIT
  ENDIF
  atone = IIF(tones=1,.T.,.F.)          && public memvar
  USE cm_setup                          && update setup database
  REPLACE err_tone WITH atone           && to retain selection
  CLOSE DATABASES
  EXIT
ENDDO
RETURN
```

Fig. 6-3. Error Tones Toggle source code.

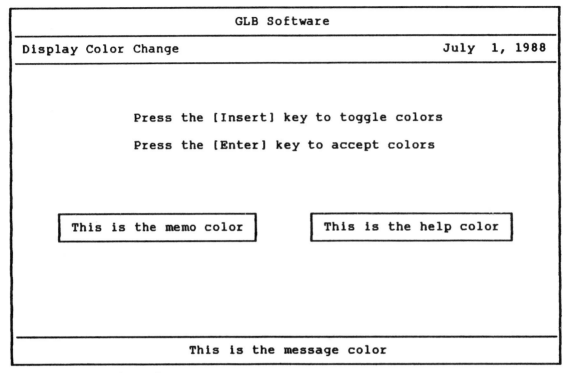

Fig. 6-4. Display Color Change screen.

BUSINESS NAME

This option allows the user to change the business name that is displayed in the screen header (line zero), and on all CM printouts. The business name change screen is shown in *Fig. 6-8,* and the module (C__NAME.PRG) code is shown in *Fig. 6-9.*

```
* Program Name .......... c_cols.prg
* Revised Date .......... 07/01/88
*
IF ! ISCOLOR()                          && must have color hardware
  RETURN
ENDIF
*
DO screen                               && screen painting procedure
*
DO WHILE .T.
  SET CURSOR(.F.)
  keypress = INKEY(0)                   && to read user selection
  SET CURSOR(.T.)
  IF keypress = 13                      && [Enter] key
    EXIT
  ELSEIF keypress = 22                  && [Insert] key
    ccode = IIF(ccode>3,1,ccode+1)      && keypress counter
    DO color WITH ccode                 && set color parameters
    DO screen                           && screen painting procedure
  ENDIF
ENDDO
USE cm_setup                            && update setup database
REPLACE col_code WITH ccode             && to retain selection
CLOSE DATABASES
RETURN
*
PROCEDURE screen                        && screen painting procedure
SETCOLOR(cnorm)
CLEAR SCREEN
SETCOLOR(clogo)
  @ 00,00 SAY SPACE(80)
  @ 00,00 SAY M_CNTR(TRIM(bname))       && display business name
SETCOLOR(cmess)
  @ 02,78-LEN(sdate) SAY sdate          && display date memvar
SETCOLOR(cline)
  @ 01,00 SAY REPLICATE("-",80)
  @ 03,00 SAY REPLICATE("-",80)
  @ 23,00 SAY REPLICATE("-",80)
SETCOLOR(cnorm)
SAYHEADER("Display Color Change")
  @ 06,00 SAY M_CNTR("Press the [Insert] key to toggle colors")
  @ 08,00 SAY M_CNTR("Press the [Enter] key to accept colors")
SETCOLOR(cline)
  @ 14,10 to 16,35
  @ 14,45 to 16,70
SETCOLOR(cmemo)
  @ 15,11 SAY " This is the memo color "
SETCOLOR(chelp)
  @ 15,46 SAY " This is the help color "
SETCOLOR(cnorm)
  @ 24,00 SAY M_CNTR("This is the message color")
RETURN
*
* end of c_cols.prg
```

Fig. 6-5. Display Color Change source code.

```
┌──────────────────────────────────────────────────────────────────┐
│                           GLB Software                             │
├──────────────────────────────────────────────────────────────────┤
│ Change Printer Configuration                      July  1, 1988    │
├──────────────────────────────────────────────────────────────────┤
│                                                                    │
│                                                                    │
│                     Expanded Print ......  ▓                       │
│                     Expanded Release ....  ▓                       │
│                     Compressed Print ....  ▓                       │
│                     Compressed Release ..  ▓                       │
│                     Form Feed ..........   ▓                       │
│                                                                    │
│                                                                    │
│                                                                    │
│                                                                    │
│                                                                    │
│                                                                    │
│                                                                    │
├──────────────────────────────────────────────────────────────────┤
│                    Press [Esc] to escape                           │
└──────────────────────────────────────────────────────────────────┘
```

Fig. 6-6. Printer Configuration Change screen.

```
* Program Name .......... c_prtr.prg
* Revised Date .......... 07/01/88
*
SAYHEADER("Change Printer Configuration")
  @ 08,28 SAY "Expanded Print ......"
  @ 09,28 SAY "Expanded Release ...."
  @ 10,28 SAY "Compressed Print ...."
  @ 11,28 SAY "Compressed Release .."
  @ 12,28 SAY "Form Feed .........."
SETCOLOR(cinve)
  @ 08,50 SAY STR(pexpa,2)              && expanded
  @ 09,50 SAY STR(prele,2)              && expanded release
  @ 10,50 SAY STR(pcprs,2)              && compressed
  @ 11,50 SAY STR(prelc,2)              && compressed release
  @ 12,50 SAY STR(pfeed,2)              && form feed
SETCOLOR(cnorm)
changing = .T.
DO WHILE changing
  ESCKEY()
    @ 08,50 GET pexpa PICTURE "##" VALID v_number(pexpa)
    @ 09,50 GET prele PICTURE "##" VALID v_number(prele)
    @ 10,50 GET pcprs PICTURE "##" VALID v_number(pcprs)
    @ 11,50 GET prelc PICTURE "##" VALID v_number(prelc)
    @ 12,50 GET pfeed PICTURE "##" VALID v_number(pfeed)
  READ
  IF LASTKEY() = 27
    EXIT
  ENDIF
  changing = .F.
  mchoice = 1
    @ 22,31 PROMPT "Update" MESSAGE "  Update file with changes"
    @ 22,38 PROMPT "Change" MESSAGE "  Change printer codes"
    @ 22,45 PROMPT "Quit"   MESSAGE "  Quit and abort"
  CLEAR TYPEAHEAD
  MENU TO mchoice
  M_CLEAR()
  DO CASE
    CASE mchoice = 1 .AND. UPDATED()
      M_WAIT()
      USE cm_setup                       && update setup database
      REPLACE prn_expa WITH pexpa, prn_rele WITH prele,;
              prn_cprs WITH pcprs, prn_relc WITH prelc,;
              prn_feed WITH pfeed
      CLOSE DATABASES
      M_CLEAR()
      EXIT
    CASE mchoice = 2
      changing = .T.
      LOOP
    CASE mchoice = 3 .OR. LASTKEY() = 27
      EXIT
  ENDCASE
ENDDO
RETURN
```

Fig. 6-7. Printer Configuration Change source code.

```
                        GLB Software
_____

Change Business Name                          July  1, 1988
_____


          Old Name .........  GLB Software

          New Name .........  ███████████████████



_____
                    Press [Esc] to escape
```

Fig. 6-8. Business Name Change screen.

```
* Program Name ......... c_name.prg
* Revised Date ......... 07/01/88
*
SAYHEADER("Change Business Name")
  @ 08,20 SAY "Old Name .........."
  @ 10,20 SAY "New Name .........."
SETCOLOR(cinve)
  @ 08,40 SAY bname                        && old business name
SETCOLOR(cnorm)
*
changing = .T.
DO WHILE changing
  ESCKEY()
    @ 10,40 GET bname VALID v_string(bname)
  READ
  IF LASTKEY() = 27
    EXIT
  ENDIF
  changing = .F.
  mchoice = 1
    @ 22,31 PROMPT "Update" MESSAGE "  Update file these changes"
    @ 22,38 PROMPT "Change" MESSAGE "  Change business name"
    @ 22,45 PROMPT "Quit"   MESSAGE "  Quit and abort"
  CLEAR TYPEAHEAD
  MENU TO mchoice
  M_CLEAR()
  DO CASE
    CASE mchoice = 1 .AND. UPDATED()
      M_WAIT()
      USE cm_setup                         && update setup database
      REPLACE bus_name WITH bname
      CLOSE DATABASES
      SETCOLOR(clogo)                      && display new business name
        @ 00,00 SAY SPACE(80)
        @ 00,00 SAY M_CNTR(TRIM(bname))
      SETCOLOR(cnorm)
      M_CLEAR()
      EXIT
    CASE mchoice = 2
      changing = .T.
      LOOP
    CASE mchoice = 3 .OR. LASTKEY() = 27
      EXIT
  ENDCASE
ENDDO
RETURN
```

Fig. 6-9. Business Name Change source code.

7

CM Analysis Reports

Cost Management includes four business report options, as shown in the *Fig. 7-1* **Reports** menu. The information in each of these reports is displayed and may be printed out.

The client, supplier, and expense type reports are very similar in structure. For each of these reports, a beginning and ending date are specified by the user. The specified information is then tabulated and a summary for each client, supplier, or expense type is displayed on the screen—along with an option to print a formal report. The screen display for the **Client Analysis Report** is shown in *Fig. 7-2*.

The partial source code for the client analysis (R_CLNT.PRG) report is shown in *Fig. 7-3*. The beginning date defaults to the first day of the current month as determined by the BEGMONTH( ) user-defined function. The ending date defaults to the current date. The entered date combination is error-checked with the general V_DATE( ) validation UDF, which compares the two dates to ensure that the ending date is always greater than, or equal to, the beginning date.

The condition for copying records from the receipts (RECEIPTS.DBF) file to a temporary report file is determined by the entered dates, and defined by a memory variable named "mcondx". Once the temporary file has been appended from the receipts file, it is then indexed on client codes, and then totalled to a second temporary file.

The full business analysis (R_FULL.PRG) report uses both the expenses (EXPENSES.DBF) file and the receipts (RECEIPTS.DBF) file to present a daily profit summary, as shown in the *Fig. 7-4* display screen.

Again, a beginning and ending date are specified by the user, as shown in the partial source code in *Fig. 7-5*. The beginning date defaults to the first day of the current month, as determined by the BEGMONTH( ) user-defined function. The ending date defaults to the current date.

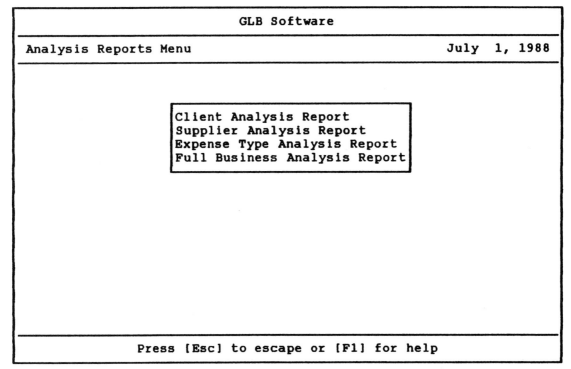

Fig. 7-1. Analysis Reports Menu screen.

The condition for appending records from the expenses (EX-PENSES.DBF) file to a temporary report file is determined by the entered dates defined by the "mcondx1" memory variable. The condition for appending records from the receipts (RECEIPTS.DBF) file to the same temporary report file is determined by the entered dates defined by the "mcondx2" memory variable.

The temporary file is created using the CREATE and CREATE FROM commands. Records are then appended from the expenses and receipts files per the respective established conditions. The DATE field in the temporary report file is then assigned either the expense date (EXPNDATE) or the receipt date (RCPTDATE), depending on the type of record entry as determined with the Clipper EMPTY function. The temporary file is then indexed on the DATE field, and then totalled to a second temporary file.

Note that the use of temporary files in report generation is much faster that using a SET FILTER command—especially when working with large database files.

```
┌─────────────────────────────────────────────────────────────┐
│                       GLB Software                            │
├─────────────────────────────────────────────────────────────┤
│ Client Analysis Report                      July  1, 1988     │
├─────────────────────────────────────────────────────────────┤
│                                                               │
│           Code        Client Name         Amount             │
│           ────     ─────────────────     ────────            │
│           ABC      ABC Corporation          800.00           │
│           FNB      First National Bank      250.00           │
│                                                               │
│                                                               │
│                                                               │
│                                                               │
│                                                               │
│               Forward Backward Top End Print                 │
├─────────────────────────────────────────────────────────────┤
│                  List the next 10 clients                     │
└─────────────────────────────────────────────────────────────┘
```

Fig. 7-2. Client Analysis Report screen.

```
* Program Name .......... r_clnt.prg
* Revised Date .......... 07/01/88
*
SAYHEADER("Client Analysis Report")
*
STORE BEGMONTH(DATE()) TO mdbeg          && first day of month UDF
STORE DATE()           TO mdend          && current date
*
HELPKEY()
  @ 08,26 SAY "Beginning Date ...." ;
          GET mdbeg PICTURE "@D"
  @ 09,26 SAY "Ending Date ......." ;
          GET mdend PICTURE "@D" VALID v_date(mdbeg,mdend)
READ
M_CLEAR()
IF LASTKEY() = 27                        && escape key
  RETURN
ENDIF
*
M_WAIT()
*
mcondx = "RCPTDATE >= mDBEG .and. RCPTDATE <= mDEND"
USE receipts
COPY TO temp1 FOR &mcondx                && condition as per above
CLOSE DATABASES
*
IF ! FILE("TEMP1.DBF")
  RETURN
ENDIF
*
USE temp1
INDEX ON clntcode TO temp1
TOTAL ON clntcode FIELDS rcptamnt TO temp2
CLOSE DATABASES
*
USE temp2
SUM rcptamnt TO alltotal                 && total of all receipts
*
SELECT 2
USE clntcode INDEX clntcode
SELECT 1
SET RELATION TO clntcode INTO b
GO TOP
*
* remainder of r_clnt.prg not included
```

Fig. 7-3. Client Analysis Report source code.

```
                            GLB Software

Full Business Analysis Report                    July  1, 1988


            Date      Expenses    Receipts     Profit
            ────────  ────────    ────────     ──────
          03/01/88        0.00      400.00      400.00
          03/03/88      210.00        0.00     -210.00
          03/12/88       25.50      200.00      174.50






                  Forward Backward Top End Print

                    List the next 10 dates
```

Fig. 7-4. Full Business Analysis Report screen.

```
* Program Name ......... r_full.prg
* Revised Date ......... 07/01/88
*
SAYHEADER("Full Business Analysis Report")
*
STORE BEGMONTH(DATE()) TO mdbeg        && first day of month UDF
STORE DATE()           TO mdend        && current date
*
HELPKEY()
   @ 08,26 SAY "Beginning Date ...." ;
           GET mdbeg PICTURE "@D"
   @ 09,26 SAY "Ending Date ......." ;
           GET mdend PICTURE "@D" VALID v_date(mdbeg,mdend)
READ
M_CLEAR()
IF LASTKEY() = 27
   RETURN
ENDIF
*
M_WAIT()
*
mcondx1 = "EXPNDATE >= mDBEG .and. EXPNDATE <= mDEND"
mcondx2 = "RCPTDATE >= mDBEG .and. RCPTDATE <= mDEND"
*
CREATE dummy                           && create a new database
STORE "DATE      D8  "  TO field1
STORE "EXPNAMNT  N8 2"  TO field2
STORE "EXPNDATE  D8  "  TO field3
STORE "RCPTAMNT  N8 2"  TO field4
STORE "RCPTDATE  D8  "  TO field5
FOR F = 1 TO 5
   fnumber = IIF(F<10,STR(F,1),STR(F,2))
   APPEND BLANK
   STORE "field" + fnumber TO fn
   REPLACE field_name WITH SUBSTR(&fn,1,10);
           field_type WITH SUBSTR(&fn,11,1);
           field_len  WITH VAL(SUBSTR(&fn,12,2));
           field_dec  WITH VAL(SUBSTR(&fn,14,1))
NEXT
CREATE templ FROM dummy
CLOSE DATABASES
ERASE dummy.dbf
*
USE templ
APPEND FROM expenses FOR &mcondx1       && fill new database file
APPEND FROM receipts FOR &mcondx2       && with expenses & receipts
REPLACE ALL DATE WITH expndate FOR ! EMPTY(expndate)
REPLACE ALL DATE WITH rcptdate FOR ! EMPTY(rcptdate)
INDEX ON DATE TO temp
TOTAL ON DATE TO temp2 FIELDS expnamnt, rcptamnt
CLOSE DATABASES
*
USE temp2
SUM rcptamnt TO mreceipts               && total of receipts
SUM expnamnt TO mexpenses               && total of expenses
*
* remainder of r_full.prg not included
```

Fig. 7-5. Full Business Analysis Report source code.

8

CM File
Utilities

The file utilities menu, as shown in *Fig. 8-1,* allows the CM user to perform various data activities including backup, recall, reindex, and data summary.

The data backup and data recall activities are very basic in the CM application. Provisions for multiple backup diskettes, for example, have not been included. The Clipper COPY command is used to copy each database (.DBF) file. The DOS COPY command is used to copy the expense memo (.TXT) files in order to utilize wildcard notations. The Cost Management data backup (D__BACK.PRG) code is shown in *Fig. 8-2.*

A user-defined function called M__STATUS( ) is used to display the current activity to the user as it occurs. This function displays the specified message, and automatically creates a box outline proportional to the message length.

The database reindexing (D__INDX.PRG) procedure uses the PACK command to permanently remove records that have been marked for deletion, as shown in the *Fig. 8-3* source code.

Again, the M__STATUS( ) function is used to notify the user as each file is being reindexed. This same procedure is also called from the top-level Cost Management module (CM.PRG) whenever index files are determined as not present.

The file summary activity is useful in determining the current status of all data files. File information displayed includes file description, number of records, file size, and last update. The file summary for Cost Management is shown in *Fig. 8-4.*

The source code for the file summary (D__SUMM.PRG) procedure is shown in *Fig. 8-5.* Note that a full description for each file is used in lieu of the actual file name.

The Clipper RECCOUNT( ) function returns the number of records in the specified database file. Note that this function includes all records, along with those that have been marked for deletion.

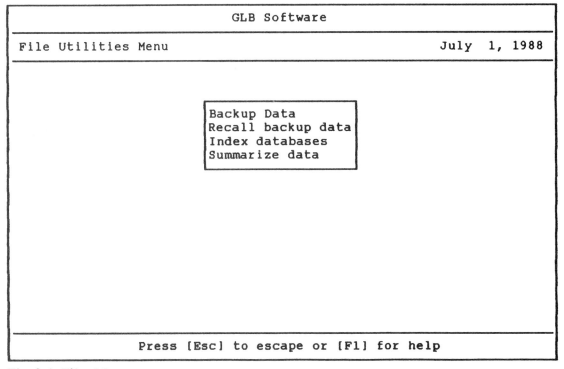

Fig. 8-1. Files Menu screen.

The database file size is determined by multiplying the number of records times the record size, and then adding the header size. The Clipper function RECSIZE( ) returns the record size, and HEADER( )+1 returns the database header size.

The last file update is returned by the Clipper LUPDATE( ) function.

```
* Program Name .......... d_back
* Revised Date .......... 07/01/88
*
SAYHEADER("Data Backup")
*
@ 09,00 SAY M_CNTR("Place backup diskette in drive A:")
@ 11,00 SAY M_CNTR("Press any key when ready.")
*
ESCKEY()
SET CURSOR(.F.)
INKEY(0)
SET CURSOR(.T.)
*
IF LASTKEY() = 27
   RETURN
ENDIF
*
M_WAIT()
*
M_STATUS("Copying Expenses data")        && status message UDF
COPY FILE expenses.dbf TO A:expenses.dbf
*
M_STATUS("Copying Receipts data")
COPY FILE receipts.dbf TO A:receipts.dbf
*
M_STATUS("Copying Client Code data")
COPY FILE clntcode.dbf TO A:clntcode.dbf
*
M_STATUS("Copying Supplier Code data")
COPY FILE suppcode.dbf TO A:suppcode.dbf
*
M_STATUS("Copying Expense Type Code data")
COPY FILE typecode.dbf TO A:typecode.dbf
*
M_STATUS("Copying CM Setup data")
COPY FILE cm_setup.dbf TO A:cm_setup.dbf
*
M_STATUS("Copying Expense Memos")
RUN COPY cm????.txt A:>nul                && DOS copy for wildcards
*
M_CLEAR()
RETURN
```

Fig. 8-2. Data Backup source code.

```
* Program Name .......... d_indx.prg
* Revised Date .......... 07/01/88
*
SAYHEADER("Reindex Databases")
M_WAIT()
*
USE expenses
M_STATUS("Indexing Expenses File")        && status message UDF
PACK                                      && delete marked records
INDEX ON expnnumb TO expenses
CLOSE DATABASES
*
USE receipts
M_STATUS("Indexing Receipts File")
PACK
INDEX ON rcptnumb TO receipts
CLOSE DATABASES
*
USE clntcode
M_STATUS("Indexing Client Codes File")
PACK
INDEX ON clntcode TO clntcode
CLOSE DATABASES
*
USE suppcode
M_STATUS("Indexing Supplier Codes File")
PACK
INDEX ON suppcode TO suppcode
CLOSE DATABASES
*
USE typecode
M_STATUS("Indexing Expense Type Codes File")
PACK
INDEX ON typecode TO typecode
CLOSE DATABASES
*
M_CLEAR()
RETURN
```

Fig. 8-3. Data Reindex source code.

```
┌──────────────────────────────────────────────────────────────┐
│                         GLB Software                           │
├──────────────────────────────────────────────────────────────┤
│ File Summary                                     July  1, 1988 │
├──────────────────────────────────────────────────────────────┤
│                                                                │
│                                                                │
│        File Description      Records      Size    Lastdate     │
│        ─────────────────     ───────     ────     ────────     │
│        Expenses                   29     2,539    07/01/88     │
│        Receipts                    3       389    07/01/88     │
│        Clients                     3       171    07/01/88     │
│        Suppliers                   4       195    07/01/88     │
│        Expense types               6       243    07/01/88     │
│                                                                │
│                                                                │
│                                                                │
│                                                                │
│                                                                │
│                                                                │
├──────────────────────────────────────────────────────────────┤
│                   Press [Esc] to escape                        │
└──────────────────────────────────────────────────────────────┘
```

Fig. 8-4. File Summary screen.

```
* Program Name ......... d_summ.prg
* Revised Date ......... 07/01/88
*
SAYHEADER("File Summary")
*
SETCOLOR(cline)
   @ 08,17 SAY " File Description    Records    Size    Lastdate"
   @ 09,17 SAY "—————————————    ———————    ————————    ————————"
SETCOLOR(cnorm)
   @ 10,17 SAY "Expenses"
   @ 11,17 SAY "Receipts"
   @ 12,17 SAY "Clients"
   @ 13,17 SAY "Suppliers"
   @ 14,17 SAY "Expense types"
*
USE expenses
@ 10,37 SAY TRAN(RECCOUNT(),"###,###")
@ 10,46 SAY TRAN(INT((RECSIZE()*RECCOUNT())+HEADER()+1),"####,###")
@ 10,56 SAY LUPDATE()
*
USE receipts
@ 11,37 SAY TRAN(RECCOUNT(),"###,###")
@ 11,46 SAY TRAN(INT((RECSIZE()*RECCOUNT())+HEADER()+1),"####,###")
@ 11,56 SAY LUPDATE()
*
USE clntcode
@ 12,37 SAY TRAN(RECCOUNT(),"###,###")
@ 12,46 SAY TRAN(INT((RECSIZE()*RECCOUNT())+HEADER()+1),"####,###")
@ 12,56 SAY LUPDATE()
*
USE suppcode
@ 13,37 SAY TRAN(RECCOUNT(),"###,###")
@ 13,46 SAY TRAN(INT((RECSIZE()*RECCOUNT())+HEADER()+1),"####,###")
@ 13,56 SAY LUPDATE()
*
USE typecode
@ 14,37 SAY TRAN(RECCOUNT(),"###,###")
@ 14,46 SAY TRAN(INT((RECSIZE()*RECCOUNT())+HEADER()+1),"####,###")
@ 14,56 SAY LUPDATE()
*
CLOSE DATABASES
ESCKEY()
SET CURSOR(.F.)
INKEY(60)
SET CURSOR(.T.)
RETURN
```

Fig. 8-5. File Summary source code.

9

CM User
Help

Cost Management includes several user-help techniques that can easily be adapted for any application. All help is contained in the single program (HELP.PRG) module and is called whenever the user presses the F1 key during a menu screen, or while awaiting data entry.

The Clipper help facility automatically passes three variables to HELP.PRG whenever F1 is pressed during a GET or MENU TO wait state. These three variables are: the calling procedure name, the memory variable name, and the procedure line number. These must always be identified at the beginning of the HELP.PRG procedure, as shown in *Fig. 9-1*. Additionally, a directive to prevent recursive calling of the help facility is shown.

When F1 is pressed during any of the menu (M__ prefix) or sub-menu (S__ prefix) procedures, as indicated in the help code of *Fig. 9-2*, the general menu help screen is displayed (see *Fig. 9-3*). The help source code simply uses the SUBSTR( ) function to determine if the calling program has an "M__" or "S__" prefix.

Fig. 9-4 contains the source code that displays HELP whenever the F1 key is pressed while awaiting any date-type memvar. Rather than listing all of the individual date memvars, the TYPE( ) function is used to simply evaluate the passed variable to see if it is a date type memvar.

Similarly, *Fig. 9-5* contains the source code that displays HELP whenever the F1 key is pressed while awaiting any logical-type memvar. In this case, however, the INKEY( ) function is actually used to retrieve the user choice, which is then forced (using the KEYBOARD( ) function) back to the calling procedure.

Fig. 9-6 shows how HELP is displayed when invoked during entry of a supplier (mSUPPCODE) code. A listing of available supplier codes is displayed on the screen in a scrollable window from which the user can select the highlighted code by pressing the Enter key. Once the user has made a selection, that supplier code is stored to the mSUPPCODE memory variable,

```
PARAMETERS prg,line,mvar              && passed parameters
*
IF prg == "HELP"                      && prevent recursive calling
   ERRORTONE()                        && error tone UDF
   RETURN
ENDIF
```

Fig. 9-1. Initial Help source code.

and is subsequently displayed on the entry screen at the supplier code GET.
The user may abort help by pressing the Escape key.

Providing maintenance code help during expense or receipt activities
can be accomplished by simply identifying the passed memory variable.
However, providing help for the maintenance activities is a little bit trickier.
Remember that common maintenance program modules were used for each
of the codes (clients, suppliers, and expense types). Actual data memvars
were defined as other GET memvars, ie.: memvar1 = "msuppcode". If a
user requested maintenance code during a maintenance activity, the variable name passed to the help module would be "memvar1", not the actual
code memvar (ie, "msuppcode", etc). This requires special methods of handling maintenance code help.

In the Cost Management initialization module (CM.PRG), a memory
variable named "hcode" was declared PUBLIC to solve this particular help
problem. When the type of code maintenance (client, supplier, or expense
type) is selected from the main menu, the common maintenance menu
(M_MNTE.PRG) assigns a value to "hcode" depending on the code type.

```
CASE SUBSTR(prg,1,2) == "M_" .OR. SUBSTR(prg,1,2) == "S_"
   SAVE SCREEN                        && save current screen
   CLS()                              && clear screen UDF
   M_HELP()                           && CM help message UDF
   SETCOLOR(cline)
   @ 07,15 TO 15,64 DOUBLE            && double-line box
   SETCOLOR(chelp)
   @ 08,16 SAY " Menu selections are scrolled by using the up    "
   @ 09,16 SAY " and down cursor keys, or the left and right      "
   @ 10,16 SAY " cursor keys. A selection is made by pressing     "
   @ 11,16 SAY " the Enter key, or by pressing the first letter "
   @ 12,16 SAY " in the name of a choice.                         "
   @ 13,16 SAY "                                                  "
   @ 14,16 SAY " Press any key to continue ...                    "
   SET CURSOR(.F.)                    && turn cursor off
   INKEY(60)                          && wait 60 sec or keypress
   SETCOLOR(cnorm)
   RESTORE SCREEN                     && restore saved screen
   RETURN
```

Fig. 9-2. Menu Help source code.

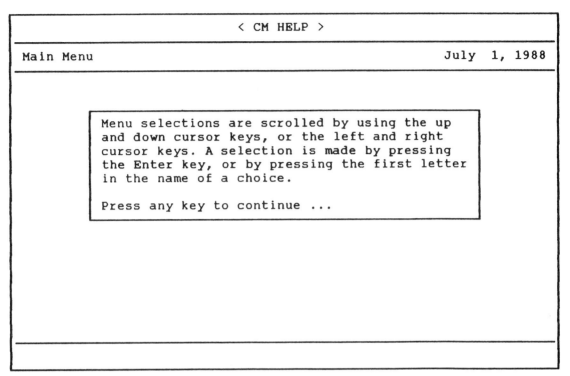

Fig. 9-3. Menu Help screen.

```
CASE TYPE(mvar) == "D"              && any date type GET memvar
   SAVE SCREEN
   M_HELP()                         && help message UDF
   SETCOLOR(cline)
     @ 06,23 TO 17,57 DOUBLE
   SETCOLOR(chelp)
     @ 07,24 SAY " Enter dates as follows:        "
     @ 08,24 SAY "                                "
     @ 09,24 SAY "    mm/dd/yy                     "
     @ 10,24 SAY "                                "
     @ 11,24 SAY "                                "
     @ 12,24 SAY "                   2-digit year "
     @ 13,24 SAY "                 2-digit day    "
     @ 14,24 SAY "             2-digit month      "
     @ 15,24 SAY "                                "
     @ 16,24 SAY " Press any key to continue ...  "
   SETCOLOR(cnorm)
   SET CURSOR(.F.)
   INKEY(10)                        && ten second delay or keypress
   SET CURSOR(.T.)
   RESTORE SCREEN
   RETURN
```

Fig. 9-4. Date Type Memvar Help source code.

```
CASE TYPE(mvar) == "L"                   && logical type
  SAVE SCREEN
  CLS()
  M_HELP()
  SETCOLOR(cline)
    @ 06,24 TO 08,56 DOUBLE
  SETCOLOR(chelp)
    @ 07,25 SAY " Press [Y] for Yes, [N] for No "
  SETCOLOR(cnorm)
  SET CURSOR(.F.)
  response = INKEY(0)                    && looking for keypress
  KEYBOARD(CHR(response)+CHR(13))        && returns choice+enter key
  SET CURSOR(.T.)
  RESTORE SCREEN
  RETURN
```

Fig. 9-5. Logical Type Memvar Help source code.

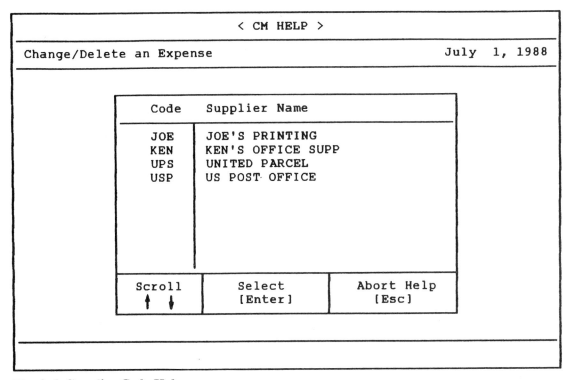

Fig. 9-6. Supplier Code Help screen.

```
CASE mvar == "MSUPPCODE" .OR. (mvar == "MEMVAR1" .AND. hcode = 5)
   SAVE SCREEN
   M_HELP()                               && help message UDF
   USE suppcode INDEX suppcode
   PRIVATE fields[2]                      && array of database fields
   PRIVATE heads[2]                       && array of column heading
   fields[1] = "SUPPCODE"
   fields[2] = "SUPPNAME"
   heads[1]  = "Code"
   heads[2]  = "Supplier Name"
   HELPBOX()                              && help box UDF
   SET CURSOR(.F.)
   DBEDIT(07,17,19,62,fields,"dbe",.T.,heads)
   SET CURSOR(.T.)
   IF LASTKEY() = 13                      && enter key
      STORE suppcode TO &mvar             && must use macro
      KEYBOARD CHR(13)                    && forced keystroke
   ENDIF
   CLOSE DATABASES
   SETCOLOR(cnorm)
   RESTORE SCREEN
   RETURN
```

Fig. 9-7. Supplier Code Help source code.

This PUBLIC variable can then be used by the help module, as shown in *Fig. 9-7,* to determine which code type GET requires the lookup-table help.

The DBEDIT( ) function is then used to help create this simple point-and-shoot capability. Clipper Summer '87 also allows headings, footings, and column separators to be defined as options to the DBEDIT( ) function. In CM, the help box outline is created with a CM function named HELP-

```
CASE mvar == "MEMVAR2" .AND. hcode = 4 && hcode signifies clients
   SAVE SCREEN
   CLS()
   M_HELP()
   SETCOLOR(cmess)
      @ 06,23 TO 11,57 DOUBLE
   SETCOLOR(chelp)
      @ 07,24 SAY " Enter a client name for this     "
      @ 08,24 SAY " field.                           "
      @ 09,24 SAY "                                  "
      @ 10,24 SAY " Press any key to continue ...    "
   SETCOLOR(cnorm)
   SET CURSOR(.F.)
   INKEY(10)
   SET CURSOR(.T.)
   RESTORE SCREEN
   RETURN
```

Fig. 9-8. Supplier Name Help source code.

BOX( ) and the field names and headings are contained in arrays and displayed by DBEDIT( ).

A user-defined function named DBE (further discussed in a later chapter) is used to evaluate the keystoke choice. In this type of point-and-shoot help, only the Enter and Escape keys are used to exit the DBEDIT( ) function.

Help for the supplier name (msuppname) memvar field can be handled similarly to that for the supplier code as shown in *Fig. 9-8*.

Help for expense number entry is provided by DBEDIT( ) as shown in *Fig. 9-9*. Three database files (EXPN.DBF, SUPP.DBF, and TYPE.DBF) are opened to provide sufficient descriptive help for expense numbers. Note how the field names array is defined using the alias file names.

```
CASE mvar == "MEXPNNR"                    && GET memvar
  SAVE SCREEN
  M_HELP()                                && help message UDF
  SELECT 3                                && workspace 3 alias C
  USE typecode INDEX typecode
  SELECT 2                                && workspace 2 alias B
  USE suppcode INDEX suppcode
  SELECT 1                                && workspace 1 alias A
  USE expenses INDEX expenses
  SET RELATION TO suppcode INTO B, TO typecode INTO C
  PRIVATE fields[4]                       && array of database fields
  PRIVATE heads[4]                        && array of column headings
  fields[1] = "EXPNNUMB"
  fields[2] = "EXPNDATE"
  fields[3] = "B->SUPPNAME"
  fields[4] = "C->TYPENAME"
  heads[1]  = "Exp #"
  heads[2]  = "Date"
  heads[3]  = "Supplier Name"
  heads[4]  = "Expense Type Name"
  HELPBOX()                               && help box UDF
  SET CURSOR(.F.)
  DBEDIT(07,17,19,62,fields,"dbe",.T.,heads)
  SET CURSOR(.T.)
  IF LASTKEY() = 13                       && enter key
    STORE VAL(expnnumb) TO mexpnnr
    KEYBOARD CHR(13)                      && forced keystroke
  ENDIF
  CLOSE DATABASES
  SETCOLOR(cnorm)
  RESTORE SCREEN
  RETURN
```

Fig. 9-9. Expense Number Help source code.

```
CASE mvar == "MMEMO"                          && from E_MEMO.PRG
  SAVE SCREEN
  numfiles = ADIR("*.TXT")                    && array size
  PRIVATE txtfiles[numfiles]                  && declare array
  ADIR("*.TXT",txtfiles)                      && fill array
  ASORT(txtfiles)                             && sort aray
  SETCOLOR(cline)
     @ 12,33 TO 20,46 DOUBLE                   && double-line box
     @ 14,33 SAY "|├────────────┤|"           && header bar
  SETCOLOR(clogo)
     @ 13,36 SAY "FileName"                    && header
  SETCOLOR(chelp)
  SET CURSOR(.F.)
  filename = txtfiles[achoice(15,34,19,45,txtfiles,"","dbt")]
  SET CURSOR(.T.)
  IF LASTKEY() = 13                            && enter key
    mmemo = filename + SPACE(10-LEN(filename))
  ELSE
    mmemo = SPACE(10)
  ENDIF
  SETCOLOR(cnorm)
  RESTORE SCREEN
  RETURN
```

Fig. 9-10. Expense Memo Name Help source code.

  User help for looking up memo file names that are required in the E__MEMO.PRG module is provided as shown in *Fig. 9-10.* Several Clipper array-handling functions are used.

  In order to declare the array of memo text file names, the total number of array elements must be determined. The ADIR( ) array function is used to find the number of *.TXT files that exist. The array is then declared using the PRIVATE command along with the ADIR( ) result. ASORT( ) is then used to alphanumerically sort the array.

  The new ACHOICE( ) function is used to actually scroll the array of memo text file names and return the selected name. The "dbt" function in ACHOICE( ) analyzes the user keystrokes as the selection process continues. This function is dicussed in a later chapter.

## 10

CM Functions

Cost Management application uses a variety of custom user-defined functions (UDF) for error messages, data validation, and error tone generation. These can easily be adapted for any application. All functions are contained in the single program (FUNC.PRG) module.

Fig. 10-1 shows the source code for the DBE function that is used by DBEDIT( ) in the CM help module. Basically, DBEDIT( ) scrolls a database until either the Escape key is pressed to abort help or the Enter key is pressed to select a displayed choice.

Fig. 10-2 shows the source code for the DBM function that is used by MEMOEDIT( ) in the expense activity modules. This function analyzes the MEMOEDIT( ) keystrokes and continually returns an editing status. DBM also displays the row and column numbers for the memo editing screen display, and provides function key equivalents for line insertion, line deletion, and memo saving. Note that a special flag (UPDATED) is used to reflect whether a displayed memo has been changed.

Fig. 10-3 shows the source code for the DBT function that is used by ACHOICE( ) in the CM help module for memo file name lookups. DBT analyzes the user keystrokes and returns a status to the ACHOICE( ) function.

The CM screen clearing function CLS( ) is shown in *Fig. 10-4*. The Clipper SCROLL( ) function is used to strategically clear the user area of the screen.

The CM activity names are always displayed using the SAY-HEADER( ) function. The name is passed to the function that not only properly displays the activity name, but also turns off the insert key using the READINSERT( ) function, and turns on the cursor using the SET CURSOR command. The SAYHEADER( ) code is shown in *Fig. 10-5*.

The CM menu box outline function MENUBOX( ) is shown in *Fig. 10-6*. All CM menus utilize this function.

```
FUNCTION DBE                            && DBEDIT() keystroke UDF
PARAMETERS mode,i                       && passed parameters
DO CASE
   CASE mode < 4                        && DBEDIT() status
     RETURN(1)                          && continue DBEDIT()
   CASE LASTKEY() = 13 .OR. LASTKEY() = 27
     RETURN(0)                          && quit DBEDIT()
   OTHERWISE
     RETURN(1)                          && continue DBEDIT()
ENDCASE
```
Fig. 10-1. DBEDIT(   ) UDF source code.

```
FUNCTION DBM                            && MEMOEDIT() keystroke UDF
PARAMETERS mode,line,col                && passed parameters
UPDATED = .F.                           && initialize memo status
IF mode = 2                             && memo has been altered
  UPDATED = .T.
ENDIF
IF mode = 0                             && idle
  @ 20,70 SAY TRAN(line,"###")          && line number display
  @ 21,70 SAY TRAN(col+1,"###")         && column number display
  RETURN(0)
ELSE
  DO CASE
    CASE LASTKEY() = 23 .OR. LASTKEY() = -9 && Ctrl-W or F10
      IF UPDATED
        M_SAVE()                        && save message UDF
        RETURN(23)                      && return Ctrl-W keycode
      ELSE
        RETURN(27)                      && return escape keycode
      ENDIF
    CASE LASTKEY() = 27                 && escape key
      IF UPDATED
        @ 24,27 SAY "Do you want to abort (y/n)?"
        response = " "
        DO WHILE ! response $ "YN"
          response = UPPER(CHR(INKEY(0)))
        ENDDO
        @ 24,00
        IF response = "Y"
          RETURN(27)                    && return escape keycode
        ELSE
          RETURN(32)                    && disable
        ENDIF
      ELSE
        RETURN(27)                      && return escape keycode
      ENDIF
    CASE LASTKEY() = -3                 && delete line
      RETURN(25)                        && return delete keycode
    CASE LASTKEY() = -5                 && insert line
      RETURN(14)                        && return insert keycode
  ENDCASE
ENDIF
```
Fig. 10-2. MEMOEDIT(   ) UDF source code.

```
FUNCTION DBT                        && ACHOICE() keystroke UDF
PARAMETERS mode,element,position    && passed parameters
DO CASE
  CASE LASTKEY() = 13               && enter key
    RETURN(1)                       && selection made
  CASE LASTKEY() = 27               && escape key
    RETURN(1)                       && selection made
  OTHERWISE
    RETURN(2)                       && continue
ENDCASE
```

Fig. 10-3. ACHOICE(   ) UDF source code.

```
FUNCTION CLS                        && strategic screen clear
SETCOLOR(CNORM)
  SCROLL(04,00,22,79,00)            && faster than CLEAR TO
  @ 24,00                           && clear message line too
RETURN("")                          && null return
```

Fig. 10-4. CLS(   ) source code.

```
FUNCTION SAYHEADER                  && activity name display UDF
PARAMETERS header                   && passed header memvar
CLS()
SETCOLOR(cmess)
  @ 02,02 SAY header+SPACE(55-LEN(header))
SETCOLOR(cnorm)
MENUTONE()
READINSERT(.F.)                     && disable insert key
SET CURSOR(.T.)                     && turn cursor on
RETURN("")                          && return null string
```

Fig. 10-5. SAYHEADER(   ) source code.

```
FUNCTION MENUBOX                    && box outline for menus
PARAMETERS TOP,LEFT,BOTTOM,RIGHT    && box coordinates
frame = " ┌─┐|┘─└|"                 && frame description
SETCOLOR(cline)
  @TOP,LEFT,BOTTOM,RIGHT BOX frame  && Clipper BOX command
SETCOLOR(cnorm)
RETURN("")
```

Fig. 10-6. MENUBOX(   ) source code.

```
FUNCTION M_CNTR                          && display message centering
PARAMETERS mmsg                          && message
RETURN(SPACE(INT(41-LEN(mmsg)/2))+mmsg)
*
FUNCTION H_CNTR                          && printed message centering
PARAMETERS hd,wid                        && message and print width
RETURN(SPACE(INT(wid/2-LEN(TRIM(hd))/2))+hd)
```
Fig. 10-7. Message Centering UDF's source code.

Two Cost Management message centering functions are shown in *Fig. 10-7*. The function M__CNTR( ) automatically centers the passed message on the screen display, while H__CNTR( ) is used to center printout headings per the width parameter that is passed with the heading text.

Fig. 10-8 shows the code for two of the user messages, M__WAIT( ) and M__SAVE( ), that are used by CM. These messages are displayed on line 24 of the screen display.

The M__PRTR( ) function uses another Clipper function named IS-PRINTER( ) to determine whether a printer is connected and on-line. If M__PRTR( ) detects a printer error, the user is notified and is given up to 10 seconds to correct the printer problem and press a key. If the printer problem is not corrected, the M__PRTR( ) function returns a logical .F. to the calling procedure (see *Fig. 10-9*).

The new Summer '87 TONE( ) function is used to create the various error tones used by Cost Management. *Fig. 10-10* shows many of these.

Shown in *Fig. 10-11* are four general functions that are used throughout Cost Management, and may be useful in any application. The

```
FUNCTION M_WAIT                          && wait message UDF
M_CLEAR()
SETCOLOR(cmess)
  @ 24,29 SAY "Working ... please wait"
SETCOLOR(cmess+"*")                      && blinking
  @ 24,29 SAY "Working"
SETCOLOR(cnorm)
SET CURSOR(.F.)                          && disable cursor
RETURN("")
*
FUNCTION M_SAVE                          && save message UDF
SETCOLOR(cmess)
  @ 24,29 SAY "Saving ... please wait"
SETCOLOR(cmess+"*")                      && blinking
  @ 24,29 SAY "Saving"
SETCOLOR(cnorm)
SET CURSOR(.F.)
RETURN("")
```
Fig. 10-8. Message UDF's source code.

```
FUNCTION M_PRTR                              && printer check UDF
IF ISPRINTER()                               && Clipper printer check UDF
  RETURN(.T.)
ELSE
  PRINTERTONE()                              && error tone
  M_CLEAR()
  SETCOLOR(cmess)
  @ 24,15 SAY "Error ... fix printer and press any key to continue"
  SETCOLOR(cmess+"*")
  @ 24,15 SAY "Error"
  SET CURSOR(.F.)
  INKEY(10)                                  && 10 sec or keypress
  SET CURSOR(.T.)
  IF LASTKEY() = 27                          && can escape print
    RETURN(.F.)
  ENDIF
  IF ISPRINTER()                             && check it again
    RETURN(.T.)
  ELSE
    RETURN(.F.)                              && last chance failed!
  ENDIF
ENDIF
RETURN("")
```

Fig. 10-9. M__PRTR( ) source code.

V__STRING( ) function ensures that a passed character string is not blank. The function V__DATE( ) checks a pair of passed dates to ensure that the second date is later than, or the same as, the first date. The V__NUMBER( ) function checks to make sure a passed number is greater than zero. And the BEGMONTH( ) function returns the date of the first day of the current month.

```
FUNCTION DONETONE                      && task completed
IF atone                               && user tones turned on?
  TONE(300,1)
  TONE(400,1)
  TONE(500,1)
ENDIF
RETURN("")
*
FUNCTION DELETETONE                    && delete warning
IF atone
  TONE(300,1)
  TONE(300,1)
  TONE(300,1)
ENDIF
RETURN("")
*
FUNCTION PRINTERTONE                   && printer error
IF atone
  TONE(400,2)
  TONE(200,2)
  TONE(400,2)
  TONE(200,2)
ENDIF
RETURN("")
*
FUNCTION ERRORTONE                     && general error
IF atone
  TONE(200,2)
ENDIF
RETURN("")
*
FUNCTION MENUTONE                      && menus
IF atone
  TONE(400,1)
ENDIF
RETURN("")
```

Fig. 10-10. Audio Tone UDF's source code.

```
FUNCTION V_STRING                        && string validation
PARAMETERS mstr                          && character string
IF EMPTY(mstr)
  ok = .F.                               && cannot be blank
  M_ERROR()
ELSE
  ok = .T.
ENDIF
RETURN(ok)
*
FUNCTION V_DATE                          && date window validation
PARAMETERS mbeg,mend                     && begin and end dates
IF EMPTY(mend) .OR. mend < mbeg
  ok = .F.
  M_ERROR()
ELSE
  ok = .T.
ENDIF
RETURN(ok)
*
FUNCTION V_NUMBER                        && number validation
PARAMETERS mnum                          && numeric value
IF EMPTY(mnum)                           && cannot be zero
  ok = .F.
  M_ERROR()
ELSE
  ok = .T.
ENDIF
RETURN(ok)
*
FUNCTION BEGMONTH                        && first day of month UDF
RETURN CTOD(STR(MONTH(DATE()),2)+"/01/"+STR(YEAR(DATE())-1900,2))
```

Fig. 10-11. Validation UDF's source code.

## 11

CM Error System

In the new Summer '87 Clipper, recoverable runtime errors have been divided into one of six different error classes:

- Database Error
- Expression error
- Miscellaneous error
- Print error
- Open error
- Undefined error

For each of the error classes, there is a runtime error-handling function that is called whenever an error occurs. The source code for the CM error-handling functions is provided in the procedure module ERRORSYS.PRG, as shown in *Fig. 11-1*.

Note that each of the functions receive error information from the calling procedure. Common to each of the error-handling functions are the parameters "name", "line", and "info". Other parameters may also be passed which contain additional information.

The "name" parameter is the character name of the procedure or function that was in process when the error occurred.

The "line" parameter is the numeric line number in the source file which caused the error. However, if the source file was compiled with the −1 option (no line numbers option), this parameter will always be zero.

The "info" parameter is the character information about the runtime error, usually containing a descriptive phrase such as "Type error", and maybe containing further information such as "(in macro)".

In addition to the recoverable errors briefly described above, and con-

```
* Program Name ......... errorsys.prg
* Revised Date ......... 07/01/88
*
FUNCTION EXPR_ERROR                    && expression error
PARAMETERS NAME,LINE,INFO,MODEL,_1,_2,_3
SET DEVICE TO SCREEN
@ 00,00
@ 00,00 SAY "PROC " + M->NAME + " LINE " + LTRIM(STR(M->LINE)) +;
  ", " + M->INFO
SETCOLOR("W")                          && reset colors
SET CURSOR(.T.)                        && turn on cursor
QUIT
RETURN .F.
*
FUNCTION UNDEF_ERROR                   && undefined error
PARAMETERS NAME,LINE,INFO,MODEL,_1
SET DEVICE TO SCREEN
@ 00,00
@ 00,00 SAY "PROC " + M->NAME + " LINE " + LTRIM(STR(M->LINE)) +;
  ", " + M->INFO + " " + M->_1
SETCOLOR("W")
SET CURSOR(.T.)
QUIT
RETURN .T.
*
FUNCTION MISC_ERROR                    && other error
PARAMETERS NAME,LINE,INFO,MODEL
SET DEVICE TO SCREEN
@ 00,00
@ 00,00 SAY "PROC " + M->NAME + " LINE " + LTRIM(STR(M->LINE)) +;
  ", " + M->INFO
SETCOLOR("W")
SET CURSOR(.T.)
QUIT
RETURN .F.
*
FUNCTION OPEN_ERROR                    && file opening error
PARAMETERS NAME,LINE,INFO,MODEL,_1
IF MODEL == "USE"
  RETURN .F.
ENDIF
SET DEVICE TO SCREEN
@ 00,00
@ 00,00 SAY "PROC " + M->NAME + " LINE " + LTRIM(STR(M->LINE)) +;
", " + M->INFO + " " + M->_1 + " (" + LTRIM(STR(DOSERROR())) + ")"
@ 00,65 SAY "RETRY? (Y/N)"             && second chance!
INKEY(0)                               && await keypress
DO WHILE ! UPPER(CHR(LASTKEY())) $ "YN"
  INKEY(0)
ENDDO
```

Fig. 11-1. CM Error-Handling source code.

```
IF ! UPPER(CHR(LASTKEY())) = "Y"          && try again
  SETCOLOR("W")
  SET CURSOR(.T.)
  QUIT
ENDIF
@ 00,00
RETURN .T.
*
FUNCTION DB_ERROR                         && data error
PARAMETERS NAME,LINE,INFO
SET DEVICE TO SCREEN
@ 00,00
@ 00,00 SAY "PROC " + M->NAME + " LINE " + LTRIM(STR(M->LINE)) +;
  ", " + M->INFO
SETCOLOR("W")
SET CURSOR(.T.)
QUIT
RETURN .F.
*
FUNCTION PRINT_ERROR                      && printer error
PARAMETERS NAME,LINE
SET DEVICE TO SCREEN
@ 00,00
@ 00,00 SAY "PROC " + M->NAME + " LINE " + LTRIM(STR(M->LINE)) +;
  ", PRINTER NOT READY"
@ 00,65 SAY "RETRY? (Y/N)"
INKEY(0)
DO WHILE ! UPPER(CHR(LASTKEY())) $ "YN"
  INKEY(0)
ENDDO
IF ! UPPER(CHR(LASTKEY())) = "Y"
  SETCOLOR("W")
  SET CURSOR(.T.)
  QUIT
ENDIF
@ 00,00
RETURN .T.
```

Fig. 11-1. Continued.

tained in the ERRORSYS.PRG code, there are several additional error messages which may also be incurred during runtime.

The error message "Internal Error" generally occurs because of a bad index file. Clipper displays the error message, and then awaits a user keypress before QUITting.

The error message "Disk Full" occurs when the disk is full during standard database file operations. Clipper displays the error message and then prompts the user to retry or quit.

The error message "Multiple Error" generally occurs when there has been an error in one of the error functions. Clipper displays the error message and then awaits a user keypress before QUITting.

The error message "Not Enough Memory" occurs when there is not enough RAM memory to load an application. Clipper displays the error message and then awaits a user keypress before QUITting.

The error message "Out of Memory" indicates that the amount of RAM memory is insufficient for an application, or even part of an application. For example, an application might load successfully, run initially, but might crash during database indexing due to lack of needed buffer space. Clipper displays the error message, and then awaits a user keypress before QUITting.

12

CM Compiling
and Linking

This chapter discusses several different methods of compiling Clipper code, and linking the resultant object files. Methods including single file, internal overlays, and external overlays are demonstrated, as is use of the Clipper Summer '87 MAKE facility.

The simplest method of compiling and linking the Cost Management application is to compile each of the four (CM, HELP, FUNC, and ER-RORSYS) high-level procedures as shown in *Fig. 12-1*. This results in four separate object (.OBJ) code files of the same base name.

The Clipper "-l" option is used in order to produce the smallest possible executable file. This option removes line numbers from the compiled code, but normally it would not be included in the compile commands until after a program has been totally completed and debugged.

Linking the resultant four object code files may be accomplished by using the PLINK86 (supplied with Clipper) linker, the DOS LINK command, or Borland's TLINK (see *Fig. 12-2*). For applications that do not utilize file overlays, LINK or TLINK will link object code files much more quickly than PLINK86.

Developing an application usually is best accomplished by dividing it into separate program code files that can be compiled individually and then linked with the other files. This saves time during development because a change in one program file means that only that file needs to be recompiled. However, in the CM application, this means keeping track of 39 different object code files.

The MAKE facility that is supplied with Clipper Summer '87 provides a means for keeping tabs on program and object code files by comparing date and time stamps with the executable file. For example, if a change was made to the D_SUMM.PRG file in CM, the MAKE file would realize that only D_SUMM.PRG needs to be recompiled and then linked with the other program files.

```
C> CLIPPER CM.PRG -l

C> CLIPPER HELP.PRG -l

C> CLIPPER FUNC.PRG -l

C> CLIPPER ERRORSYS.PRG -l
```

Fig. 12-1. CM Single File Compile commands.

The MAKE file (CM.MAK) for CM is shown in *Fig. 12-3*. Twelve macros are defined according to the activity type. For example, all of the expense program files are defined as being in object code macro number four. The number and decription of macros is strictly up to the programmer.

The compile command used in CM.MAK file simply instructs MAKE to compile all program files using the Clipper "-m" and "-l" options, meaning that only specified program files (ie. no dependents) are compiled — with line numbers excluded. The corresponding object code file must also be defined for each program file as shown in the MAKE file code.

The link command instructs MAKE to use TLINK along with the CM link (CM__TLINK.LNK) file, which is shown in *Fig. 12-4*. The link command can be changed to utilize the Clipper-supplied Phoenix linker by specifying PLINK86 and the PLINK link (CM__PLINK.LNK) file, which is shown in *Fig. 12-5*.

Cost Management can also be linked using internal overlays by specifying PLINK86 and the PLINK internal overlay link (CM__INT.LNK) file as shown in *Fig. 12-6*. In this example, internal overlays are created based on similarity of activities — expense activities are overlaid, receipt activities are overlaid, etc.

Cost Management can also be linked using an external overlay by specifying PLINK86 and the PLINK external overlay link (CM__EXT.LNK) file, as shown in *Fig. 12-7*. In this example, an external overlay named CM.OVL is created to hold all of the CM activity modules for expenses, receipts, maintenance, reports, operations, and file utilities. Note that program modules which may be common to all other modules (HELP, FUNC, and ERRORSYS) must not be placed in the external overlay.

Fig. 12-8 summarizes the different compile and link methods. Note that the smallest executable (CM.EXE) file is obtained with the use of an external overlay.

```
C> PLINK86 FI CM,HELP,FUNC,ERRORSYS LIB CLIPPER,EXTEND
```

-OR-

```
C> TLINK CM+HELP+FUNC+ERRORSYS,,,CLIPPER+EXTEND
```

Fig. 12-2. CM PLINK/LINK/TLINK commands.

```
# MAKE Utility for Cost Management (CM)
# =====================================
# Object code macros
# -----------------
obj01 = cm.obj
obj02 = d_inst.obj
obj03 = m_main.obj
obj04 = m_expn.obj e_expn.obj c_expn.obj v_expn.obj /
        s_expn.obj l_expn.obj
obj05 = m_rcpt.obj e_rcpt.obj c_rcpt.obj v_rcpt.obj /
        s_rcpt.obj l_rcpt.obj
obj06 = m_rprt.obj r_clnt.obj r_supp.obj r_type.obj /
        r_full.obj
obj07 = m_mnte.obj e_mnte.obj c_mnte.obj v_mnte.obj /
        l_mnte.obj
obj08 = m_oper.obj c_tone.obj c_cols.obj c_prtr.obj /
        c_name.obj
obj09 = m_file.obj d_back.obj d_rcll.obj d_indx.obj /
        d_summ.obj
obj10 = help.obj
obj11 = func.obj
obj12 = errorsys.obj

# Compile command
# ---------------
.prg.obj:
  CLIPPER $* -m -l

# Program files
# --------------
cm.obj              :cm.prg
  d_inst.obj        :d_inst.prg
  m_main.obj        :m_main.prg
    m_expn.obj      :m_expn.prg
      e_expn.obj    :e_expn.prg
      c_expn.obj    :c_expn.prg
      v_expn.obj    :v_expn.prg
      s_expn.obj    :s_expn.prg
      l_expn.obj    :l_expn.prg
    m_rcpt.obj      :m_rcpt.prg
      e_rcpt.obj    :e_rcpt.prg
      c_rcpt.obj    :c_rcpt.prg
      v_rcpt.obj    :v_rcpt.prg
      s_rcpt.obj    :s_rcpt.prg
      l_rcpt.obj    :l_rcpt.prg
    m_rprt.obj      :m_rprt.prg
      r_clnt.obj    :r_clnt.prg
      r_supp.obj    :r_supp.prg
      r_type.obj    :r_type.prg
      r_full.obj    :r_full.prg
```

Fig. 12-3. MAKE (CM.MAK) file.

```
     m_mnte.obj       :m_mnte.prg
       e_mnte.obj     :e_mnte.prg
       c_mnte.obj     :c_mnte.prg
       v_mnte.obj     :v_mnte.prg
       l_mnte.obj     :l_mnte.prg
     m_oper.obj       :m_oper.prg
       c_tone.obj     :c_tone.prg
       c_cols.obj     :c_cols.prg
       c_prtr.obj     :c_prtr.prg
       c_name.obj     :c_name.prg
     m_file.obj       :m_file.prg
       d_back.obj     :d_back.prg
       d_rcll.obj     :d_rcll.prg
       d_indx.obj     :d_indx.prg
       d_summ.obj     :d_summ.prg
help.obj              :help.prg
func.obj              :func.prg
errorsys.obj          :errorsys.prg

# Execute file
# ------------
cm.exe :$(obj01) $(obj02) $(obj03) $(obj04) $(obj05) /
       $(obj06) $(obj07) $(obj08) $(obj09) $(obj10) /
       $(obj11) $(obj12)

# Link command
# ------------
TLINK @CM_TLINK.LNK
```

Fig. 12-3. Continued.

```
CM+
D_INST+
M_MAIN+
M_EXPN+
E_EXPN+
C_EXPN+
V_EXPN+
S_EXPN+
L_EXPN+
M_RCPT+
E_RCPT+
C_RCPT+
V_RCPT+
S_RCPT+
L_RCPT+
M_RPRT+
R_CLNT+
R_SUPP+
R_TYPE+
R_FULL+
M_MNTE+
E_MNTE+
C_MNTE+
V_MNTE+
L_MNTE+
M_OPER+
C_TONE+
C_COLS+
C_PRTR+
C_NAME+
M_FILE+
D_BACK+
D_RCLL+
D_INDX+
D_SUMM+
HELP+
FUNC+
ERRORSYS
CM.EXE
NULL
CLIPPER+
EXTEND
```

Fig. 12-4. CM__TLINK.LNK link file for LINK/TLINK.

```
FI CM
FI D_INST
FI M_MAIN
FI M_EXPN
FI E_EXPN
FI C_EXPN
FI V_EXPN
FI S_EXPN
FI L_EXPN
FI M_RCPT
FI E_RCPT
FI C_RCPT
FI V_RCPT
FI S_RCPT
FI L_RCPT
FI M_RPRT
FI R_CLNT
FI R_SUPP
FI R_TYPE
FI R_FULL
FI M_MNTE
FI E_MNTE
FI C_MNTE
FI V_MNTE
FI L_MNTE
FI M_OPER
FI C_TONE
FI C_COLS
FI C_PRTR
FI C_NAME
FI M_FILE
FI D_BACK
FI D_RCLL
FI D_INDX
FI D_SUMM
FI HELP
FI FUNC
FI ERRORSYS
OUTPUT CM.EXE
LIB CLIPPER
LIB EXTEND
```

Fig. 12-5. CM_PLINK.LNK link file for PLINK86.

```
FI CM
FI D_INST,M_MAIN
FI HELP,FUNC,ERRORSYS
LIB CLIPPER,EXTEND,OVERLAY
OUTPUT CM.EXE
BEGINAREA
   SECTION FI M_EXPN,E_EXPN,C_EXPN,V_EXPN,S_EXPN,L_EXPN
   SECTION FI M_RCPT,E_RCPT,C_RCPT,V_RCPT,S_RCPT,L_RCPT
   SECTION FI M_RPRT,R_CLNT,R_SUPP,R_TYPE,R_FULL
   SECTION FI M_MNTE,E_MNTE,C_MNTE,V_MNTE,R_MNTE
   SECTION FI M_OPER,C_TONE,C_COLS,C_PRTR,C_NAME
   SECTION FI M_FILE,D_BACK,D_RCLL,D_INDX,D_SUMM
ENDAREA
```

Fig. 12-6. CM__INT.LNK internal overlay PLINK file.

```
FI CM
FI D_INST,M_MAIN
FI HELP,FUNC,ERRORSYS
LIB CLIPPER,EXTEND,OVERLAY
OUTPUT CM.EXE
BEGINAREA
   SECTION INTO CM FI M_EXPN,E_EXPN,C_EXPN,V_EXPN,S_EXPN,L_EXPN
   SECTION INTO CM FI M_RCPT,E_RCPT,C_RCPT,V_RCPT,S_RCPT,L_RCPT
   SECTION INTO CM FI M_RPRT,R_CLNT,R_SUPP,R_TYPE,R_FULL
   SECTION INTO CM FI M_MNTE,E_MNTE,C_MNTE,V_MNTE,R_MNTE
   SECTION INTO CM FI M_OPER,C_TONE,C_COLS,C_PRTR,C_NAME
   SECTION INTO CM FI M_FILE,D_BACK,D_RCLL,D_INDX,D_SUMM
ENDAREA
```

Fig. 12-7. CM__EXT.LNK external overlay PLINK file.

```
     Compile & Link Method          CM.EXE      CM.OVL
------------------------------      ----------  ----------
Compile CM,HELP,FUNC,ERRORSYS         256K         xxx
MAKE Utility                          267K         xxx
MAKE Utility Internal Overlays        270K         xxx
MAKE Utility External Overlay         232K         38K

Note: CLIPPER -l (no line numbers) used in all compilations
```

Fig. 12-8. Compile and Link summary.

## 13

Using DBU

Clipper Summer '87 includes a file manipulating tool called DBU which can be used to edit database files, as well as perform other direct file maintenance. DBU can be used during the application development cycle to create and modify database structures, index, browse, and edit as required. A comprehensive interface allows the programmer to perform database activities via pull-down menus and point-and-shoot selections. *Fig. 13-1* shows the initial DBU screen. The function keys are used to select the primary list of options.

The F1 key invokes a context-sensitive help system that provides assistance throughout a DBU session.

The F2 key activates a pull-down menu that allows the programmer to open a database, index, or view file as shown in *Fig. 13-2*. If the database option is selected, then a list of database files is displayed which may be scrolled to select the file to open. Alternatively, the programmer may also type-in the file to be opened.

The F3 key allows the programmer to create a database or index file, as well as modify an existing database file.

The F4 key allows the programmer to save a created or modified database file, as well as save the current view. DBU uses an environment approach that allows a group of files, indexes, fields, and relations to be retained in a view file for later recall and use. For example, the DBU environment shown in *Fig. 13-3* can be saved to a .VEW file for later recall and use.

The F5 key provides browse capability for individual database files and environment view files that have been previously set. It should be noted that accessing DBU from the DOS prompt, and specifying a file name, will automatically put DBU in the browse mode for that file.

The F6 key provides various database file utilities including COPY, APPEND, PACK, ZAP, and RUN. DBU's pull-down menu system only allows legitimate activities to be selected — a database must be opened before

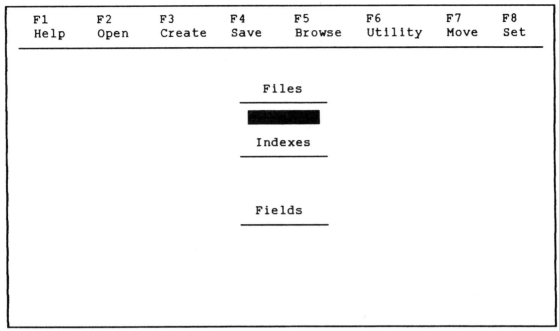

Fig. 13-1. DBU opening screen.

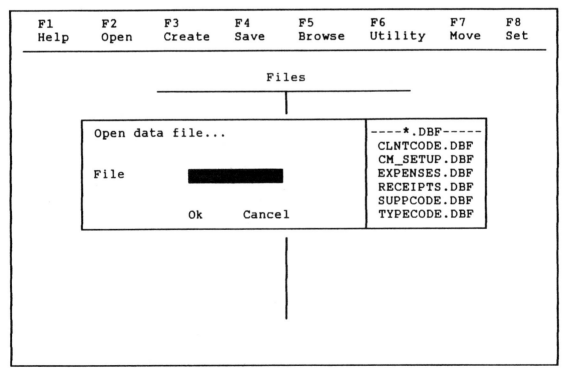

Fig. 13-2. DBU File Selection screen.

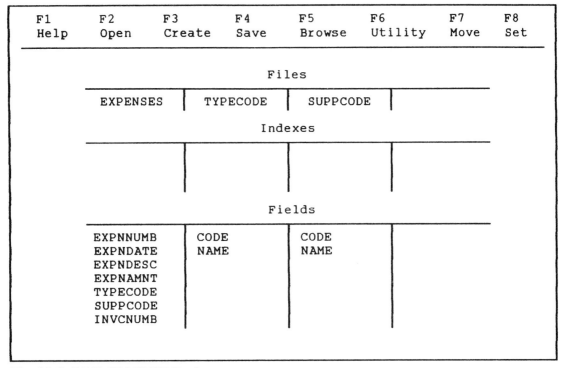

F1	F2	F3	F4	F5	F6	F7	F8
Help	Open	Create	Save	Browse	Utility	Move	Set

Files

EXPENSES	TYPECODE	SUPPCODE	

Indexes

Fields

EXPNNUMB	CODE	CODE	
EXPNDATE	NAME	NAME	
EXPNDESC			
EXPNAMNT			
TYPECODE			
SUPPCODE			
INVCNUMB			

Fig. 13-3. DBU CM.VEW Environment screen.

the ZAP option can be selected. DBU also displays warning/verification messages before a database command, such as PACK or ZAP, is executed.

The F7 key is used to manipulate the record pointer of an opened database file. Commands supported by DBU include SEEK, GOTO, LOCATE, and SKIP.

The F8 key allows various database SET commands to be executed, including SET FILTER and SET RELATION.

The source code for DBU is included with Clipper Summer '87 and must be compiled and linked to create the DBU.EXE file. A MAKEDBU.BAT batch file is also included to facilitate the compiling and linking.

14

Clipper
Telecommunications

Telecommunications capability can be added to Clipper applications by using the *SilverComm* library from SilverWare, Incorporated. This library contains over 65 communications functions that can be linked with a Clipper application to provide full-service telecommunications for a variety of purposes. The *SilverComm* library has been used in database applications for terminal emulation, file transfer, and bar-code reading.

The *SilverComm* library has even been used in conjunction with Clipper Summer '87 to develop a complete remote bulletin board system (RBBS). The *Silver Bullet,* authored by Larry Stewart and John Halovanic, is a fully-functional BBS that includes such features as private mail, multi-protocol file upload/download, user bulletins, message conferencing, and remote sysop utilities.

The *SilverComm* library contains low-level functions that provide full control over hardware communications ports. Many of the functions are specific solutions to unique programming situations; it is highly unlikely that one would need to use all of the available library functions in a given application.

SILVERCOMM DESCRIPTION
Several *SilverComm* functions are designed to be communications status indicators. The STATUSCD( ) function would be commonly used in any application, as it returns the status of the communications carrier detect signal. If a carrier is detected at the specified comm port, STATUSCD( ) will return a logical true (.T.).

The DEVICEPRES( ) function determines whether or not communications hardware is installed in the specified port. OPENCOMM( ) opens a port for communications with predetermined transmit and receive buffer sizes. The SETBAUD( ) function sets the operating parameters of a comm-

port, including baud rate, parity, stop bits, and data bits. CLOSECOMM( )
closes a communications port and releases the memory allocated by OPEN-
COMM( ).

Many functions are designed to evaluate and control the contents of the
receive buffer. Some of the functions are quite similar in the task that they
perform, but the *SilverComm* library is designed to provide all of the functions that might be needed to solve any programming problem.

For example, RXEMPTY( ) determines if the receive buffer is empty,
while RXFULL( ) determines if it is full. RXCOUNT( ) returns the
number of characters in the receive buffer, and RXFREE( ) returns the
amount of free space in the buffer, while RXOVFLOW( ) determines
whether or not there has been a receive buffer overflow.

Character strings are also handled with a variety of specific functions.
RXCHARLOOK( ) peeks at the next character in the receive buffer.
RXECHOCHAR( ) not only peeks at the next character, but also returns it
to the display screen. The RXSTRING( ) function is used to receive a
string transmitted by a remote terminal, and includes options for specified
timeout and backspace editing.

Similarly, many functions are designed to the status and control of the
transmit buffers. For example, TXEMPTY( ) determines if the transmit
buffer is empty, while TXFULL( ) determines if it is full. TXCOUNT( )
returns the number of characters in the transmit buffer and TXFREE( )
returns the amount of free space in the buffer. TXBLOCK( ) determines
whether the transmit buffer is blocked and, if so, why it is blocked. The
TXCHAR( ) function places a character in the transmit buffer.
TXSTRING( ) places a string of characters in the buffer.

SWTXMORE( ) is a powerful function that transmits a string of characters per a defined format. For example, a text file can be transmitted ten
lines at a time, with the receiving user prompted (by the library function) to
continue at the end of each ten lines before another ten lines are transmitted.

Two functions are provided for interactive terminal emulation. SWE-
MANSI( ) provides ANSI emulation, while SWEMTTY( ) provides
standard TTY terminal emulation.

SilverComm contains various functions for controlling smart
MODEMs. The ones that would most likely be used in any application are
SMDIAL( ) and SMRESET( ). The SMDIALMODE( ) function can be
used to set the dial mode (tone or pulse).

The *SilverComm* library also includes three screen display functions.
The SCROLLUP( ) function can be used for window scrolling, and is
similar to the Clipper SCROLL( ) function. SETCURPOS( ) sets the
cursor position at a specified row and column, and SWPUTCHAR( )
displays a specified character at the current row and column.

```
STATUS/CONTROL
   CHECKLSTAT( )     Has line status interrup occurred?
   CHECKMSTAT( )     Has MODEM status interrupt occurred?
   CHECKRING( )      Has phone rung?
   CLRRINGCNT( )     Get value of internal ring counter and clear it
   CONTROLDTR( )     Control DTR signal
   CONTROLRTS( )     Control RTS signal
   ENRTSCTS( )       Enable/disable RTS/CTS flow control
   GETRINGCNT( )     Get number of times phone rang
   STATUSBI( )       Get status of break interrupt bit
   STATUSCD( )       Get status of carier detect signal
   STATUSCTS( )      Get status of CTS signal
   STATUSDSR( )      Get status of DSR signal
   STATUSFE( )       Status of UART framing bit error
   STATUSOR( )       Status of UART overrun bit
   STATUSPE( )       Status of UART parity error bit
   STATUSRI( )       Get status of RI signal
GENERAL PORT CONTROL
   CLOSECOMM( )      Close comm port
   DEVICEPRES( )     Is COMM device installed?
   OPENCOMM( )       Open comm port
   SETBAUD( )        Set baud rate, parity, stop bits, & data bits
RECEIVE DATA
   RXCHAR( )         Get a character from the receive buffer
   RXCHARDLY( )      Wait specified seconds for specified characters
   RXCHRLOOK( )      Look at next character in receive buffer
   RXCOUNT( )        Number of characters in receive buffer
   RXECHOCHAR( )     Get character from recv buff and echo to screen
   RXEMPTY( )        Is receive buffer empty?
   RXFLUSH( )        Empty receive buffer
   RXFREE( )         Free space in receive buffer
   RXFULL( )         Is receive buffer full?
   RXOVFLOW( )       Has receive buffer overflowed?
   RXSTRING( )       Receive a string (editing & timeout options)
   RXSTRINGER( )     Returns status of last RXSTRING( ) call
TRANSMIT DATA
   SWTXMORE( )       Transmit a string (with prompt for more)
   TXBLOCKED( )      Is transmitter blocked and why?
   TXBREAK( )        Transmit a break signal
   TXCHAR( )         Put a character in the transmit buffer
   TXCOUNT( )        Number of characters in transmit buffer
   TXEMPTY( )        Is transmit buffer empty?
   TXFLUSH( )        Empty transmit buffer
   TXFREE( )         Free space in transmit buffer
   TXFULL( )         Is transmit buffer full?
   TXSTRING( )       Transmit a string
TERMINAL EMULATION
   SWEANSI( )        ANSI terminal emulation
   SWEMTTY( )        TTY terminal emulation
```

Fig. 14-1. SilverComm Functions summary.

```
SMARTMODEM
  SMAUTOANSW()      Control Smart MODEM auto-answer
  SMDIAL()          Dial a number on smart MODEM
  SMDIALMODE()      Set smart MODEM dialing mode (tone or pulse)
  SMESCAPE()        Send escape command to smart MODEM
  SMFULLHALF()      Enable/disable smart MODEM full/half duplex
  SMQUIET()         Enable/disable smart MODEM result codes
  SMREADREG()       Send command to query internal registers
  SMRESET()         Reset smart MODEM
  SMSETREG()        Set smart MODEM internal register
  SMSWHOOK()        Set smart MODEM on/off hook
  SMVERBOSE()       Enable/disable verbose smart MODEM result codes
GENERAL
  SWASYNCREV()      Returns SilverComm revison
  SWASYNCVER()      Returns SilverComm version
  SWDELAY().        Delays the specified number of .0549 seconds
  SWFILESIZE()      Gets the size (in bytes) of a file
  SWGTIME()         Gets the number of seconds since 01/01/1970
SCREEN DISPLAY
  SCROLLUP()        Scroll a window
  SETCURPOS()       Set cursor position
  SWPUTCHAR()       Write a character to the screen
XMODEM
  RXXMODEM()        Receive a file using XMODEM protocol
  TXXBLOCKS()       Number of 128 byte blocks in a file
  TXXMODEM()        Transmit a file using XMODEM protocol
  TXXTIME()         Calculate approximate transfer time using XMODEM
```

Fig. 14-1. Continued.

SilverComm provides functions that are useful in XMODEM protocol file transfers. The function TXXMODEM(   ) is used to transmit a file via XMODEM, and RXXMODEM(   ) is used to receive a file via XMODEM.

Fig. 14-1 shows a summary and brief description of all *SilverComm* library functions.

CMX TERMINAL OPTION

The example program in *Fig. 14-2* shows how *SilverComm* functions can be used with Clipper to provide data communications. The CMX terminal program is designed for MODEM communications between the CM user and a remote terminal. It is a simple-to-use terminal application in that the user simply presses D to dial the remote terminal, or Q to quit.

CMX only accomodates a single phone number entry which, in a typical business operating environment, would probably be all that is needed. Communications parameters may be changed to match the user's hardware configuration, as shown in the CMX setup screen of *Fig. 14-3.* The setup screen is obtained by entering CMX followed by a space and any other

```
* Program Name .......... cmx.prg
* Revised Date .......... 04/01/88
* Description .......... CMX Communications Terminal Program -
*                        Written entirely in Clipper Summer '87
*                        using SilverComm communications library
*
*
*
*
*
*
*
*
*
*
*
*
*
*
*
*
*
*
```

Structure for CMX.DBF			
Field	Field Name	Type	Width
01	CMXPHONE	Char	16
02	COMMINIT	Char	30
03	CALLINIT	Char	30
04	COMMPORT	Num	1
05	STOPBITS	Num	1
06	DATABITS	Num	1
07	PARTYBIT	Num	1
08	BAUDRATE	Num	4
09	ANSIGRAF	Log	1
10	COLORSET	Log	1

```
PARAMETERS passed
CLEAR
SET SCOREBOARD(.F.)
SET CONFIRM(.T.)
SET BELL(.F.)
SET WRAP(.T.)
SET MESSAGE TO
*
IF ! FILE("CMX.DBF")
   SETCOLOR("W+*")
     @ 10,33 SAY "Installing ..."
   SETCOLOR("W")
   SET CURSOR(.F.)
   CREATE dummy
   STORE "CMXPHONEC16 " TO field1
   STORE "COMMINITC30 " TO field2
   STORE "CALLINITC30 " TO field3
   STORE "COMMPORTN1 0" TO field4
   STORE "STOPBITSN1 0" TO field5
   STORE "DATABITSN1 0" TO field6
   STORE "PARTYBITN1 0" TO field7
   STORE "BAUDRATEN4 0" TO field8
   STORE "ANSIGRAFL1  " TO field9
   STORE "COLORSETL1  " TO field10
```

Fig. 14-2. CMX Comm Terminal source code.

```
  FOR i = 1 TO 10
    IF i < 10
      STORE "field"+str(i,1) TO fn
    ELSE
      STORE "field"+str(i,2) TO fn
    ENDIF
    APPEND BLANK
    REPLACE field_name WITH SUBSTR(&fn,1,8)
    REPLACE field_type WITH SUBSTR(&fn,9,1)
    REPLACE field_len  WITH VAL(substr(&fn,10,2))
    REPLACE field_dec  WITH VAL(substr(&fn,12,1))
  NEXT
  CREATE cmx.dbf FROM dummy
  CLOSE DATABASES
  ERASE dummy.dbf
  USE cmx
  APPEND BLANK
  REPLACE cmxphone WITH " -1-713-251-3319"
  REPLACE comminit WITH "&C1&D2&W", callinit WITH "ATM1"
  REPLACE commport WITH 2, stopbits WITH 1, databits WITH 8,;
          partybit WITH 0, baudrate WITH 1200
  REPLACE ansigraf WITH .F., colorset WITH .F.
  CLOSE DATABASES
  SET CURSOR(.T.)
  CLEAR
ENDIF
*
PUBLIC mcmxphone, mcomminit, mcallinit, mcommport, mstopbits,;
       mdatabits, mpartybit, mbaudrate, mansigraf, mcolorset
PUBLIC cnorm, cinve, cblnk
*
USE cmx
STORE cmxphone TO mcmxphone
STORE comminit TO mcomminit
STORE callinit TO mcallinit
STORE commport TO mcommport
STORE stopbits TO mstopbits
STORE databits TO mdatabits
STORE partybit TO mpartybit
STORE baudrate TO mbaudrate
STORE ansigraf TO mansigraf
STORE colorset TO mcolorset
CLOSE DATABASES
*
DO setcols
*
```

Fig. 14-2. Continued.

```
IF pcount() > 0                    && if a parameter is passed,
  DO commset                       && do setup
ENDIF
*
SETCOLOR(cblnk)
  @ 10,28 SAY "Initializing equipment..."
SETCOLOR(cnorm)
SET CURSOR(.F.)
*
IF ! DEVICEPRES(mcommport)         && is a COMM device installed?
  ? CHR(7)
  CLEAR
  SET CURSOR(.T.)
  QUIT
ENDIF
*
error = OPENCOMM(mcommport,2000,400)        && open comm port
SWDELAY(1 * 18)
IF error <> 0
  ? CHR(7)
  CLEAR
  SET CURSOR(.T.)
  QUIT
ENDIF
*
error = SMRESET(mcommport)         && reset MODEM and then ...
SWDELAY(1 * 18)
IF error <> 0
  ? CHR(7)
  CLEAR
  SET CURSOR(.T.)
  QUIT
ENDIF
*
IF RXEMPTY(mcommport)              && should get MODEM response
  ? CHR(7)
  CLEAR
  SET CURSOR(.T.)
  QUIT
ENDIF
*
error = SETBAUD(mcommport,mbaudrate,mpartybit,mstopbits,mdatabits)
SWDELAY(1 * 18)
IF error <> 0
  ? CHR(7)
  CLEAR
  SET CURSOR(.T.)
  QUIT
ENDIF
*
```

Fig. 14-2. Continued.

```
RXFLUSH(mcommport)                      && flush (empty) rx buffer
TXSTRING(mcommport,ALLTRIM(mcomminit)+CHR(13))
*
RXFLUSH(mcommport)                      && flush (empty) rx buffer
TXSTRING(mcommport,ALLTRIM(mcallinit)+CHR(13))
*
RXFLUSH(mcommport)                      && flush (empty) rx buffer
TXCHAR(mcommport,CHR(12))
*
SET CURSOR(.T.)
*
DO terminal WITH mcommport,mbaudrate,mpartybit,mstopbits,mdatabits
*
CLEAR
SETCOLOR(cnorm)
  @ 00,00 SAY SPACE(80)
SETCOLOR(cblnk)
  @ 10,29 SAY "Resetting equipment..."
SETCOLOR(cnorm)
SET CURSOR(.F.)
SMESCAPE(mcommport)                     && send escape command
SMSWHOOK(mcommport,"0")                 && go on-hook
SWDELAY(1 * 18)
CLOSECOMM(mcommport)                    && close comm port
SWDELAY(1 * 18)
RELEASE ALL
CLEAR
SET CURSOR(.T.)
QUIT
*
PROCEDURE terminal
PARAMETERS mcommport,mbaudrate,mpartybit,mstopbits,mdatabits
CLEAR
DO WHILE .T.
  @ 00,00
  mtask = 1
  SETCOLOR(cinve)
  IF STATUSCD(mcommport)            && carrier detect
    @ 00,00 SAY SPACE(29)+"[D]isconnect    [Q]uit"+SPACE(29)
  ELSE
    @ 00,00 SAY SPACE(29)+"[D]ial          [Q]uit"+SPACE(29)
  ENDIF
    @ 00,30 PROMPT "D"
    @ 00,46 PROMPT "Q"
  MENU TO mtask
  SETCOLOR(cnorm)
```

Fig. 14-2. Continued.

```
      DO CASE
        CASE mtask = 1
          IF STATUSCD(mcommport)        && carrier detect
            ? CHR(7)
            SETCOLOR(cinve)
              @ 00,00
            SETCOLOR(cinve+"*")
              @ 00,32 SAY "Disconnecting..."
            SETCOLOR(cnorm)
            SMESCAPE(mcommport)         && send escape command
            SMSWHOOK(mcommport,"0")     && go on-hook
            SWDELAY(1 * 18)
          ELSE
            SMDIAL(mcommport,mcmxphone)          && dial number
            IF ! mansigraf
              commexit = "Alt-F10"
              DO statline WITH mcommport,mbaudrate,commexit
              SWEMTTY(mcommport,1,24,7,7)        && standard TTY
            ELSE
              commexit = "Esc"
              DO statline WITH mcommport,mbaudrate,commexit
              SWEMANSI(mcommport,27)             && ANSI
            ENDIF
            CLEAR
          ENDIF
        CASE mtask = 2
          EXIT
      ENDCASE
ENDDO
CLEAR
RETURN
*
PROCEDURE statline
PARAMETERS mcommport,mbaudrate,commexit
SETCOLOR(cinve)
  @ 00,00
  @ 00,00 SAY "    "+commexit+" = Exit"
  @ 00,40 SAY "Comm Port = "+STR(mcommport,1)
  @ 00,61 SAY "Baud Rate = "+LTRIM(STR(mbaudrate,4))
SETCOLOR(cnorm)
SETCURPOS(1,0)
RETURN
*
```

Fig. 14-2. Continued.

```
PROCEDURE commset
SETCOLOR(cnorm)
   @ 02,27 SAY "CMX Terminal Software Setup"
   @ 03,27 SAY "―――――――――――――――――――――――――"
   @ 05,10 TO 18,70 DOUBLE
   @ 07,12 SAY "CMX Number ........"
   @ 08,12 SAY "Comm Prefix ......."
   @ 09,12 SAY "Call Prefix ......."
   @ 10,12 SAY "Comm Port ........."
   @ 11,12 SAY "Stop Bits ........."
   @ 12,12 SAY "Data Bits ........."
   @ 13,12 SAY "Parity ............"
   @ 14,12 SAY "Baud Rate ........."
   @ 15,12 SAY "ANSI Graphics ....."
   @ 16,12 SAY "Color Display ....."
SETCOLOR(cinve)
   @ 07,32 SAY mcmxphone
   @ 08,32 SAY mcomminit
   @ 09,32 SAY mcallinit
   @ 10,32 SAY "COM"+STR(mcommport,1)
   @ 11,32 SAY STR(mstopbits,1)
   @ 12,32 SAY STR(mdatabits,1)
DO CASE
   CASE mpartybit = 0
     @ 13,32 say "None"
   CASE mpartybit = 1
     @ 13,32 say "Odd "
   CASE mpartybit = 2
     @ 13,32 say "Even"
ENDCASE
   @ 14,32 SAY STR(mbaudrate,4)
   @ 15,32 SAY IF(mansigraf,"Yes","No ")
   @ 16,32 SAY IF(mcolorset,"Yes","No ")
SETCOLOR(cnorm)

DO WHILE .T.

   @ 07,32 GET mcmxphone PICTURE "#-#-###-###-####"
   @ 08,32 GET mcomminit PICTURE "@!"
   @ 09,32 GET mcallinit PICTURE "@!"
   READ

   mchoice = IIF(mcommport=1,1,2)
   @ 10,37 SAY "<- use || to scan choices"
   @ 10,32 PROMPT "COM1"
   @ 10,32 PROMPT "COM2"
   CLEAR TYPEAHEAD
   MENU TO mchoice
   mcommport = mchoice
```

Fig. 14-2. Continued.

```
mchoice = IIF(mstopbits=0,1,2)
@ 10,37 SAY SPACE(25)
@ 11,37 SAY "<- use || to scan choices"
@ 11,32 PROMPT "0"
@ 11,32 PROMPT "1"
CLEAR TYPEAHEAD
MENU TO mchoice
mstopbits = IIF(mchoice=1,0,1)

mchoice = IIF(mdatabits=7,1,2)
@ 11,37 SAY SPACE(25)
@ 12,37 SAY "<- use || to scan choices"
@ 12,32 PROMPT "7"
@ 12,32 PROMPT "8"
CLEAR TYPEAHEAD
MENU TO mchoice
mdatabits = IIF(mchoice=1,7,8)

mchoice = mpartybit + 1
@ 12,37 SAY SPACE(25)
@ 13,37 SAY "<- use || to scan choices"
@ 13,32 PROMPT "None"
@ 13,32 PROMPT "Odd "
@ 13,32 PROMPT "Even"
CLEAR TYPEAHEAD
MENU TO mchoice
mpartybit = mchoice - 1

mchoice = IIF(mbaudrate=1200,1,2)
@ 13,37 SAY SPACE(25)
@ 14,37 SAY "<- use || to scan choices"
@ 14,32 PROMPT "1200"
@ 14,32 PROMPT "2400"
CLEAR TYPEAHEAD
MENU to mchoice
mbaudrate = IIF(mchoice=1,1200,2400)

mchoice = IIF(mansigraf,1,2)
@ 14,37 SAY SPACE(25)
@ 15,37 SAY "<- use || to scan choices"
@ 15,32 PROMPT "Yes"
@ 15,32 PROMPT "No "
CLEAR TYPEAHEAD
MENU to mchoice
mansigraf = IIF(mchoice=1,.t.,.f.)
```

Fig. 14-2. Continued.

```
mchoice = IIF(mcolorset,1,2)
@ 15,37 SAY SPACE(25)
@ 16,37 SAY "<- use || to scan choices"
@ 16,32 PROMPT "Yes"
@ 16,32 PROMPT "No "
CLEAR TYPEAHEAD
MENU to mchoice
mcolorset = IIF(mchoice=1,.t.,.f.)
@ 16,37 SAY SPACE(25)

mchoice = 1
@ 22,32 PROMPT "Save"
@ 22,37 PROMPT "Revise"
@ 22,44 PROMPT "Abort"
CLEAR TYPEAHEAD
MENU to mchoice
@ 22,00 CLEAR
DO CASE
   CASE mchoice = 1
     USE cmx
     REPLACE cmxphone WITH mcmxphone, comminit WITH mcomminit,;
             callinit WITH mcallinit
     REPLACE commport WITH mcommport, databits WITH mdatabits,;
             partybit WITH mpartybit, baudrate WITH mbaudrate,;
             ansigraf WITH mansigraf, colorset WITH mcolorset
     CLOSE DATABASES
     DO setcols
     EXIT
   CASE mchoice = 2
     LOOP
   CASE mchoice = 3 .or. LASTKEY() = 27
     EXIT
   ENDCASE
ENDDO
CLEAR
RETURN

PROCEDURE setcols
IF ! mcolorset
  cnorm = "W/N,N/W,N,,N/W"
  cinve = "N/W"
  cblnk = "W+*/N"
ELSE
  cnorm = "GR+/N,W+/GR,N,,W+/GR"
  cinve = "W+/GR"
  cblnk = "GR+*/N"
ENDIF
RETURN
```

Fig. 14-2. Continued.

CMX Terminal Software Setup

```
CMX Number ........  -1-713-251-3319
COMM Prefix .......  &C1&D2&W
CallPrefix ........  ATM1
Comm Port .........  COM2
Stop Bits .........  1
Data Bits .........  8
Parity ...........  None
Baud Rate .........  1200
ANSI Graphics .....  Yes
Color Display .....  Yes
```

Fig. 14-3. CMX Comm Terminal setup screen.

```
TLINK CMX,,,CLIPPER EXTEND SWASYNC

*    where CLIPPER, EXTEND, and SWASYNC libraries are in the
*    directory path
```

Fig. 14-4. Linking CMX.

character (i.e. entering CMX X from the DOS prompt activates the setup screen).

CMX may be used as a stand-alone communcations program, or may be integrated within another Clipper application. Other options could be easily incorporated using *SilverComm* and Clipper, such as a dialing directory and file transfer capability.

Using the SilverComm library simply requires linking SWASYNC.LIB with Clipper libraries, as shown in *Fig. 14-4* for the communications terminal (CMX) example. CMX could be easily incorporated into the Cost Management application to provide remote terminal communications.

## 15

Clipper Graphics

The same company that authored the *SilverComm* communications library for Clipper also has available a video enhancement library for Clipper called *SilverPaint.* This library contains over 25 functions that can be used to develop graphics presentations, animations, and even sound effects. *Silver-Paint* supports CGA, EGA, VGA, and Hercules, and includes an interface that allows picture files, such as those created with Microsoft's *Paintbrush,* to be displayed by a Clipper application. *Silverpaint* also supports a powerful XOR function whereby a graphic can be displayed on top of another graphic, without disturbing the original design.

SILVERPAINT DESCRIPTION

The graphics functions in *SilverPaint* are used much like any other Clipper user-defined functions. Parameters must be defined and then passed to the graphics library function. In most cases, screen location parameters are defined by picture element (pixel) x and y coordinates. A medium resolution (CGA-4 color) graphic screen is normally 320 pixels wide (x) by 200 pixels high (y), while Hercules is 720 by 348, EGA (16-colors) is 640 by 350, and VGA (16-colors) is 640 by 480. Each pixel is capable of creating a single color dot on the graphics display screen.

SilverPaint allows the Clipper programmer to display lines, boxes, and circles by calling a library function with the pixel and color information. For example, to display a solid line on the video display, the starting and ending pixels are defined with x and y coordinates and then passed, along with a color parameter, to the *SilverPaint* function SWLINE( ). The example of *Fig. 15-1* shows the function syntax and illustrates how to display a horizontal line. A similar line function in *SilverPaint* is SWLINETO( ) which draws a line from the specified x and y pixel coordinates to the specified SWSETORIGEN( ) origin coordinates.

```
startmode = SWSETVMODE(-1)      && store current video mode
SWSETVMODE(4)                   && set graphics video mode (CGA)
x1 = 0                          && starting pixel x coordinate
y1 = 0                          && starting pixel y coordinate
x2 = 319                        && ending pixel x coordinate
y2 = 199                        && ending pixel y coordinate
color = 1                       && line color
SWLINE(x1,y1,x2,y2,color)       && draw the line
SWSETVMODE(startmode)           && restore original video mode
```

Fig. 15-1. SWLINE( ) function.

Drawing a box is accomplished by passing the four corner-pixel coordinates, color parameter, and fill (yes or no) option to the *SilverPaint* SWBOX( ) function, as shown in *Fig. 15-2*. Remember that because pixels are used to specify x and y coordinates, the resulting box is not limited to only row and column displacement, nor is it limited to only horizontal and vertical sides.

Circles and ellipses may be displayed with the SWCIRCLE( ) function. The center-pixel x and y coordinates, radius, color, and aspect ratio are passed to the *SilverPaint* function as shown in *Fig. 15-3*. In medium resolution, an aspect ration of 5/6 produces a circle, while an aspect ratio less than 5/6 produces an ellipse that is wider than it is high.

A single-color dot pixel may be displayed using the SWWRITE-DOT( ) function, and the color attribute of a displayed pixel can be found with the SWREADDOT( ) function. The SWPALETTE( ) function can be used to set or change the foreground and background colors of the current palette.

A character string may be displayed using the SWCOATSAY( ) function which, unlike most other *SilverPaint* graphics functions, uses the standard row and column parameter syntax to display the information. SWCOATSAY( ) results in a 40-column display of text, in medium resolution, at the specified row and column as shown in the *Fig. 15-4* example.

Picture files that have been created with Microsoft's *PaintBrush* or ZSoft's *PC Paintbrush* can be displayed with *SilverPaint's* SWPOP-

```
startmode = SWSETVMODE(-1)        && store current video mode
SWSETVMODE(4)                     && set graphics video mode (CGA)
ulx = 100                         && upper left pixel x coordinate
uly = 60                          && upper left pixel y coordinate
lrx = 200                         && lower right pixel x coordinate
lry = 150                         && lower right pixel y coordinate
color = 1                         && box outline color
fill = 1                          && box fill (yes)
SWBOX(ulx,uly,lrx,lry,color,fill) && draw and fill the box
SWSETVMODE(startmode)             && restore original video mode
```

Fig. 15-2. SWBOX( ) function.

```
startmode = SWSETVMODE(-1)          && store current video mode
SWSETVMODE(4)                       && set graphics video mode (CGA)
x = 160                             && center pixel x coordinate
y = 100                             && center pixel y coordinate
rad = 50                            && radius in pixels
color = 1                           && circle color
num = 5                             && aspect ration numerator
den = 6                             && aspect ratio denominator
SWCIRCLE(x,y,rad,color,num,den)     && draw the circle
SWSETVMODE(startmode)               && restore original video mode
```

Fig. 15-3. SWCIRCLE( ) function.

```
startmode = SWSETVMODE(-1)          && store current video mode
SWSETVMODE(4)                       && set graphics video mode (CGA)
row = 10                            && row number
col = 10                            && column number
color = 1                           && text color
str = "SilverPaint"                 && text
SWCOATSAY(row,col,color,str)        && display the text (40 col mode)
SWSETVMODE(startmode)               && restore original video mode
```

Fig. 15-4. SWCOATSAY( ) function.

```
i = 1
freq = 200                          && beginning frequency
fcount = 10                         && freq counts
lcount = 130                        && loop counts
dur = 500                           && duration
SWSETSOUND(1)                       && presets sound durations
DO WHILE i < 6
   SWFORSOUND(beg,end,fcount,lcount,dur)
   i = i + 1
ENDDO
SWSETSOUND(0)
```

Fig. 15-5. SWFORSOUND( ) function.

```
x = 0
i = 1
SWSRAND(i)                            && seeds the swrand() function
DO WHILE i < 100
  x = SWRAND()%1999                   && random number generation
  IF x = 32
    SWSOUND(x,1)                      && freq = x
  ENDIF
  i = i + 1
ENDDO
```

Fig. 15-6. SWSOUND( ) function.

SLIDE( ) function. This lets the artistic programmer design custom front-ends, such as company headings and logos, for use in Clipper applications.

As if the graphics functions were not enough, *Silverpaint* also includes a library of sound functions that can be used to generate just about any type of noise. Sirens, warbles, tick-tocks, and water-in-the-floppy sounds can be easily created using *Silverpaint*.

```
SWBOX()         Draws a box or rectangle
SWCIRCLE()      Draws a circle or an ellipse
SWCOATSAY()     Displays a character string
SWDELAY()       Delays the specified number of .0549 seconds
SWFORSOUND()    Generates complex, high-speed tones
SWGCLS()        Clears the graphics screen
SWGETMAXC()     Returns the maximum color value for current video
SWGETMAXX()     Gets the maximum value of x for a set video mode
SWGETMAXY()     Gets the maximum value of y for a set video mode
SWGETVMODE()    Gets the current video mode
SWGETXORV()     Returns the XOR offset value
SWISEGA()       Detects EGA video hardware
SWISHERC()      Detects Hercules video hardware
SWISVGA()       Detects VGA video hardware
SWLINE()        Draws a line
SWLINETO()      Draws a line from a specified origin point
SWPAINTREV()    Returns the SWPAINT revision
SWPAINTVER()    Returns the SWPAINT version
SWPALETTE()     Sets the color palette
SWPOPSLIDE()    Reads a picture file (MS or PC Paintbrush)
SWQDELAY()      Delays the specified number of .000015 seconds
SWRAND()        Generates a random number
SWREADDOT()     Reads the color attribute of the specified pixel
SWSETORIGN()    Sets the origin point for SWLINETO()
SWSETSOUND()    Sets the internal timer duration using DMA timebase
SWSETVMODE()    Sets the video mode
SWSOUND()       Generates a sound of defined frequency and duration
SWSOUNDOFF()    Turns sound off
SWSOUNDON()     Generates a sound of defined frequency
SWSRAND()       Seeds the random number generator SWRAND()
SWWRITEDOT()    Writes a dot at the specified pixel coordinates
```

Fig. 15-7. SilverPaint functions summary.

```
TLINK FILES,,,CLIPPER EXTEND SWPAINT
```

```
*   where the CLIPPER, EXTEND, and SWPAINT libraries are in the
*   directory path, and FILES includes the object code filenames
```

Fig. 15-8. **Linking SilverPaint.**

The *Silverpaint* SWFORSOUND( ) functions by passing parameters to an internal complex of C and assembler logic that simulates a Clipper FOR..NEXT loop. The assembler routine actually calls low-level sound routines resulting in very high-speed, complex tone generation. The starting frequency, frequency step, loop step, and duration are defined as shown in the *Fig. 15-5* example.

The SWSOUND( ) function can be used to generate a tone at the defined frequency and duration. This function may be combined with the *SilverPaint* random number generating function, SWRAND( ), to create sounds of random frequency and duration, as shown in the *Fig. 15-6* example.

SWSETSOUND( ) is used to pre-define the tone delay duration for both SWSOUND( ) and SWFORSOUND( ). It uses the DMA controller as the time base, allowing *SilverPaint* to create complex sounds that other sound libraries cannot match.

Fig. 15-7 shows a summary and brief description of all *SilverPaint* functions.

Using the *SilverPaint* library requires linking SWPAINT.LIB with other Clipper libraries, as shown in *Fig. 15-8.*

CM OPENING LOGO OPTION

The source code shown in *Fig. 15-9* utilizes *SilverPaint* graphics and sounds to create an alternate opening logo for the Cost Management application example. Comments inserted in the code listing further explain the use of *SilverPaint's* functions.

```
* Program Name ......... logo.prg
* Revised Date ......... 07/01/88
* Description .......... Optional Opening Logo for CM (requires
*                       (requires SilverPaint Library)
*
startmode = SWSETVMODE(-1) && returns current video mode
clear

PRIVATE string[18]         && declare an array
string[01] = " "
string[02] = "C"
string[03] = "O"
string[04] = "S"
string[05] = "T"
string[06] = "-"
string[07] = "M"
string[08] = "A"
string[09] = "N"
string[10] = "A"
string[11] = "G"
string[12] = "E"
string[13] = "M"
string[14] = "E"
string[15] = "N"
string[16] = "T"
string[17] = " "

SWSETVMODE(4)              && sets video mode at 320x200 CGA

SWCOATSAY(03,14,1,"GLB SOFTWARE")

SWDELAY(2*18)             && a two second delay

SWCOATSAY(07,16,1,"presents")

SWDELAY(2*18)             && a two second delay

SWBOX(020,100,300,170,2,0) && draws a box
SWBOX(030,110,290,160,2,1) && draws a box and fills it

FOR i = 1 TO 17
   SWCOATSAY(15,10+i,3," ")         && displays COSTS-MANAGEMENT one
   SWCOATSAY(16,10+i,3,string[i]) && character at a time with a
   SWCOATSAY(17,10+i,3," ")         && chirp between each character
   SWSOUND(2500,1)
NEXT

SWDELAY(5*18)             && a five second delay
SWSETVMODE(startmode)     && reset video mode
RETURN
```

Fig. 15-9. CM Logo.

## 16

Clipper Function Libraries

Maybe one of the greatest advantages of using Clipper, aside from it's speed and open architecture, is the amount of third-party support it has received. Chapters 14 and 15 have already discussed add-on libraries for communications and graphics. But there are many, many more Clipper add-ons in the form of low-cost, specialized function libraries that are readily available to the Clipper programmer. This chapter will briefly focus on two of them, both of which have versions compatible with the new Clipper Summer '87 version.

PROFESSIONAL CLIPPER LIBRARY (PROCLIP)

One popular functions library is *Professional Clipper* by Jason Matthews. ProClip contains various cursor and display functions, as well as a few keyboard and file functions.

A dynamic clock function, named CLOCK( ), can continuously display real time anywhere on the screen per a selected color and format. For example, to continuously display a clock on the screen using 2400 format (with seconds) and a red-on-white color combination, the following function syntax is used:

@ 00,00 SAY CLOCK("ON","24 HOUR","SECONDS","R/W")

The file attributes function FILEATTR( ) can be used to set, or reset, a file's attributes, which can be useful in applications as a means of helping to prevent unauthorized (or unwanted) file erasure. For example, at the start of an application, in order to remove the write-protect attribute of a database file, the following function syntax is used:

FILEATTR("EXPENSES.DBF ","-R/O")

At the close of an application, in order to add write-protection to the same file, the following function syntax is used:

FILEATTR("EXPENSES.DBF","+R/O")

A real handy function to place in many Clipper applications is ProClip's UNRESET( ) function. This function is capable of intercepting the Control – Alternate – Delete keyboard reset — either diabling it or providing a warning to the user as to whether this is really what the user wants to do. The following use of UNRESET( ) totally disables the Control – Alternate – Delete sequence reset:

UNRESET("ON")

A complete listing of ProClip functions, along with a brief description of each, is shown in *Fig. 16-1.*

BREEZE WINDOWS LIBRARY

A very popular windows library for Clipper is produced by a company called Logitek. *The Breeze* library contains over 30 windowing functions that can enhance an application's user-interface. With *The Breeze,* programmers can do both full and partial screen saves, move both full and partial windows, and write directly to both displayed and non-displayed windows. Up to 99 different windows can be defined using *The Breeze.*

A window select area must first be determined in order to create and display a window. Remembering that up to 99 different select areas may be initialized, the following BREEZE function keeps it simple by starting with area number 1:

WSELECT(01)

Now, in order to create a window that is 10 rows high, 50 columns wide, positioned at row 5 column 5 (upper left-hand corner of the window), and is colored white on a blue background, the following *Breeze* function is used:

WUSE(10,50,05,05,"W/B")

So far, a window has been created and placed in a window select area, but has not yet been displayed. To do so means using the following function and syntax:

WDISPLAY(01)

This displays the window at the predefined coordinates. The function parameters can be modified, however, to display the same window but at different (row 6, column 6) screen coordinates, as follows:

WDISPLAY(01,06,06)

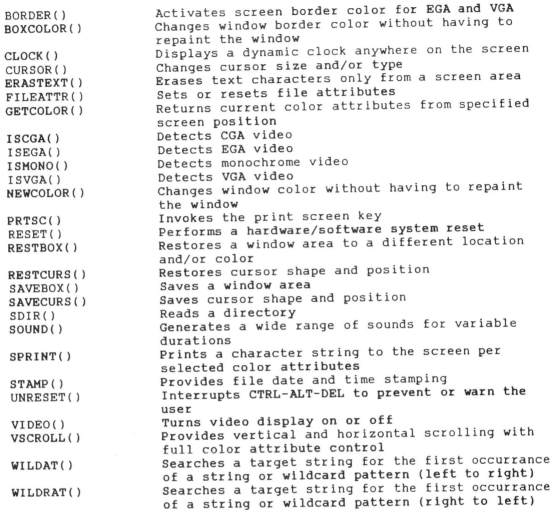

BORDER( )	Activates screen border color for EGA and VGA
BOXCOLOR( )	Changes window border color without having to repaint the window
CLOCK( )	Displays a dynamic clock anywhere on the screen
CURSOR( )	Changes cursor size and/or type
ERASTEXT( )	Erases text characters only from a screen area
FILEATTR( )	Sets or resets file attributes
GETCOLOR( )	Returns current color attributes from specified screen position
ISCGA( )	Detects CGA video
ISEGA( )	Detects EGA video
ISMONO( )	Detects monochrome video
ISVGA( )	Detects VGA video
NEWCOLOR( )	Changes window color without having to repaint the window
PRTSC( )	Invokes the print screen key
RESET( )	Performs a hardware/software system reset
RESTBOX( )	Restores a window area to a different location and/or color
RESTCURS( )	Restores cursor shape and position
SAVEBOX( )	Saves a window area
SAVECURS( )	Saves cursor shape and position
SDIR( )	Reads a directory
SOUND( )	Generates a wide range of sounds for variable durations
SPRINT( )	Prints a character string to the screen per selected color attributes
STAMP( )	Provides file date and time stamping
UNRESET( )	Interrupts CTRL-ALT-DEL to prevent or warn the user
VIDEO( )	Turns video display on or off
VSCROLL( )	Provides vertical and horizontal scrolling with full color attribute control
WILDAT( )	Searches a target string for the first occurrence of a string or wildcard pattern (left to right)
WILDRAT( )	Searches a target string for the first occurrence of a string or wildcard pattern (right to left)

Fig. 16-1. PROCLIP library functions.

Note that the area of the screen that has been overwritten with the window has also been saved to memory.

The Breeze includes a variety of other functions that may be applied to any created window, such as WCOLOR( ) to change the color of a window, WSAVE( ) to save a window to disk, and WSHIFT( ) to move a window one space at a time. Text can be included in any created window using WPRINT( ) whose text printing coordinates are relative to the window itself, not the display screen.

```
BOX()                     Draws five different types of boxes to memory
CLEARSCR()                Clears a rectangle and optionally refills it
                          with any character
KEYCODE()                 Returns scan code when a key is pressed
LINE()                    Draws two different types of lines to memory
PRINTSTR()                Prints a string to memory
SCRMODE()                 Returns current display video mode
SETSCR()                  Changes active display memory page
SOUND()                   Generates sounds per frequency and duration
TOGSCR()                  Toggles video monitor on and off
WCLEAR()                  Clears a window
WCLOSE()                  Closes a window and restores overwritten area
WCOLOR()                  Changes a window color
WCOLUMN()                 Returns number of columns in a window
WCOLSCR()                 Returns default screen column of a window
WCOPY()                   Copies a window
WDISPLAY()                Displays a window
WFILL()                   Changes color in part of a window
WFIND()                   Returns next free window area
WFRAME()                  Frames a window
WEXIST()                  Returns whether a window is in use
WLINE()                   Draws to types of lines in a window
WMOVEFROM()               Moves a portion of a window to screen
WMOVETO()                 Moves a portion of screen to a window
WPRINT()                  Prints a string to a window
WRELEASE()                Releases a window from memory
WRESTORE()                Restores a window from disk
WROW()                    Returns number of rows in a window
WROWSCR()                 Returns default screen row of a window
WSAVE()                   Saves a window to disk
WSCROLL()                 Scrolls a displayed window
WSELECT()                 Selects one of up to 99 windows
WSHIFT()                  Moves a displayed window one space at a time
WUPDATE()                 Updates a window in memory
WUSE()                    Creates a window
```

Fig. 16-2. THE BREEZE library functions.

Fig. 16-2 lists and briefly describes the windowing functions found in *The Breeze*. The library uses a combination of C (90%) and Assembly to provide speed and flexibility. Logitek includes source code for both the library and demo programs.

## 17

Clipper Development Tools

There are other Clipper development tools that may not necessarily be in the form of a linkable library, but which can significantly increase programming efficiency and reduce development time.

POWERTOOLS

One of the handiest Clipper development tools has to be *PowerTools* from SilverWare Incorporated. Consisting of over 20 Clipper tools (see *Fig. 17-1*), this package contains many useful commands all of which are executable from the DOS prompt.

For example, the RENDIR command can be used to rename a file directory from CM to CM__NEW as follows:

RENDIR D:\CM D:\CM__NEW

Familiar to most programmers is the TOUCH command, which updates specified files to a current date and time stamp. *PowerTools* also includes a command called STAMP which updates specified files to a specified date and time stamp. For example, to stamp all the current directory .PRG files to 12/27/88 2:00, the following command syntax is used:

STAMP 12/27/88 2:00 *.PRG

Maybe the real power tool for Clipper programmers is the SilverMake (SM) utility system which allows programmers to automatically create both MAKE and LINK files in just a matter of seconds. SMLIST looks at all of the .PRG files in the specified subdirectory and creates a MAKE file. SM then uses the MAKE file to create a LINK file, and proceed to compiles and link the program. A nice advantage to using SILVERMAKE is that it will stop and report any module errors before continuing the compile process.

```
ASCII.EXE              Full Screen ASCII display tool
CHMOD.EXE              Modifies file and directory attributes
DUMP.EXE               Hex/ASCII dump tool
ET.EXE                 Program timing tool
EZCODE.EXE             Code generator and outpus .DBF file statistics
GREP.EXE               Search tool to find text in file(s)
KEYBOARD.EXE           A full screen keyboard code response tool to
                       display documented INKEY() values (dBASE/Clipper)
LEFTY.EXE              Source file manipulator
LOCATE.EXE             A recursive global locator tool, with optional
                       delete
LPTSWAP.EXE            Swap physical to logical printer ports
LS.EXE                 List files in alphabetical order, by date,
                       reverse alphabetical, or reverse date
MENU.EXE               MS/PC DOS system level point and shoot menu for
                       combining physical .EXE files into one logical
                       system
RENDIR.EXE             Renames directories
SHOWINTS.EXE           Displays interrupt vectors
SM.EXE                 SilverMake, maintains Clipper source, object,
                       and executable files
SMLIST.EXE             Builds script files for SilverMake
SPRINT.EXE             Prints file(s) adding line and page numbers
STAMP.EXE              Modifies date and time stamp of file(s) as
                       specified on the command line
TOUCH.EXE              Updates file(s) to the current date and time
WC.EXE                 Counts words, lines, characters in file(s)
```

Fig. 17-1. PowerTools commands.

Shown in *Fig. 17-2* is the MAKE file that was created using *SilverMake* for the Cost Management example. With all of the CM .PRG files in the current directory, the following *PowerTools* command was executed:

SMLIST −o CM.EXE *.PRG > CM.MAK

The −o refers to the final compiled and linked file name that must be specified. The DOS redirection simply outputs the results of SMLIST into the desired CM.MAK file.

Once the MAKE file has been created, it is just a matter of text-editing the file to name the highest-level program module (CM.PRG) as well as identifying the compile switch options, linker type, and add-on object or library files. Even this process can be simplified by placing a SET CLIPLIB environment command in the AUTOEXEC.BAT file to pre-define link libraries.

Once the MAKE file has been created using SMLIST, the SM command can be used to actually compile and link an application. SM operates like any other MAKE facility: compiling only those program code files that have been updated since the last compile and link. SilverMake offers various

```
* File list for SM (SilverMake)
*
* Created by SMLIST.EXE,  Fri Jul 01 02:00:00 1988
*
:CMP clipper
:COP -m -l
:LNK tlink
:LIB c:\clipper\clipper c:\clipper\extend
:OUT CM.EXE
** Main Program (.PRG) goes here **
cm.prg
** External Object (.OBJ) files **
** Program (.PRG) files **
c_cols.prg
c_expn.prg
c_mnte.prg
c_name.prg
c_prtr.prg
c_rcpt.prg
c_tone.prg
d_back.prg
d_indx.prg
d_inst.prg
d_rcll.prg
d_summ.prg
errorsys.prg
e_expn.prg
e_memo.prg
e_mnte.prg
e_rcpt.prg
func.prg
help.prg
l_expn.prg
l_mnte.prg
l_rcpt.prg
m_expn.prg
m_file.prg
m_main.prg
m_mnte.prg
m_oper.prg
m_rcpt.prg
m_rprt.prg
r_clnt.prg
r_full.prg
r_supp.prg
r_type.prg
s_expn.prg
s_rcpt.prg
v_expn.prg
v_mnte.prg
v_rcpt.prg
```

Fig. 17-2. CM MAKE file created with SilverMake.

options to the SM command syntax, including an option to automatically create the LINK file based on the linker type specified in the MAKE file. For example, to compile and link CM using CM.MAK, and letting SilverMake create a CM.LNK file, the following SM command syntax is used:

SM −n CM.LNK CM.MAK

If the application requires a special LINK file, as would be needed if using overlays, then the "− n" would be replaced with "−l" which notifies SM that an existing LINK file must be used.

INSTAHLP SYSTEM

Creating user-help screens for Clipper applications can be a rather tedious and time-consuming task. INSTAHLP from XEC Development Incorporated can help ease the burden by allowing the programmer to create sophisticated help screens while the application is actually being executed. Imagine testing a new application, discovering that general user-help was not included for a data entry or menu prompt, and then just pressing Alt−H to add the needed user-help on-the-fly.

To enable INSTAHLP within a program, the following commands must be included, normally in the top-level program module:

```
EXTERNAL HELP, INSTAHLP        && For making help screens
SET KEY 291 TO INSTAHLP        && Alt−H triggers creating help
```

These commands cause the linker (TLINK/LINK/PLINK) to look for the modules INSTAHLP.OBJ and HELP.OBJ during link, and set Alt−H to INSTAHLP. When an application is completed and ready to give to the customer, these commands may then be deleted or commented out.

With INSTAHLP enabled, whenever Alt−H is pressed at a Clipper "wait" state, a box will appear in the upper-left corner of the screen display. Enter the number of the help screen to edit (1-9), as well as whether the help screen is generic or variable-specific.

Next, a parameters screen (see *Fig. 17-3*) will be displayed so that help screen-specific information may be determined. If the selected help screen already exists, the help text will appear for editing first. Pressing Alt−F5 allows editing of the parameters.

The parameters screen is further explained as follows:

Program   The name of the program when Alt−H was pressed.

Variable   The name of the variable when Alt−H was pressed. Valid entries are: the variable name calling INSTAHLP; or an empty field. There are different uses for this parameter. By leaving this information blank, the help screen will be a

```
Program:     IN20DEMO
Variable:    VAR1
Box Chars:   ▓▓▓▓▓▓▓▓▓▓▓▓
Box Color:   B/B;W/W
Text Color:  G+/N;W/N
Header:      [ Help for scre
Footer:      [ PgDn, Or any
Head Color:  W+/N;W/N
Foot Color:  W+/N;W/N
Shadow:      Y
Sh. Color:   B/N;W/N
Overlay:     Y
Pause Time:  0

*** Press ALT+F1 For Help ***
```

Fig. 17-3. INSTAHLP parameters screen.

GENERIC help screen for that procedure. This can provide a combination of specific and non-specific help for that screen.

Box Chars   Characters for the help box outline.

Box Color   Color for the help box.

Text Color   Color for text inside the box.

Header   Message to be displayed at the top of the help box.

Footer   Message to be displayed at the bottom of the help box.

Head Color   Color for header message.

Foot Color   Color for footer message.

Shadow   Box shadow (Y/N).

Sh. Color   Color for box shadow.

Overlay   Overlay help boxes (Y/N).

Pause Time   Amount of time to wait for a user keypress.

Once the specific information is filled in and confirmed, the cursor is moved to the location for the upper-left corner of the help box to appear. Pressing Enter locks that position. Then the cursor is moved to where the lower-right corner is to appear. Pressing Enter locks that position. The defined help box will be drawn followed by actual help text editing.

During help text editing, the following special keys are also available to the programmer:

Help Screen (Alt–F1)   displays the keys that may be pressed during editing of the help text.

Toggle Screens (Alt–F2)	toggles between writing help and viewing the application screen.
Delete (Alt–F3)	deletes current help screen.
Move Window (Alt–F4)	uses the cursor keys to move your help window to another part of the screen.
Edit Parameters (Alt–F5)	calls up the Parameters screen to edit the colors, header, footer, etc.
Re-size (Alt–F6)	moves the cursor to define the upper-left corner of the help screen, and then the lower-right corner.
Print Help (Alt–F7)	produces a report listing the current systems help screens.
Dump Info (Alt–F8)	allows the developer to write the parameters and help text to a file to read into another screen, or into another completely different development system!
Read Info (Alt–F9)	reads a file composed of commands from Alt–F8 to read in a help screen and parameters from another screen.
Save/Exit (Alt–H)	saves the current help screen and returns back to the application.
Abort/Exit (Esc)	aborts current editing of help and returns back to the application.

INSTAHLP, written in 100% Clipper code, is shareware and can be downloaded (for evaluation) from most Clipper bulletin board systems.

STEVE STRALEY's *TOOLKIT*

The name Steve Straley is synonymous with quality Clipper products. The *Steve Straley ToolKit* (aka SST) for Clipper Summer '87 is no exception. This collection of over 300 user-defined functions and Clipper procedures contains a wealth of programming solutions and ideas. Each is written in pure 100% Clipper code.

SST consists of a manual which describes each function and procedure, plus a diskette containing all of the procedure and function Clipper source code. SST contains 20 programs that may be compiled and linked to demonstrate most of the kit's tools, procedures, and functions.

Some of the many useful programming procedures in the *Steve Straley ToolKit* include:

BACKUP   a generic backup routine with windows that can acco-
                      modate multi-diskette backup.

RESTORE   a generic routine to restore data saved to disk with
                      BACKUP.

WORD_PRO   on-line Clipper word processor that includes mail-
                      merge, hot-keys, headers, and footers.

SAVEARRAY   saves array elements to a file.

RESTARRAY   restores array elements from a SAVEARRAY file.

REPORTER   on-line report generator.

The wide range of SST functions include string functions, array functions, math and statistical functions, date functions, database functions, and
many others. Just a few examples include:

MAKE_EMPTY( )   creates an empty variable based on the variable
                      type.

OCCURRENCE( )   returns the number of times one expression
                      occurs in another.

UPPERLOWER( )   returns a string with the first character capital-
                      ized, and the rest in lower case.

SIN( )   returns the sine.

COS( )   returns the cosine.

DEP_RATE( )   returns the simple depreciation rate.

FV( )   returns the future value.

FILEDATE( )   returns a file's date stamp.

FILETIME( )   returns a file's time stamp.

MAKEMENU( )   menu generator.

SHOW_REC( )   returns record number during COPY, AP-
                      PEND, etc.

Obviously, this is just a very brief sampling of the 300-plus procedures
and functions contained in SST. Because all source code is included in the
ToolKit, specific procedures and functions may easily be used directly in any
application.

Appendix A

CM Application Source Code

Appendix A contains all of the source code for the Cost Management application example discussed in this book. The program code modules are listed in alphabetical as follows:

```
* Program Name ......... CM.PRG
* Revised Date ......... 07/01/88
*
CLEAR
SET BELL(.F.)
SET WRAP(.T.)
SET DELETED(.T.)
SET CONFIRM(.T.)
SET SCOREBOARD(.T.)
SET SAFETY OFF
SET MESSAGE TO 24 CENTER
sdate = CMONTH(DATE())+" "+STR(DAY(DATE()),2)+ ;
        ", "+STR(YEAR(DATE()),4)
hcode = 0
*
PUBLIC pexpa,pcprs,pfeed,prele,prelc
PUBLIC ccode,cnorm,cinve,cline,chelp,cmemo,cmess,clogo
PUBLIC atone,bname,scode,hcode
*
PRIVATE dbffile[6]
dbffile[1] = "EXPENSES"
dbffile[2] = "RECEIPTS"
dbffile[3] = "CLNTCODE"
dbffile[4] = "SUPPCODE"
dbffile[5] = "TYPECODE"
dbffile[6] = "CM_SETUP"
FOR n = 1 TO 6
   IF ! FILE(dbffile[n]+".DBF")
     DO d_inst WITH n
   ENDIF
NEXT
*
USE cm_setup
STORE bus_name TO bname
STORE prn_expa TO pexpa
STORE prn_cprs TO pcprs
STORE prn_rele TO prele
STORE prn_relc TO prelc
STORE prn_feed TO pfeed
STORE col_code TO ccode
STORE err_tone TO atone
STORE sys_code TO scode
CLOSE DATABASES
*
DO COLOR WITH ccode
*
SETCOLOR(cnorm)
CLEAR
SETCOLOR(clogo)
```

```
  @ 02,25 SAY "
  @ 03,25 SAY "
  @ 04,25 SAY "
  @ 05,25 SAY "
  @ 06,25 SAY "
  @ 07,25 SAY "
  @ 08,25 SAY "
  @ 09,25 SAY "
  @ 11,00 SAY "
  @ 12,00 SAY "
  @ 13,00 SAY "
  @ 14,00 SAY "
  @ 15,00 SAY "
  @ 16,00 SAY "
  @ 11,41 SAY "
  @ 12,41 SAY "
  @ 13,41 SAY "
  @ 14,41 SAY "
  @ 15,41 SAY "
  @ 16,41 SAY "
```

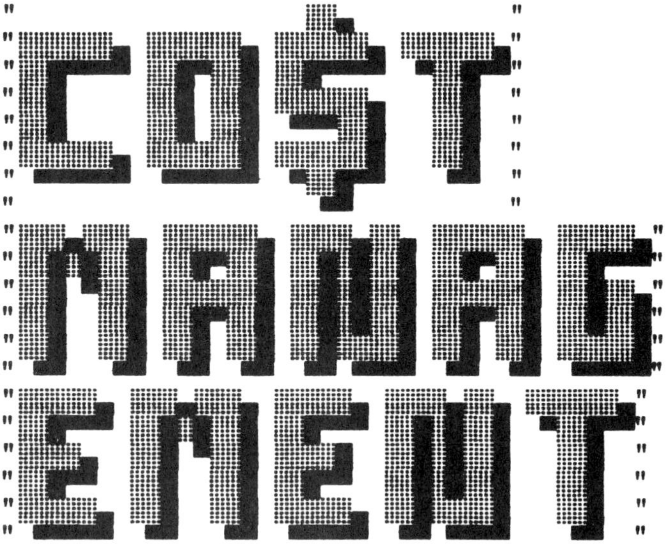

```
SETCOLOR(cline)
  @ 19,23 SAY "   Cost Management version 1.20   "
  @ 20,23 SAY "Copyright (c) 1988 by GLB SOFTWARE"
  @ 21,23 SAY "       All Rights Reserved        "
SETCOLOR(cmess)
  @ 24,23 SAY "         Press any key ...        "
SETCOLOR(cnorm)
*
SET CURSOR(.F.)
INKEY(60)
SET CURSOR(.T.)
*
CLEAR
SETCOLOR(clogo)
  @ 00,00 SAY M_CNTR(TRIM(bname))
SETCOLOR(cmess)
  @ 02,78-LEN(sdate) SAY sdate
SETCOLOR(cline)
  @ 01,00 SAY REPLICATE("-",80)
  @ 03,00 SAY REPLICATE("-",80)
  @ 23,00 SAY REPLICATE("-",80)
SETCOLOR(cnorm)
*
PRIVATE ntxfile[5]
ntxfile[1] = "EXPENSES"
ntxfile[2] = "RECEIPTS"
ntxfile[3] = "CLNTCODE"
ntxfile[4] = "SUPPCODE"
ntxfile[5] = "TYPECODE"
FOR n = 1 TO 5
```

```
    IF ! FILE(ntxfile[n]+".NTX")
      DO d_indx
      EXIT
    ENDIF
  NEXT
  *
  DO WHILE .T.
    SAYHEADER("Password Entry")
    HELPKEY()
    STORE SPACE(10) TO mpassword
    SETCOLOR(cline+",x")
      @ 12,23 SAY "Enter your password ...." ;
              GET mpassword PICTURE "@!"
    READ
    SETCOLOR(cnorm)
    IF LASTKEY() = 27
      SET CURSOR ON
      SETCOLOR("w/n")
      CLEAR
      QUIT
    ENDIF
    IF mpassword == scode
      DO m_main
    ELSE
      M_ERROR()
      LOOP
    ENDIF
  ENDDO
  RETURN
  *
  PROCEDURE color
  PARAMETERS ccode
  DO CASE
    CASE ccode = 1
      cnorm = "GR+/B,W/R,B,,R/W"
      cinve = "R/W"
      cline = "W+/B"
      chelp = "BG+/B"
      cmemo = "G+/B"
      cmess = "G+/B"
      clogo = "R+/B"
    CASE ccode = 2
      cnorm = "G/N,W/R,N,,R/W"
      cinve = "R/W"
      cline = "W/N"
      chelp = "BG+/N"
      cmemo = "BG+/N"
      cmess = "G+/N"
      clogo = "R+/N"
    CASE ccode = 3
```

```
      cnorm = "GR+/N,N/GR,N,,GR/N"
      cinve = "GR/N"
      cline = "W/N"
      chelp = "N/W"
      cmemo = "N/W"
      cmess = "G+/N"
      clogo = "R+/N"
   CASE ccode = 4
      cnorm = "W/N,N/W,N,,N/W"
      cinve = "N/W"
      cline = "W+/N"
      chelp = "N/W"
      cmemo = "W+/N"
      cmess = "W+/N"
      clogo = "W+/N"
ENDCASE
RETURN
```

```
* Program Name ......... c_cols.prg
* Revised Date ......... 07/01/88
*
IF ! ISCOLOR()
  RETURN
ENDIF
*
DO screen
*
DO WHILE .T.
  SET CURSOR(.F.)
  keypress = INKEY(0)
  SET CURSOR(.T.)
  IF keypress = 13
    EXIT
  ELSEIF keypress = 22
    ccode = IIF(ccode>3,1,ccode+1)
    DO color WITH ccode
    DO screen
  ENDIF
ENDDO
USE cm_setup
REPLACE col_code WITH ccode
CLOSE
RETURN
*
PROCEDURE screen
SETCOLOR(cnorm)
CLEAR SCREEN
SETCOLOR(clogo)
  @ 00,00 SAY SPACE(80)
  @ 00,00 SAY M_CNTR(TRIM(bname))
```

```
SETCOLOR(cmess)
  @ 02,78-LEN(sdate) SAY sdate
SETCOLOR(cline)
  @ 01,00 SAY REPLICATE("-",80)
  @ 03,00 SAY REPLICATE("-",80)
  @ 23,00 SAY REPLICATE("-",80)
SETCOLOR(cnorm)
SAYHEADER("Display Color Change")
  @ 06,00 SAY M_CNTR("Press the [Insert] key to toggle colors")
  @ 08,00 SAY M_CNTR("Press the [Enter] key to accept colors")
SETCOLOR(cline)
  @ 14,10 to 16,35
  @ 14,45 to 16,70
SETCOLOR(cmemo)
  @ 15,11 SAY " This is the memo color "
SETCOLOR(chelp)
  @ 15,46 SAY " This is the help color "
SETCOLOR(cnorm)
  @ 24,00 SAY M_CNTR("This is the message color")
RETURN
```

```
* Program Name ......... c_expn.prg
* Revised Date ......... 07/01/88
*
SAYHEADER("Change/Delete an Expense")
  @ 07,00 SAY "Expense Number ...."
  @ 07,40 SAY "Expense Date ......"
  @ 08,00 SAY "Expense Amount ...."
  @ 08,40 SAY "Description ......."
  @ 10,00 SAY "Type Code ........."
  @ 10,40 SAY "Description ......."
  @ 11,00 SAY "Supplier Code ....."
  @ 11,40 SAY "Description ......."
  @ 13,00 SAY "Invoice Number ...."
  @ 14,00 SAY "Check Number ......"
  @ 14,40 SAY "Date Paid ........."
  @ 16,00 SAY "Comment (y/n) ....."
SETCOLOR(cline)
  @ 09,00 SAY repl("-",80)
  @ 12,00 SAY repl("-",80)
  @ 15,00 SAY repl("-",80)
SETCOLOR(cnorm)
*
STORE 0 TO mexpnnr
HELPKEY()
  @ 07,20 GET mexpnnr PICTURE "####" VALID vc_expn1(mexpnnr)
READ
M_CLEAR()
IF LASTKEY() = 27
  RETURN
```

```
ENDIF
*
STORE STR(mexpnnr,4) TO mexpnnumb
USE expenses INDEX expenses
SEEK mexpnnumb
STORE expndate TO mexpndate
STORE expndesc TO mexpndesc
STORE expnamnt TO mexpnamnt
STORE typecode TO mtypecode
STORE suppcode TO msuppcode
STORE invcnumb TO minvcnumb
STORE paiddate TO mpaiddate
STORE cheknumb TO mcheknumb
STORE expnmemo TO mexpnmemo
CLOSE DATABASES
*
USE typecode INDEX typecode
SEEK mtypecode
mtypename = IIF(FOUND(),typename,SPACE(20))
CLOSE DATABASES
*
USE suppcode INDEX suppcode
SEEK msuppcode
msuppname = IIF(FOUND(),suppname,SPACE(20))
CLOSE DATABASES
*
SETCOLOR(cinve)
  @ 07,60 SAY mexpndate
  @ 08,20 SAY tran(mexpnamnt,"##,###.##")
  @ 08,60 SAY mexpndesc
  @ 10,20 SAY mtypecode
  @ 10,60 SAY mtypename
  @ 11,20 SAY msuppcode
  @ 11,60 SAY msuppname
  @ 13,20 SAY minvcnumb
  @ 14,20 SAY mcheknumb
  @ 14,60 SAY mpaiddate
  @ 16,20 SAY IIF(mexpnmemo,"Y","N")
SETCOLOR(cnorm)
*
mchoice = 1
  @ 22,31 PROMPT "Change" MESSAGE "  Change this expense"
  @ 22,38 PROMPT "Delete" MESSAGE "  Delete this expense"
  @ 22,45 PROMPT "Quit"   MESSAGE "  Quit and abort"
CLEAR TYPEAHEAD
MENU TO mchoice
M_CLEAR()
DO CASE
  CASE mchoice = 2
    DELETETONE()
```

```
      STORE "N" TO msure
        @ 24,31 SAY "Are you sure (y/n)?" GET msure PICTURE "Y"
      READ
      M_CLEAR()
      IF LASTKEY() = 27
        RETURN
      ENDIF
      IF msure = "Y"
        M_WAIT()
        USE expenses INDEX expenses
        SEEK mexpnnumb
        REPLACE expnnumb WITH "     "
        DELETE
        CLOSE DATABASES
        STORE "CM"+LTRIM(mexpnnumb)+".TXT" TO mfilename
        IF FILE(mfilename)
          ERASE(mfilename)
        ENDIF
        M_CLEAR()
      ENDIF
      RETURN
    CASE mchoice = 3 .OR. LASTKEY() = 27
      RETURN
ENDCASE
*
changing = .T.
DO WHILE changing
  HELPKEY()
    @ 07,60 GET mexpndate PICTURE "@D"
    @ 08,20 GET mexpnamnt PICTURE "##,###.##"
    @ 08,60 GET mexpndesc
    @ 10,20 GET mtypecode PICTURE "@!" VALID ve_expn1(mtypecode)
    @ 11,20 GET msuppcode PICTURE "@!" VALID ve_expn2(msuppcode)
    @ 13,20 GET minvcnumb PICTURE "@!"
    @ 14,20 GET mcheknumb PICTURE "@!"
    @ 14,60 GET mpaiddate PICTURE "@D"
    @ 16,20 GET mexpnmemo PICTURE "Y"
  READ
  M_CLEAR()
  IF LASTKEY() = 27
    RETURN
  ENDIF
  changing = .F.
  mchoice = 1
    @ 22,31 PROMPT "Update" MESSAGE "  Update file with changes"
    @ 22,38 PROMPT "Change" MESSAGE "  Change this expense"
    @ 22,45 PROMPT "Quit"   MESSAGE "  Quit and abort"
  CLEAR TYPEAHEAD
  MENU TO mchoice
  M_CLEAR()
```

```
    DO CASE
      CASE mchoice = 1
        IF UPDATED()
          M_WAIT()
          USE expenses INDEX expenses
          SEEK mexpnnumb
          REPLACE expndate WITH mexpndate,;
                  expndesc WITH mexpndesc, expnamnt WITH mexpnamnt,;
                  typecode WITH mtypecode, suppcode WITH msuppcode
          REPLACE invcnumb WITH minvcnumb, paiddate WITH mpaiddate,;
                  cheknumb WITH mcheknumb, expnmemo WITH mexpnmemo
          CLOSE DATABASES
          M_CLEAR()
        ENDIF
        STORE "CM"+LTRIM(mexpnnumb)+".TXT" TO mfilename
        IF mexpnmemo
          MEMOBOX1()
          SETCOLOR(cmemo)
          IF FILE(mfilename)
            MEMOWRIT(mfilename,MEMOEDIT;
                    (MEMOREAD(mfilename),05,04,18,75,.T.,"dbm"))
          ELSE
            STORE SPACE(1) TO memo
            MEMOWRIT(mfilename,MEMOEDIT(memo,05,04,18,75,.T.,"dbm"))
          ENDIF
          SETCOLOR(cnorm)
        ELSE
          IF FILE(mfilename)
            ERASE mfilename
          ENDIF
        ENDIF
        EXIT
      CASE mchoice = 2
        changing = .T.
        LOOP
      CASE mchoice = 3 .OR. LASTKEY() = 27
        EXIT
    ENDCASE
ENDDO
RETURN
*
FUNCTION vc_expn1
PARAMETERS mexpnnr
STORE STR(mexpnnr,4) TO mexpnnumb
USE expenses INDEX expenses
SEEK mexpnnumb
IF FOUND()
  ok = .T.
ELSE
  ok = .F.
```

```
   M_ERROR()
ENDIF
CLOSE DATABASES
RETURN(ok)
```

```
* Program Name ......... c_mnte.prg
* Revised Date ......... 07/01/88
*
PARAMETERS m_main
*
DO CASE
  CASE m_main = 4
    SAYHEADER("Change/Delete a Client Code")
    prompt1 = "Client Code ......."
    prompt2 = "Client Name ......."
    memvar1 = "mCLNTCODE"
    memvar2 = "mCLNTNAME"
    dbfvar1 = "CLNTCODE"
    dbfvar2 = "CLNTNAME"
    dbfname = "CLNTCODE"
    ntxname = "CLNTCODE"
  CASE m_main = 5
    SAYHEADER("Change/Delete a Supplier Code")
    prompt1 = "Supplier Code ....."
    prompt2 = "Supplier Name......"
    memvar1 = "mSUPPCODE"
    memvar2 = "mSUPPNAME"
    dbfvar1 = "SUPPCODE"
    dbfvar2 = "SUPPNAME"
    dbfname = "SUPPCODE"
    ntxname = "SUPPCODE"
  CASE m_main = 6
    SAYHEADER("Change/Delete an Expense Type Code")
    prompt1 = "Type Code ........."
    prompt2 = "Type Name ........."
    memvar1 = "mTYPECODE"
    memvar2 = "mTYPENAME"
    dbfvar1 = "TYPECODE"
    dbfvar2 = "TYPENAME"
    dbfname = "TYPECODE"
    ntxname = "TYPECODE"
ENDCASE
*
STORE SPACE(03) TO memvar1
*
HELPKEY()
  @ 07,20 SAY prompt1 GET memvar1 PICTURE "@!" ;
          VALID vc_mnte(memvar1,dbfname,ntxname)
  @ 08,20 SAY prompt2
READ
```

```
M_CLEAR()
IF LASTKEY() = 27
  RETURN
ENDIF
*
USE (dbfname) INDEX (ntxname)
SEEK memvar1
STORE &dbfvar2 TO memvar2
CLOSE DATABASES
*
SETCOLOR(cinve)
  @ 08,40 SAY memvar2
SETCOLOR(cnorm)
*
mchoice = 1
  @ 22,31 PROMPT "Change" MESSAGE "  Change this code"
  @ 22,38 PROMPT "Delete" MESSAGE "  Delete this code"
  @ 22,45 PROMPT "Quit"   MESSAGE "  Quit and abort"
CLEAR TYPEAHEAD
MENU TO mchoice
M_CLEAR()
DO CASE
  CASE mchoice = 2
    DELETETONE()
    STORE "N" TO msure
      @ 24,31 SAY "Are you sure (y/n)?" GET msure PICTURE "Y"
    READ
    IF LASTKEY() = 27
      RETURN
    ENDIF
    IF msure = "Y"
      M_WAIT()
      USE (dbfname) INDEX (ntxname)
      SEEK memvar1
      REPLACE &dbfvar1 WITH "    "
      DELETE
      CLOSE DATABASES
      M_CLEAR()
    ENDIF
    RETURN
  CASE mchoice = 3 .OR. LASTKEY() = 27
    RETURN
ENDCASE
*
changing = .T.
DO WHILE changing
  HELPKEY()
    @ 08,40 GET memvar2 VALID v_string(memvar2)
  READ
  M_CLEAR()
```

```
IF LASTKEY() = 27
  EXIT
ENDIF
changing = .F.
mchoice = 1
ESCKEY()
  @ 22,31 PROMPT "Update" MESSAGE "  Update file with changes"
  @ 22,38 PROMPT "Change" MESSAGE "  Change this code"
  @ 22,45 PROMPT "Quit"   MESSAGE "  Quit and abort"
CLEAR TYPEAHEAD
MENU TO mchoice
M_CLEAR()
DO CASE
  CASE mchoice = 1 .AND. UPDATED()
    M_WAIT()
    USE (dbfname) INDEX (ntxname)
    SEEK memvar1
    REPLACE &dbfvar2 WITH memvar2
    M_CLEAR()
    EXIT
  CASE mchoice = 2
    changing = .T.
    LOOP
  CASE mchoice = 3 .OR. LASTKEY() = 27
    EXIT
  ENDCASE
ENDDO
RETURN
*
FUNCTION vc_mnte
PARAMETERS memvar1,dbfname,ntxname
USE (dbfname) INDEX (ntxname)
SEEK memvar1
IF FOUND()
  ok = .T.
ELSE
  ok = .F.
  M_ERROR()
ENDIF
CLOSE DATABASES
RETURN(ok)
```

```
* Program Name .......... c_name.prg
* Revised Date .......... 07/01/88
*
SAYHEADER("Change Business Name")
  @ 08,20 SAY "Old Name .........."
  @ 10,20 SAY "New Name .........."
SETCOLOR(cinve)
  @ 08,40 SAY bname
```

```
SETCOLOR(cnorm)
*
changing = .T.
DO WHILE changing
  ESCKEY()
    @ 10,40 GET bname VALID v_string(bname)
  READ
  IF LASTKEY() = 27
    EXIT
  ENDIF
  changing = .F.
  mchoice = 1
    @ 22,31 PROMPT "Update" MESSAGE "  Update file with these changes"
    @ 22,38 PROMPT "Change" MESSAGE "  Change this business name"
    @ 22,45 PROMPT "Quit"   MESSAGE "  Quit and abort"
  CLEAR TYPEAHEAD
  MENU TO mchoice
  M_CLEAR()
  DO CASE
    CASE mchoice = 1 .AND. UPDATED()
      M_WAIT()
      USE cm_setup
      REPLACE bus_name WITH bname
      CLOSE DATABASES
      SETCOLOR(clogo)
        @ 00,00 SAY SPACE(80)
        @ 00,00 SAY M_CNTR(TRIM(bname))
      SETCOLOR(cnorm)
      M_CLEAR()
      EXIT
    CASE mchoice = 2
      changing = .T.
      LOOP
    CASE mchoice = 3 .OR. LASTKEY() = 27
      EXIT
  ENDCASE
ENDDO
RETURN

* Program Name .......... c_prtr.prg
* Revised Date .......... 07/01/88
*
SAYHEADER("Change Printer Configuration")
  @ 08,28 SAY "Expanded Print ......"
  @ 09,28 SAY "Expanded Release ...."
  @ 10,28 SAY "Compressed Print ...."
  @ 11,28 SAY "Compressed Release .."
  @ 12,28 SAY "Form Feed .........."
SETCOLOR(cinve)
  @ 08,50 SAY STR(pexpa,2)
```

```
  @ 09,50 SAY STR(prele,2)
  @ 10,50 SAY STR(pcprs,2)
  @ 11,50 SAY STR(prelc,2)
  @ 12,50 SAY STR(pfeed,2)
SETCOLOR(cnorm)
*
changing = .T.
DO WHILE changing
  ESCKEY()
    @ 08,50 GET pexpa PICTURE "##" VALID v_number(pexpa)
    @ 09,50 GET prele PICTURE "##" VALID v_number(prele)
    @ 10,50 GET pcprs PICTURE "##" VALID v_number(pcprs)
    @ 11,50 GET prelc PICTURE "##" VALID v_number(prelc)
    @ 12,50 GET pfeed PICTURE "##" VALID v_number(pfeed)
  READ
  IF LASTKEY() = 27
    EXIT
  ENDIF
  changing = .F.
  mchoice = 1
    @ 22,31 PROMPT "Update" MESSAGE "  Update file with these changes"
    @ 22,38 PROMPT "Change" MESSAGE "  Change these printer codes"
    @ 22,45 PROMPT "Quit"   MESSAGE "  Quit and abort"
  CLEAR TYPEAHEAD
  MENU TO mchoice
  M_CLEAR()
  DO CASE
    CASE mchoice = 1 .AND. UPDATED()
      M_WAIT()
      USE cm_setup
      REPLACE prn_expa WITH pexpa, prn_rele WITH prele,;
              prn_cprs WITH pcprs, prn_relc WITH prelc,;
              prn_feed WITH pfeed
      CLOSE DATABASES
      M_CLEAR()
      EXIT
    CASE mchoice = 2
      changing = .T.
      LOOP
    CASE mchoice = 3 .OR. LASTKEY() = 27
      EXIT
  ENDCASE
ENDDO
RETURN
```

```
* Program Name ......... c_rcpt.prg
* Revised Date ......... 07/01/88
*
SAYHEADER("Change/Delete a Receipt")
  @ 07,00 SAY "Receipt Number ...."
```

```
  @ 07,40 SAY "Receipt Date ......"
  @ 08,00 SAY "Receipt Amount ...."
  @ 08,40 SAY "Description ......."
  @ 10,00 SAY "Client Code ......."
  @ 10,40 SAY "Description ......."
  @ 12,00 SAY "Check Number ......"
SETCOLOR(cline)
  @ 09,00 SAY repl("—",80)
  @ 11,00 SAY repl("—",80)
SETCOLOR(cnorm)
*
STORE 0 TO mrcptnr
HELPKEY()
  @ 07,20 GET mrcptnr PICTURE "####" VALID vc_rcpt(mrcptnr)
READ
M_CLEAR()
IF LASTKEY() = 27
  RETURN
ENDIF
*
STORE STR(mrcptnr,4) TO mrcptnumb
USE receipts INDEX receipts
SEEK mrcptnumb
STORE rcptdate TO mrcptdate
STORE rcptdesc TO mrcptdesc
STORE rcptamnt TO mrcptamnt
STORE clntcode TO mclntcode
STORE cheknumb TO mcheknumb
CLOSE DATABASES
*
USE clntcode INDEX clntcode
SEEK mclntcode
mclntname = IIF(FOUND(),clntname,SPACE(20))
*
SETCOLOR(cinve)
  @ 07,60 SAY mrcptdate
  @ 08,20 SAY TRAN(mrcptamnt,"##,###.##")
  @ 08,60 SAY mrcptdesc
  @ 10,20 SAY mclntcode
  @ 10,60 SAY mclntname
  @ 12,20 SAY mcheknumb
SETCOLOR(cnorm)
*
mchoice = 1
  @ 22,31 PROMPT "Change" MESSAGE "  Change this receipt"
  @ 22,38 PROMPT "Delete" MESSAGE "  Delete this receipt"
  @ 22,45 PROMPT "Quit"   MESSAGE "  Quit and abort"
CLEAR TYPEAHEAD
MENU TO mchoice
M_CLEAR()
```

```
DO CASE
  CASE mchoice = 2
    DELETETONE()
    STORE "N" TO msure
      @ 24,31 SAY "Are you sure (y/n)?" GET msure PICTURE "Y"
    READ
    M_CLEAR()
    IF LASTKEY() = 27
      RETURN
    ENDIF
    IF msure = "Y"
      M_WAIT()
      USE receipts INDEX receipts
      SEEK mrcptnumb
      REPLACE rcptnumb WITH "      "
      DELETE
      CLOSE DATABASES
      M_CLEAR()
    ENDIF
    RETURN
  CASE mchoice = 3 .OR. LASTKEY() = 27
    RETURN
ENDCASE
*
changing = .T.
DO WHILE changing
  HELPKEY()
    @ 07,60 GET mrcptdate PICTURE "@D"
    @ 08,20 GET mrcptamnt PICTURE "##,###.##"
    @ 08,60 GET mrcptdesc
    @ 10,20 GET mclntcode PICTURE "@!" VALID ve_rcpt(mclntcode)
    @ 12,20 GET mcheknumb PICTURE "@!"
  READ
  M_CLEAR()
  IF LASTKEY() = 27
    RETURN
  ENDIF
  changing = .F.
  mchoice = 1
    @ 22,31 PROMPT "Update" MESSAGE "  Update file with changes"
    @ 22,38 PROMPT "Change" MESSAGE "  Change this receipt"
    @ 22,45 PROMPT "Quit"   MESSAGE "  Quit and abort"
  CLEAR TYPEAHEAD
  MENU TO mchoice
  M_CLEAR()
  DO CASE
    CASE mchoice = 1 .AND. UPDATED()
      M_WAIT()
      USE receipts INDEX receipts
      SEEK mrcptnumb
```

```
       REPLACE rcptdate WITH mrcptdate,;
               rcptdesc WITH mrcptdesc, rcptamnt WITH mrcptamnt,;
               clntcode WITH mclntcode, cheknumb WITH mcheknumb
      CLOSE DATABASES
      EXIT
      M_CLEAR()
    CASE mchoice = 2
      changing = .T.
      LOOP
    CASE mchoice = 3 .OR. LASTKEY() = 27
      EXIT
  ENDCASE
ENDDO
RETURN
*
FUNCTION vc_rcpt
PARAMETERS mrcptnr
STORE STR(mrcptnr,4) TO mrcptnumb
USE receipts INDEX receipts
SEEK mrcptnumb
IF FOUND()
  ok = .T.
ELSE
  ok = .F.
  M_ERROR()
ENDIF
CLOSE DATABASES
RETURN(ok)
```

```
* Program Name ......... c_tone.prg
* Revised Date ......... 07/01/88
*
DO WHILE .T.
  SAYHEADER("Error Tones Toggle")
  HELPKEY()
  MENUBOX(07,24,10,55)
    @ 08,25 PROMPT "Yes, turn audio error tones ON"
    @ 09,25 PROMPT "No, turn audio error tones OFF"
  tones = IIF(atone,1,2)
  CLEAR TYPEAHEAD
  MENU TO tones
  IF LASTKEY() = 27
    EXIT
  ENDIF
  atone = IIF(tones=1,.T.,.F.)
  USE cm_setup
  REPLACE err_tone WITH atone
  CLOSE DATABASES
  EXIT
ENDDO
RETURN
```

```
* Program Name ......... d_back.prg
* Revised Date ......... 07/01/88
*
SAYHEADER("Data Backup")
*
@ 09,00 SAY M_CNTR("Place backup diskette in drive A:")
@ 11,00 SAY M_CNTR("Press any key when ready.")
*
ESCKEY()
SET CURSOR(.F.)
INKEY(0)
SET CURSOR(.T.)
*
IF LASTKEY() = 27
  RETURN
ENDIF
*
CLS()
M_WAIT()
*
M_STATUS("Copying Expenses data")
COPY FILE expenses.dbf TO A:expenses.dbf
*
M_STATUS("Copying Receipts data")
COPY FILE receipts.dbf TO A:receipts.dbf
*
M_STATUS("Copying Client Code data")
COPY FILE clntcode.dbf TO A:clntcode.dbf
*
M_STATUS("Copying Supplier Code data")
COPY FILE suppcode.dbf TO A:suppcode.dbf
*
M_STATUS("Copying Expense Type Code data")
COPY FILE typecode.dbf TO A:typecode.dbf
*
M_STATUS("Copying CM Setup data")
COPY FILE cm_setup.dbf TO A:cm_setup.dbf
*
M_STATUS("Copying Expense Memos")
RUN COPY cm????.txt A:>nul
*
RETURN
```

```
* Program Name ......... d_indx.prg
* Revised Date ......... 07/01/88
*
SAYHEADER("Reindex Databases")
M_WAIT()
```

```
*
USE expenses
M_STATUS("Indexing Expenses File")
PACK
INDEX ON expnnumb TO expenses
CLOSE DATABASES
*
USE receipts
M_STATUS("Indexing Receipts File")
PACK
INDEX ON rcptnumb TO receipts
CLOSE DATABASES
*
USE clntcode
M_STATUS("Indexing Client Codes File")
PACK
INDEX ON clntcode TO clntcode
CLOSE DATABASES
*
USE suppcode
M_STATUS("Indexing Supplier Codes File")
PACK
INDEX ON suppcode TO suppcode
CLOSE DATABASES
*
USE typecode
M_STATUS("Indexing Expense Type Codes File")
PACK
INDEX ON typecode TO typecode
CLOSE DATABASES
*
M_CLEAR()
RETURN
```

```
* Program Name ......... d_inst.prg
* Revised Date .......... 04/01/88
*
PARAMETERS n
*
SETCOLOR("W+*")
  @ 10,00 SAY m_cntr("Installation")
SETCOLOR("W")
SET CURSOR(.F.)
*
DO CASE
  CASE n = 1
    CREATE dummy
    STORE "EXPNNUMB   C4  "  TO field1
    STORE "EXPNDATE   D8  "  TO field2
    STORE "EXPNDESC   C20 "  TO field3
```

```
      STORE "EXPNAMNT   N8 2"   TO field4
      STORE "TYPECODE   C3  "   TO field5
      STORE "SUPPCODE   C3  "   TO field6
      STORE "INVCNUMB   C10 "   TO field7
      STORE "PAIDDATE   D8  "   TO field8
      STORE "CHEKNUMB   C10 "   TO field9
      STORE "EXPNMEMO   L1  "   TO field10
      FOR F = 1 TO 10
         fnumber = IIF(F<10,STR(F,1),STR(F,2))
         APPEND BLANK
         STORE "field" + fnumber TO fn
         REPLACE field_name WITH SUBSTR(&fn,1,10);
                 field_type WITH SUBSTR(&fn,11,1);
                 field_len  WITH VAL(SUBSTR(&fn,12,2));
                 field_dec  WITH VAL(SUBSTR(&fn,14,1))
      NEXT
      CREATE expenses FROM dummy
      CLOSE DATABASES
      ERASE dummy.DBF
   CASE n = 2
      CREATE dummy
      STORE "RCPTNUMB   C4  "   TO field1
      STORE "RCPTDATE   D8  "   TO field2
      STORE "RCPTDESC   C20 "   TO field3
      STORE "RCPTAMNT   N8 2"   TO field4
      STORE "CLNTCODE   C3  "   TO field5
      STORE "CHEKNUMB   C10 "   TO field6
      FOR F = 1 TO 6
         fnumber = STR(F,1)
         APPEND BLANK
         STORE "field" + fnumber TO fn
         REPLACE field_name WITH SUBSTR(&fn,1,10);
                 field_type WITH SUBSTR(&fn,11,1);
                 field_len  WITH VAL(SUBSTR(&fn,12,2));
                 field_dec  WITH VAL(SUBSTR(&fn,14,1))
      NEXT
      CREATE receipts FROM dummy
      CLOSE DATABASES
      ERASE dummy.DBF
   CASE n = 3
      CREATE dummy
      STORE "CLNTCODE   C3  "   TO field1
      STORE "CLNTNAME   C20 "   TO field2
      FOR F = 1 TO 2
         fnumber = STR(F,1)
         APPEND BLANK
         STORE "field" + fnumber TO fn
         REPLACE field_name WITH SUBSTR(&fn,1,10);
                 field_type WITH SUBSTR(&fn,11,1);
                 field_len  WITH VAL(SUBSTR(&fn,12,2));
```

```
                    field_dec   WITH VAL(SUBSTR(&fn,14,1))
  NEXT
  CREATE clntcode FROM dummy
  CLOSE DATABASES
  ERASE dummy.DBF
CASE n = 4
  CREATE dummy
  STORE "SUPPCODE   C3  "   TO field1
  STORE "SUPPNAME   C20 "   TO field2
  FOR F = 1 TO 2
    fnumber = STR(F,1)
    APPEND BLANK
    STORE "field" + fnumber TO fn
    REPLACE field_name WITH SUBSTR(&fn,1,10);
            field_type WITH SUBSTR(&fn,11,1);
            field_len  WITH VAL(SUBSTR(&fn,12,2));
            field_dec  WITH VAL(SUBSTR(&fn,14,1))
  NEXT
  CREATE suppcode FROM dummy
  CLOSE DATABASES
  ERASE dummy.DBF
CASE n = 5
  CREATE dummy
  STORE "TYPECODE   C3  "   TO field1
  STORE "TYPENAME   C20 "   TO field2
  FOR F = 1 TO 2
    fnumber = STR(F,1)
    APPEND BLANK
    STORE "field" + fnumber TO fn
    REPLACE field_name WITH SUBSTR(&fn,1,10);
            field_type WITH SUBSTR(&fn,11,1);
            field_len  WITH VAL(SUBSTR(&fn,12,2));
            field_dec  WITH VAL(SUBSTR(&fn,14,1))
  NEXT
  CREATE typecode FROM dummy
  CLOSE DATABASES
  ERASE dummy.DBF
CASE n = 6
  CREATE dummy
  STORE "BUS_NAME   C20 "   TO field1
  STORE "SYS_CODE   C10 "   TO field2
  STORE "COL_CODE   N1  "   TO field3
  STORE "ERR_TONE   L1  "   TO field4
  STORE "PRN_EXPA   N2  "   TO field5
  STORE "PRN_RELE   N2  "   TO field6
  STORE "PRN_CPRS   N2  "   TO field7
  STORE "PRN_RELC   N2  "   TO field8
  STORE "PRN_FEED   N2  "   TO field9
  FOR F = 1 TO 9
    fnumber = STR(F,1)
```

```
      APPEND BLANK
      STORE "field" + fnumber TO fn
      REPLACE field_name WITH SUBSTR(&fn,1,10)
      REPLACE field_type WITH SUBSTR(&fn,11,1)
      REPLACE field_len  WITH VAL(SUBSTR(&fn,12,2))
      REPLACE field_dec  WITH VAL(SUBSTR(&fn,14,1))
   NEXT
   CREATE cm_setup FROM dummy
   APPEND BLANK
   REPLACE bus_name WITH "GLB Software", sys_code WITH "CM",;
           prn_expa WITH 14, prn_rele WITH 20,;
           prn_cprs WITH 15, prn_relc WITH 18,;
           prn_feed WITH 12
   REPLACE col_code WITH IIF(ISCOLOR(),1,4);
           err_tone WITH .T.
   CLOSE DATABASES
   ERASE dummy.DBF
ENDCASE
*
SET CURSOR(.T.)
RETURN
```

```
* Program Name .......... d_rcll
* Revised Date .......... 07/01/88
*
SAYHEADER("Data Recall")
*
@ 09,00 SAY M_CNTR("Place backup diskette in drive A:")
@ 11,00 SAY M_CNTR("Press any key when ready.")
*
ESCKEY()
SET CURSOR(.F.)
INKEY(0)
SET CURSOR(.T.)
*
IF LASTKEY() = 27
   RETURN
ENDIF
*
CLS()
M_WAIT()
*
IF FILE("A:EXPENSES.dbf")
   M_STATUS("Recalling Expenses data")
   COPY FILE A:expenses.dbf TO expenses.dbf
ENDIF
*
IF FILE("A:RECEIPTS.dbf")
   M_STATUS("Recalling Receipts data")
   COPY FILE A:receipts.dbf TO receipts.dbf
```

```
ENDIF
*
IF FILE("A:CLNTCODE.dbf")
  M_STATUS("Recalling Client Code data")
  COPY FILE A:clntcode.dbf TO clntcode.dbf
ENDIF
*
IF FILE("A:SUPPCODE.dbf")
  M_STATUS("Recalling Supplier Code data")
  COPY FILE A:suppcode.dbf TO suppcode.dbf
ENDIF
*
IF FILE("A:TYPECODE.dbf")
  M_STATUS("Recalling Expense Type Code data")
  COPY FILE A:typecode.dbf TO typecode.dbf
ENDIF
*
IF FILE("A:CM_SETUP.dbf")
  M_STATUS("Recalling CM Setup data")
  COPY FILE A:cm_setup.dbf TO cm_setup.dbf
ENDIF
*
M_STATUS("Recalling Expense Memos")
RUN COPY A:cm????.txt>nul
*
DO d_indx
*
RETURN
```

```
* Program Name ......... d_summ.prg
* Revised Date ......... 07/01/88
*
SAYHEADER("File Summary")
*
SETCOLOR(cline)
  @ 08,17 SAY " File Description      Records      Size      Lastdate"
  @ 09,17 SAY "_____   _____   _____   _____"
SETCOLOR(cnorm)
  @ 10,17 SAY "Expenses"
  @ 11,17 SAY "Receipts"
  @ 12,17 SAY "Clients"
  @ 13,17 SAY "Suppliers"
  @ 14,17 SAY "Expense types"
*
USE expenses
  @ 10,37 SAY TRAN(RECCOUNT(),"###,###")
  @ 10,46 SAY TRAN(INT((RECSIZE()*reccount())+header()+1),"####,###")
  @ 10,56 SAY LUPDATE()
*
USE receipts
```

```
  @ 11,37 SAY TRAN(RECCOUNT(),"###,###")
  @ 11,46 SAY TRAN(INT((RECSIZE()*reccount())+header()+1),"####,###")
  @ 11,56 SAY LUPDATE()
*
USE clntcode
  @ 12,37 SAY TRAN(RECCOUNT(),"###,###")
  @ 12,46 SAY TRAN(INT((RECSIZE()*reccount())+header()+1),"####,###")
  @ 12,56 SAY LUPDATE()
*
USE suppcode
  @ 13,37 SAY TRAN(RECCOUNT(),"###,###")
  @ 13,46 SAY TRAN(INT((RECSIZE()*reccount())+header()+1),"####,###")
  @ 13,56 SAY LUPDATE()
*
USE typecode
  @ 14,37 SAY TRAN(RECCOUNT(),"###,###")
  @ 14,46 SAY TRAN(INT((RECSIZE()*reccount())+header()+1),"####,###")
  @ 14,56 SAY LUPDATE()
*
CLOSE DATABASES
ESCKEY()
SET CURSOR(.F.)
INKEY(60)
SET CURSOR(.T.)
RETURN
```

```
* Program Name .......... errorsys.prg
* Revised Date .......... 07/01/88
*
FUNCTION EXPR_ERROR
PARAMETERS NAME,LINE,INFO,MODEL,_1,_2,_3
SET DEVICE TO SCREEN
@ 00,00
@ 00,00 SAY "PROC " + M->NAME + " LINE " + LTRIM(STR(M->LINE)) +;
  ", " + M->INFO
SETCOLOR("W")
SET CURSOR(.T.)
QUIT
RETURN .F.
*
FUNCTION UNDEF_ERROR
PARAMETERS NAME,LINE,INFO,MODEL,_1
SET DEVICE TO SCREEN
@ 00,00
@ 00,00 SAY "PROC " + M->NAME + " LINE " + LTRIM(STR(M->LINE)) +;
  ", " + M->INFO + " " + M->_1
SETCOLOR("W")
SET CURSOR(.T.)
QUIT
RETURN .T.
```

```
*
FUNCTION MISC_ERROR
PARAMETERS NAME,LINE,INFO,MODEL
SET DEVICE TO SCREEN
@ 00,00
@ 00,00 SAY "PROC " + M->NAME + " LINE " + LTRIM(STR(M->LINE)) +;
  ", " + M->INFO
SETCOLOR("W")
SET CURSOR(.T.)
QUIT
RETURN .F.
*
FUNCTION OPEN_ERROR
PARAMETERS NAME,LINE,INFO,MODEL,_1
IF MODEL == "USE"
  RETURN .F.
ENDIF
SET DEVICE TO SCREEN
@ 00,00
@ 00,00 SAY "PROC " + M->NAME + " LINE " + LTRIM(STR(M->LINE)) +;
  ", " + M->INFO + " " + M->_1 + " (" + LTRIM(STR(DOSERROR())) + ")"
@ 00,65 SAY "RETRY? (Y/N)"
INKEY(0)
DO WHILE ! UPPER(CHR(LASTKEY())) $ "YN"
  INKEY(0)
ENDDO
IF ! UPPER(CHR(LASTKEY())) = "Y"
  SETCOLOR("W")
  SET CURSOR(.T.)
  QUIT
ENDIF
@ 00,00
RETURN .T.
*
FUNCTION DB_ERROR
PARAMETERS NAME,LINE,INFO
SET DEVICE TO SCREEN
@ 00,00
@ 00,00 SAY "PROC " + M->NAME + " LINE " + LTRIM(STR(M->LINE)) +;
  ", " + M->INFO
SETCOLOR("W")
SET CURSOR(.T.)
QUIT
RETURN .F.
*
FUNCTION PRINT_ERROR
PARAMETERS NAME,LINE
SET DEVICE TO SCREEN
@ 00,00
@ 00,00 SAY "PROC " + M->NAME + " LINE " + LTRIM(STR(M->LINE)) +;
  ", PRINTER NOT READY"
```

```
@ 00,65 SAY "RETRY? (Y/N)"
INKEY(0)
DO WHILE ! UPPER(CHR(LASTKEY())) $ "YN"
  INKEY(0)
ENDDO
IF ! UPPER(CHR(LASTKEY())) = "Y"
  SETCOLOR("W")
  SET CURSOR(.T.)
  QUIT
ENDIF
@ 00,00
RETURN .T.
```

```
* Program Name ......... e_expn.prg
* Revised Date ......... 07/01/88
*
SAYHEADER("Enter a New Expense")
  @ 07,00 SAY "Expense Number ...."
  @ 07,40 SAY "Expense Date ......"
  @ 08,00 SAY "Expense Amount ...."
  @ 08,40 SAY "Description ......."
  @ 10,00 SAY "Type Code ........."
  @ 10,40 SAY "Description ......."
  @ 11,00 SAY "Supplier Code ....."
  @ 11,40 SAY "Description ......."
  @ 13,00 SAY "Invoice Number ...."
  @ 14,00 SAY "Check Number ......"
  @ 14,40 SAY "Date Paid ........."
  @ 16,00 SAY "Comment (y/n) ....."
SETCOLOR(cline)
  @ 09,00 SAY repl("—",80)
  @ 12,00 SAY repl("—",80)
  @ 15,00 SAY repl("—",80)
SETCOLOR(cnorm)
*
STORE SPACE(03)        TO mtypecode, msuppcode
STORE SPACE(04)        TO mexpnnumb
STORE SPACE(10)        TO minvcnumb, mcheknumb
STORE SPACE(20)        TO mexpndesc
STORE DATE()           TO mexpndate
STORE CTOD("  /  /  ") TO mpaiddate
STORE 0                TO mexpnamnt
STORE .F.              TO mexpnmemo
*
USE expenses INDEX expenses
GO BOTTOM
STORE STR(VAL(expnnumb)+1,4) TO mexpnnumb
CLOSE DATABASES
*
```

```
SETCOLOR(cinve)
  @ 07,20 SAY mexpnnumb
SETCOLOR(cnorm)
*
entering = .T.
DO WHILE entering
  HELPKEY()
    @ 07,60 GET mexpndate PICTURE "@D"
    @ 08,20 GET mexpnamnt PICTURE "##,###.##"
    @ 08,60 GET mexpndesc
    @ 10,20 GET mtypecode PICTURE "@!" VALID ve_expn1(mtypecode)
    @ 11,20 GET msuppcode PICTURE "@!" VALID ve_expn2(msuppcode)
    @ 13,20 GET minvcnumb PICTURE "@!"
    @ 14,20 GET mcheknumb PICTURE "@!"
    @ 14,60 GET mpaiddate PICTURE "@D"
    @ 16,20 GET mexpnmemo PICTURE "Y"
  READ
  M_CLEAR()
  IF LASTKEY() = 27
    RETURN
  ENDIF
  entering = .F.
  mchoice = 1
    @ 22,31 PROMPT "Append" MESSAGE "  Add this expense to the file"
    @ 22,38 PROMPT "Change" MESSAGE "  Change this expense"
    @ 22,45 PROMPT "Quit"   MESSAGE "  Quit and abort"
  CLEAR TYPEAHEAD
  MENU TO mchoice
  M_CLEAR()
  DO CASE
    CASE mchoice = 1
      M_WAIT()
      USE expenses INDEX expenses
      SET DELETED OFF
      SEEK "      "
      IF ! FOUND()
        APPEND BLANK
      ELSE
        RECALL
      ENDIF
      REPLACE expnnumb WITH mexpnnumb, expndate WITH mexpndate,;
              expndesc WITH mexpndesc, expnamnt WITH mexpnamnt,;
              typecode WITH mtypecode, suppcode WITH msuppcode
      REPLACE invcnumb WITH minvcnumb, paiddate WITH mpaiddate,;
              cheknumb WITH mcheknumb, expnmemo WITH mexpnmemo
      SET DELETED ON
      CLOSE DATABASES
      M_CLEAR()
      IF mexpnmemo
        MEMOBOX1()
```

```
        STORE SPACE(1) TO memo
        STORE "CM"+LTRIM(mexpnnumb)+".TXT" TO mfilename
        SETCOLOR(cmemo)
        MEMOWRIT(mfilename,MEMOEDIT(memo,05,04,18,75,.T.,"dbm"))
        SETCOLOR(cnorm)
      ENDIF
      EXIT
    CASE mchoice = 2
      entering = .T.
      LOOP
    CASE mchoice = 3 .OR. LASTKEY() = 27
      EXIT
  ENDCASE
ENDDO
RETURN
*
FUNCTION ve_expn1
PARAMETERS mtypecode
USE typecode INDEX typecode
SEEK mtypecode
IF ! FOUND()
  ok = .F.
  M_ERROR()
ELSE
  ok = .T.
  SETCOLOR(cinve)
    @ 10,60 SAY typename
  SETCOLOR(cnorm)
ENDIF
CLOSE DATABASES
RETURN(ok)
*
FUNCTION ve_expn2
PARAMETERS msuppcode
USE suppcode INDEX suppcode
SEEK msuppcode
IF ! FOUND()
  ok = .F.
  M_ERROR()
ELSE
  ok = .T.
  SETCOLOR(cinve)
    @ 11,60 SAY suppname
  SETCOLOR(cnorm)
ENDIF
CLOSE DATABASES
RETURN(ok)
```

```
* Program Name .......... e_memo.prg
* Revised Date .......... 07/01/88
*
SAYHEADER("Review/Edit an Expense Memo")
*
HELPKEY()
M_BLANK()
STORE 0 TO mexpnnr
  @ 07,25 SAY "Expense Number ...."
  @ 09,25 SAY "Memo Name ........."
  @ 07,45 GET mexpnnr PICTURE "####" VALID ve_memo1(mexpnnr)
READ
IF LASTKEY() = 27
  RETURN
ENDIF
STORE "CM"+LTRIM(STR(mexpnnr,4))+".TXT" TO mmemo
*
IF mexpnnr = 0
  M_CLEAR()
  HELPKEY()
  STORE SPACE(10) to mmemo
    @ 09,45 GET mmemo PICTURE "@!" VALID ve_memo2(mmemo)
  READ
  IF LASTKEY() = 27
    RETURN
  ENDIF
ENDIF
*
SAYHEADER("Editing Expense Memo "+mmemo)
MEMOBOX1()
SETCOLOR(cmemo)
MEMOWRIT(mmemo,MEMOEDIT(MEMOREAD(mmemo),05,04,18,75,.T.,"dbm"))
SETCOLOR(cnorm)
RETURN
*
FUNCTION ve_memo1
PARAMETERS mexpnnr
IF mexpnnr = 0
  ok = .T.
ELSE
  STORE "CM"+LTRIM(STR(mexpnnr,4))+".TXT" TO mmemo
  IF FILE(mmemo)
    ok = .T.
  ELSE
    ok = .F.
    M_ERROR()
  ENDIF
ENDIF
RETURN(ok)
*
FUNCTION ve_memo2
PARAMETERS mmemo
```

```
IF FILE(mmemo)
  ok = .T.
ELSE
  ok = .F.
  M_ERROR()
ENDIF
RETURN(ok)
```

```
* Program Name .......... e_mnte.prg
* Revised Date .......... 07/01/88
*
PARAMETERS m_main
*
DO CASE
  CASE m_main = 4
    SAYHEADER("Enter a new Client Code")
    prompt1 = "Client Code ......."
    prompt2 = "Client Name ......."
    memvar1 = "mCLNTCODE"
    memvar2 = "mCLNTNAME"
    dbfvar1 = "CLNTCODE"
    dbfvar2 = "CLNTNAME"
    dbfname = "CLNTCODE"
    ntxname = "CLNTCODE"
  CASE m_main = 5
    SAYHEADER("Enter a new Supplier Code")
    prompt1 = "Supplier Code ....."
    prompt2 = "Supplier Name......"
    memvar1 = "mSUPPCODE"
    memvar2 = "mSUPPNAME"
    dbfvar1 = "SUPPCODE"
    dbfvar2 = "SUPPNAME"
    dbfname = "SUPPCODE"
    ntxname = "SUPPCODE"
  CASE m_main = 6
    SAYHEADER("Enter a new Expense Type Code")
    prompt1 = "Type Code ........."
    prompt2 = "Type Name ........."
    memvar1 = "mTYPECODE"
    memvar2 = "mTYPENAME"
    dbfvar1 = "TYPECODE"
    dbfvar2 = "TYPENAME"
    dbfname = "TYPECODE"
    ntxname = "TYPECODE"
ENDCASE
*
STORE SPACE(03) TO memvar1
STORE SPACE(20) TO memvar2
*
entering = .T.
```

```
DO WHILE entering
  HELPKEY()
    @ 07,20 SAY prompt1 GET memvar1 PICTURE "@!" ;
            VALID ve_mnte(memvar1,dbfname,ntxname)
    @ 08,20 SAY prompt2 GET memvar2 VALID v_string(memvar2)
  READ
  M_CLEAR()
  IF LASTKEY() = 27
    EXIT
  ENDIF
  entering = .F.
  mchoice = 1
    @ 22,31 PROMPT "Append" MESSAGE "  Add this code to the file"
    @ 22,38 PROMPT "Change" MESSAGE "  Change this code"
    @ 22,45 PROMPT "Quit"   MESSAGE "  Quit and abort"
  CLEAR TYPEAHEAD
  MENU TO mchoice
  M_CLEAR()
  DO CASE
    CASE mchoice = 1
      M_WAIT()
      USE (dbfname) INDEX (ntxname)
      SET DELETED OFF
      SEEK "    "
      IF FOUND()
        RECALL
      ELSE
        APPEND BLANK
      ENDIF
      REPLACE &dbfvar1 WITH memvar1, &dbfvar2 WITH memvar2
      SET DELETED ON
      CLOSE DATABASES
      M_CLEAR()
    CASE mchoice = 2
      entering = .T.
      LOOP
    CASE mchoice = 3 .OR. LASTKEY() = 27
      EXIT
  ENDCASE
ENDDO
RETURN
*
FUNCTION ve_mnte
PARAMETERS memvar1,dbfname,ntxname
IF EMPTY(memvar1)
  ok = .F.
  M_ERROR()
ELSE
  USE (dbfname) INDEX (ntxname)
  SEEK memvar1
```

```
  IF FOUND()
    ok = .F.
    M_INFILE()
  ELSE
    ok = .T.
  ENDIF
  CLOSE DATABASES
ENDIF
RETURN(ok)
```

```
* Program Name ......... e_rcpt.prg
* Revised Date ......... 07/01/88
*
SAYHEADER("Enter a New Receipt")
  @ 07,00 SAY "Receipt Number ...."
  @ 07,40 SAY "Receipt Date ......"
  @ 08,00 SAY "Receipt Amount ...."
  @ 08,40 SAY "Description ......."
  @ 10,00 SAY "Client Code ......."
  @ 10,40 SAY "Description ......."
  @ 12,00 SAY "Check Number ......"
SETCOLOR(cline)
  @ 09,00 SAY repl("-",80)
  @ 11,00 SAY repl("-",80)
SETCOLOR(cnorm)
*
STORE SPACE(03) TO mclntcode
STORE SPACE(04) TO mrcptnumb
STORE SPACE(10) TO mcheknumb
STORE SPACE(20) TO mrcptdesc
STORE DATE()    TO mrcptdate
STORE 0         TO mrcptamnt
*
USE receipts INDEX receipts
GO BOTTOM
STORE STR(VAL(rcptnumb)+1,4) TO mrcptnumb
CLOSE DATABASES
*
SETCOLOR(cinve)
  @ 07,20 SAY mrcptnumb
SETCOLOR(cnorm)
*
entering = .T.
DO WHILE entering
  HELPKEY()
    @ 07,60 GET mrcptdate PICTURE "@D"
    @ 08,20 GET mrcptamnt PICTURE "##,###.##"
    @ 08,60 GET mrcptdesc
    @ 10,20 GET mclntcode PICTURE "@!" VALID ve_rcpt(mclntcode)
    @ 12,20 GET mcheknumb PICTURE "@!"
```

```
READ
M_CLEAR()
IF LASTKEY() = 27
  RETURN
ENDIF
entering = .F.
mchoice = 1
ESCKEY()
  @ 22,31 PROMPT "Append" MESSAGE "  Add this receipt to the file"
  @ 22,38 PROMPT "Change" MESSAGE "  Change this receipt"
  @ 22,45 PROMPT "Quit"   MESSAGE "  Quit and abort"
CLEAR TYPEAHEAD
MENU TO mchoice
M_CLEAR()
DO CASE
  CASE mchoice = 1
    M_WAIT()
    USE receipts INDEX receipts
    SET DELETED OFF
    SEEK "      "
    IF ! FOUND()
      APPEND BLANK
    ELSE
      RECALL
    ENDIF
    REPLACE rcptnumb WITH mrcptnumb, rcptdate WITH mrcptdate,;
            rcptdesc WITH mrcptdesc, rcptamnt WITH mrcptamnt,;
            clntcode WITH mclntcode, cheknumb WITH mcheknumb
    SET DELETED ON
    CLOSE DATABASES
    M_CLEAR()
    EXIT
  CASE mchoice = 2
    entering = .T.
    LOOP
  CASE mchoice = 3 .OR. LASTKEY() = 27
    EXIT
  ENDCASE
ENDDO
RETURN
*
FUNCTION ve_rcpt
PARAMETERS mclntcode
USE clntcode INDEX clntcode
SEEK mclntcode
IF ! FOUND()
  ok = .F.
  M_ERROR()
ELSE
  ok = .T.
```

```
  SETCOLOR(cinve)
     @ 10,60 SAY clntname
  SETCOLOR(cnorm)
ENDIF
CLOSE DATABASES
RETURN(ok)
```

```
* Program Name ......... func.prg
* Revised Date ......... 07/01/88
*
FUNCTION DBE
PARAMETERS mode,i
cur_field = fields[i]
DO CASE
  CASE mode < 4
    RETURN(1)
  CASE LASTKEY() = 13 .OR. LASTKEY() = 27
    RETURN(0)
  OTHERWISE
    RETURN(1)
ENDCASE
*
FUNCTION DBM
PARAMETERS mode,line,col
UPDATED = .F.
IF mode = 2
  UPDATED = .T.
ENDIF
IF mode = 0 && idle
  @ 20,70 SAY TRAN(line,"###")
  @ 21,70 SAY TRAN(COL+1,"###")
  RETURN(0)
ELSE
  DO CASE
    CASE LASTKEY() = 23 .OR. LASTKEY() = -9 && save
      IF UPDATED
        M_SAVE()
        RETURN(23)
      ELSE
        RETURN(27)
      ENDIF
    CASE LASTKEY() = 27 && escape
      IF UPDATED
        @ 24,27 SAY "Do you want to abort (y/n)?"
        response = " "
        DO WHILE ! response $ "YN"
          response = UPPER(CHR(INKEY(0)))
        ENDDO
        @ 24,00
        IF response = "Y"
```

```
                          RETURN(27)
                    ELSE
                          RETURN(32)
                    ENDIF
              ELSE
                    RETURN(27)
              ENDIF
         CASE LASTKEY() = -3 && delete line
              RETURN(25)
         CASE LASTKEY() = -5 && insert line
              RETURN(14)
      ENDCASE
ENDIF
*
FUNCTION DBT
PARAMETERS mode,element,position
DO CASE
   CASE LASTKEY() = 13
        RETURN(1)
   CASE LASTKEY() = 27
        RETURN(1)
   OTHERWISE
        RETURN(2)
ENDCASE
*
FUNCTION CLS
SETCOLOR(CNORM)
SCROLL(04,00,22,79,00)
   @ 24,00
RETURN("")
*
FUNCTION SAYHEADER
PARAMETERS header
CLS()
SETCOLOR(cmess)
   @ 02,02 SAY header+SPACE(55-LEN(header))
SETCOLOR(cnorm)
MENUTONE()
READINSERT(.F.)
SET CURSOR(.T.)
RETURN("")
*
FUNCTION ESCKEY
SETCOLOR(cmess)
   @ 24,00
   @ 24,00 SAY M_CNTR("Press [Esc] to escape")
SETCOLOR(cnorm)
RETURN("")
*
FUNCTION HELPKEY
```

```
SETCOLOR(cmess)
   @ 24,00
   @ 24,00 SAY M_CNTR("Press [Esc] to escape or [F1] for help")
SETCOLOR(cnorm)
RETURN("")
*
FUNCTION MENUBOX
PARAMETERS TOP,LEFT,BOTTOM,RIGHT
frame = "┌─┐||┘─└|"
SETCOLOR(cline)
   @TOP,LEFT,BOTTOM,RIGHT BOX frame
SETCOLOR(cnorm)
RETURN("")
*
FUNCTION M_CNTR
PARAMETERS mmsg
RETURN(SPACE(INT(41-LEN(mmsg)/2))+mmsg)
*
FUNCTION H_CNTR
PARAMETERS hd,wid
RETURN(SPACE(INT(wid/2-LEN(TRIM(hd))/2))+hd)
*
FUNCTION HELPBOX
SETCOLOR(cmess)
   @ 05,19 TO 21,60 DOUBLE
   @ 18,19 SAY "┌─────────────┬─────────────┬──────────────┐"
   @ 19,19 SAY "│   Scroll | | │   Select    │  Abort Help  │"
   @ 20,19 SAY "│   Pan  <- -> │   Choice <─┘│     [Esc]    │"
   @ 21,19 SAY "└─────────────┴─────────────┴──────────────┘"
SETCOLOR(clogo)
   @ 19,21 SAY "Scroll | |"
   @ 19,34 SAY "Select"
   @ 19,48 SAY "Abort Help"
   @ 20,21 SAY "Pan  <- ->"
   @ 20,34 SAY "Choice <─┘"
   @ 20,50 SAY "[Esc]"
SETCOLOR(cnorm)
RETURN("")
*
FUNCTION MEMOBOX1
SETCOLOR(cmess)
   @ 04,03 TO 22,76 DOUBLE
   @ 19,03 SAY;
"┌────────────────────┬────────────────────┬──────────────────────┐"
   @ 20,03 SAY;
"│    Esc => Abort    │  F4 => delete a line  │   Current line      │"
   @ 21,03 SAY;
"│    F10 => Save     │  F6 => insert a line  │   Current column    │"
   @ 22,03 SAY;
"└────────────────────┴────────────────────┴──────────────────────┘"
```

```
SETCOLOR(clogo)
   @ 20,07 SAY "Esc => Abort"
   @ 21,07 SAY "F10 => Save"
   @ 20,26 SAY "F4 => delete a line"
   @ 21,26 SAY "F6 => insert a line"
   @ 20,52 SAY "Current line"
   @ 21,52 SAY "Current column"
SETCOLOR(cnorm)
RETURN("")
*
FUNCTION MEMOBOX2
SETCOLOR(cmess)
   @ 04,03 TO 22,76 DOUBLE
   @ 19,03 SAY;
"|---------------------------------------------------------------------|"
   @ 20,03 SAY;
"|    Esc => Abort       |                    |  Current line        |"
   @ 21,03 SAY;
"|                       |                    |  Current column      |"
   @ 22,03 SAY;
"|_____|_____|_____|"
SETCOLOR(clogo)
   @ 20,07 SAY "Esc => Abort"
   @ 20,52 SAY "Current line"
   @ 21,52 SAY "Current column"
SETCOLOR(cnorm)
RETURN("")
*
FUNCTION M_WAIT
M_CLEAR()
SETCOLOR(cmess)
   @ 24,29 SAY "Working ... please wait"
SETCOLOR(cmess+"*")
   @ 24,29 SAY "Working"
SETCOLOR(cnorm)
SET CURSOR(.F.)
RETURN("")
*
FUNCTION M_SAVE
SETCOLOR(cmess)
   @ 24,29 SAY "Saving ... please wait"
SETCOLOR(cmess+"*")
   @ 24,29 SAY "Saving"
SETCOLOR(cnorm)
SET CURSOR(.F.)
RETURN("")
*
FUNCTION M_ERROR
SAVE SCREEN
```

```
M_CLEAR()
ERRORTONE()
SETCOLOR(cmess)
  @ 24,29 SAY "Error ... invalid entry"
SETCOLOR(cmess+"*")
  @ 24,29 SAY "Error"
SETCOLOR(cnorm)
SET CURSOR(.F.)
INKEY(3)
SET CURSOR(.T.)
RESTORE SCREEN
RETURN("")
*
FUNCTION M_INFILE
SAVE SCREEN
M_CLEAR()
ERRORTONE()
SETCOLOR(cmess)
  @ 24,28 SAY "Error ... duplicate entry"
SETCOLOR(cmess+"*")
  @ 24,28 SAY "Error"
SETCOLOR(cnorm)
SET CURSOR(.F.)
INKEY(3)
SET CURSOR(.T.)
RESTORE SCREEN
RETURN("")
*
FUNCTION M_PRINT
M_CLEAR()
SETCOLOR(cmess)
  @ 24,24 SAY "Printing ... press [Esc] to abort"
SETCOLOR(cmess+"*")
  @ 24,24 SAY "Printing"
SETCOLOR(cnorm)
SET CURSOR(.F.)
RETURN("")
*
FUNCTION M_BLANK
SETCOLOR(cmess)
  @ 22,00
  @ 22,00 SAY M_CNTR("You may leave this entry blank")
SETCOLOR(cnorm)
RETURN("")
*
FUNCTION M_CLEAR
SETCOLOR(cnorm)
  @ 22,00 SAY SPACE(80)
  @ 24,00
SET CURSOR(.T.)
RETURN("")
```

```
*
FUNCTION M_STATUS
PARAMETERS mmsg
M_CLEAR()
SETCOLOR(cmess)
  @ 24,00 SAY M_CNTR(mmsg)
SETCOLOR(cnorm)
SET CURSOR(.F.)
RETURN("")
*
FUNCTION M_PRTR
IF ISPRINTER()
  RETURN(.T.)
ELSE
  PRINTERTONE()
  M_CLEAR()
  SETCOLOR(cmess)
    @ 24,15 SAY "Error ... fix printer and press any key to continue"
  SETCOLOR(cmess+"*")
    @ 24,15 SAY "Error"
  SET CURSOR(.F.)
  INKEY(10)
  SET CURSOR(.T.)
  IF LASTKEY() = 27
    RETURN(.F.)
  ENDIF
  IF ISPRINTER()
    RETURN(.T.)
  ELSE
    RETURN(.F.)
  ENDIF
ENDIF
RETURN("")
*
FUNCTION M_HELP
@ 00,00
SETCOLOR(clogo+"*")
  @ 00,00 SAY M_CNTR("< CM Help >")
SETCOLOR(cnorm)
RETURN("")
*
FUNCTION DONETONE
IF atone
  TONE(300,1)
  TONE(400,1)
  TONE(500,1)
ENDIF
RETURN("")
*
```

```
FUNCTION FILETONE
IF atone
   TONE(500,1)
ENDIF
RETURN("")
*
FUNCTION DELETETONE
IF atone
   TONE(300,1)
   TONE(300,1)
   TONE(300,1)
ENDIF
RETURN("")
*
FUNCTION PRINTERTONE
IF atone
   TONE(400,2)
   TONE(200,2)
   TONE(400,2)
   TONE(200,2)
ENDIF
RETURN("")
*
FUNCTION ERRORTONE
IF atone
   TONE(200,2)
ENDIF
RETURN("")
*
FUNCTION MENUTONE
IF atone
   TONE(400,1)
ENDIF
RETURN("")
*
FUNCTION V_STRING
PARAMETERS mstr
IF EMPTY(mstr)
   ok = .F.
   M_ERROR()
ELSE
   ok = .T.
ENDIF
RETURN(ok)
*
FUNCTION V_DATE
PARAMETERS mbeg,mend
IF EMPTY(mend) .OR. mend < mbeg
   ok = .F.
   M_ERROR()
```

```
ELSE
   ok = .T.
ENDIF
RETURN(ok)
*
FUNCTION V_NUMBER
PARAMETERS mnum
IF EMPTY(mnum)
   ok = .F.
   M_ERROR()
ELSE
   ok = .T.
ENDIF
RETURN(ok)
*
FUNCTION BEGMONTH
RETURN CTOD(STR(MONTH(DATE()),2)+"/01/"+STR(YEAR(DATE())-1900,2))
```

```
* Program Name ......... help.prg
* Revised Date ......... 07/01/88
*
PARAMETERS prg,line,mvar
*
IF prg = "HELP"
   ERRORTONE()
   RETURN
ENDIF
*
DO CASE
*
CASE prg = "CM"
   SAVE SCREEN
   CLS()
   M_HELP()
   SETCOLOR(cline)
   @ 07,15 TO 15,64 DOUBLE
   SETCOLOR(chelp)
   @ 08,16 SAY " Welcome to Cost Management, designed to track  "
   @ 09,16 SAY " business expenses and receipts. If this is the "
   @ 10,16 SAY " first time use of CM, a system password has     "
   @ 11,16 SAY " yet to be assigned. Therefore, at password      "
   @ 12,16 SAY " entry, just enter CM to get started.            "
   @ 13,16 SAY "                                                 "
   @ 14,16 SAY " Press any key to continue ...                   "
   SET CURSOR(.F.)
   INKEY(60)
   SET CURSOR(.T.)
   SETCOLOR(cline+",x")
   RESTORE SCREEN
   RETURN
```

```
*
CASE SUBSTR(prg,1,2) == "M_" .OR. SUBSTR(prg,1,2) == "S_"
  SAVE SCREEN
  CLS()
  M_HELP()
  SETCOLOR(cline)
  @ 07,15 TO 15,64 DOUBLE
  SETCOLOR(chelp)
  @ 08,16 SAY " Menu selections are scrolled by using the up   "
  @ 09,16 SAY " and down cursor keys, or the left and right     "
  @ 10,16 SAY " cursor keys. A selection is made by pressing    "
  @ 11,16 SAY " the Enter key, or by pressing the first letter  "
  @ 12,16 SAY " in the name of a choice.                        "
  @ 13,16 SAY "                                                 "
  @ 14,16 SAY " Press any key to continue ...                   "
  SET CURSOR(.F.)
  INKEY(60)
  SETCOLOR(cnorm)
  RESTORE SCREEN
  RETURN
*
CASE mvar == "MMEMO"
  SAVE SCREEN
  numfiles = ADIR("*.TXT")
  PRIVATE txtfiles[numfiles]
  ADIR("*.TXT",txtfiles)
  ASORT(txtfiles)
  SETCOLOR(cline)
    @ 12,33 TO 20,46 DOUBLE
    @ 14,33 SAY "|---------------|"
  SETCOLOR(clogo)
    @ 13,36 SAY "FileName"
  SETCOLOR(chelp)
  SET CURSOR(.F.)
  filename = txtfiles[achoice(15,34,19,45,txtfiles,"","dbt")]
  SET CURSOR(.T.)
  IF LASTKEY() = 13
    mmemo = filename + SPACE(10-LEN(filename))
  ELSE
    mmemo = SPACE(10)
  ENDIF
  SETCOLOR(cnorm)
  RESTORE SCREEN
  RETURN
*
CASE mvar == "MCLNTCODE" .OR. (mvar == "MEMVAR1" .AND. hcode = 4)
  SAVE SCREEN
  CLS()
  M_HELP()
  USE clntcode INDEX clntcode
```

```
      DECLARE fields[2]
      DECLARE heads[2]
      fields[1] = "CLNTCODE"
      fields[2] = "CLNTNAME"
      heads[1]  = "Code"
      heads[2]  = "Client Name"
      HELPBOX()
      SET CURSOR(.F.)
      DBEDIT(06,20,17,59,fields,"dbe",.T.,heads)
      SET CURSOR(.T.)
      IF LASTKEY() = 13
        STORE clntcode TO &mvar
        KEYBOARD CHR(13)
      ENDIF
      CLOSE DATABASES
      SETCOLOR(cnorm)
      RESTORE SCREEN
      RETURN
*
CASE mvar == "MSUPPCODE" .OR. (mvar == "MEMVAR1" .AND. hcode = 5)
      SAVE SCREEN
      CLS()
      M_HELP()
      USE suppcode INDEX suppcode
      DECLARE fields[2]
      DECLARE heads[2]
      fields[1] = "SUPPCODE"
      fields[2] = "SUPPNAME"
      heads[1]  = "Code"
      heads[2]  = "Supplier Name"
      HELPBOX()
      SET CURSOR(.F.)
      DBEDIT(06,20,17,59,fields,"dbe",.T.,heads)
      SET CURSOR(.T.)
      IF LASTKEY() = 13
        STORE suppcode TO &mvar
        KEYBOARD CHR(13)
      ENDIF
      CLOSE DATABASES
      SETCOLOR(cnorm)
      RESTORE SCREEN
      RETURN
*
CASE mvar == "MTYPECODE" .OR. (mvar == "MEMVAR1" .AND. hcode = 6)
      SAVE SCREEN
      CLS()
      M_HELP()
      USE typecode INDEX typecode
      DECLARE fields[2]
      DECLARE heads[2]
```

```
  fields[1] = "TYPECODE"
  fields[2] = "TYPENAME"
  heads[1]  = "Code"
  heads[2]  = "Type Name"
  HELPBOX()
  SET CURSOR(.F.)
  DBEDIT(06,20,17,59,fields,"dbe",.T.,heads)
  SET CURSOR(.T.)
  IF LASTKEY() = 13
    STORE typecode TO &mvar
    KEYBOARD CHR(13)
  ENDIF
  CLOSE DATABASES
  SETCOLOR(cnorm)
  RESTORE SCREEN
  RETURN
*
CASE mvar == "MEXPNNR"
  SAVE SCREEN
  CLS()
  M_HELP()
  SELECT 3
  USE typecode INDEX typecode
  SELECT 2
  USE suppcode INDEX suppcode
  SELECT 1
  USE expenses INDEX expenses
  SET RELATION TO suppcode INTO B, TO typecode INTO C
  DECLARE fields[4]
  DECLARE heads[4]
  fields[1] = "EXPNNUMB"
  fields[2] = "EXPNDATE"
  fields[3] = "B->SUPPNAME"
  fields[4] = "C->TYPENAME"
  heads[1]  = "Expn#"
  heads[2]  = "Date"
  heads[3]  = "Supplier Name"
  heads[4]  = "Expense Type Name"
  HELPBOX()
  SET CURSOR(.F.)
  DBEDIT(06,20,17,59,fields,"dbe",.T.,heads)
  SET CURSOR(.T.)
  IF LASTKEY() = 13
    STORE VAL(expnnumb) TO mexpnnr
    KEYBOARD CHR(13)
  ENDIF
  CLOSE DATABASES
  SETCOLOR(cnorm)
  RESTORE SCREEN
  RETURN
```

```
*
CASE mvar == "MRCPTNR"
  SAVE SCREEN
  CLS()
  M_HELP()
  SELECT 2
  USE clntcode INDEX clntcode
  SELECT 1
  USE receipts INDEX receipts
  SET RELATION TO clntcode INTO B
  DECLARE fields[3]
  DECLARE heads[3]
  fields[1] = "RCPTNUMB"
  fields[2] = "RCPTDATE"
  fields[3] = "B->CLNTNAME"
  heads[1]  = "Rcpt#"
  heads[2]  = "Date"
  heads[3]  = "Client Name"
  HELPBOX()
  SET CURSOR(.F.)
  DBEDIT(06,20,17,59,fields,"dbe",.T.,heads)
  SET CURSOR(.T.)
  IF LASTKEY() = 13
    STORE VAL(rcptnumb) TO mrcptnr
    KEYBOARD CHR(13)
  ENDIF
  CLOSE DATABASES
  SETCOLOR(cnorm)
  RESTORE SCREEN
  RETURN
*
CASE mvar == "MEMVAR2" .AND. hcode = 4
  SAVE SCREEN
  CLS()
  M_HELP()
  SETCOLOR(cmess)
    @ 06,23 TO 11,57 DOUBLE
  SETCOLOR(chelp)
    @ 07,24 SAY " Enter a client name for this   "
    @ 08,24 SAY " field.                         "
    @ 09,24 SAY "                                "
    @ 10,24 SAY " Press any key to continue ...  "
  SETCOLOR(cnorm)
  SET CURSOR(.F.)
  INKEY(10)
  SET CURSOR(.T.)
  RESTORE SCREEN
  RETURN
*
CASE mvar == "MEMVAR2" .AND. hcode = 5
```

```
  SAVE SCREEN
  CLS( )
  M_HELP( )
  SETCOLOR(cmess)
    @ 06,23 TO 11,57 DOUBLE
  SETCOLOR(chelp)
    @ 07,24 SAY " Enter a supplier name for this  "
    @ 08,24 SAY " field.                          "
    @ 09,24 SAY "                                 "
    @ 10,24 SAY " Press any key to continue ...   "
  SETCOLOR(cnorm)
  SET CURSOR(.F.)
  INKEY(10)
  SET CURSOR(.T.)
  RESTORE SCREEN
  RETURN
*
CASE mvar == "MEMVAR2" .AND. hcode = 6
  SAVE SCREEN
  CLS( )
  M_HELP( )
  SETCOLOR(cmess)
    @ 06,23 TO 11,57 DOUBLE
  SETCOLOR(chelp)
    @ 07,24 SAY " Enter an expense type name or   "
    @ 08,24 SAY " description for this field.      "
    @ 09,24 SAY "                                 "
    @ 10,24 SAY " Press any key to continue ...   "
  SETCOLOR(cnorm)
  SET CURSOR(.F.)
  INKEY(10)
  SET CURSOR(.T.)
  RESTORE SCREEN
  RETURN
*
CASE TYPE(mvar) == "D"
  SAVE SCREEN
  CLS( )
  M_HELP( )
  SETCOLOR(cline)
    @ 06,23 TO 17,57 DOUBLE
  SETCOLOR(chelp)
    @ 07,24 SAY " Enter dates as follows:         "
    @ 08,24 SAY "                                 "
    @ 09,24 SAY "      mm/dd/yy                    "
    @ 10,24 SAY "      ⎩ ⎩ ⎩                      "
    @ 11,24 SAY "                                 "
    @ 12,24 SAY "          └ 2-digit year         "
    @ 13,24 SAY "        └ 2-digit day            "
    @ 14,24 SAY "      └ 2-digit month            "
```

```
      @ 15,24 SAY "                                          "
      @ 16,24 SAY " Press any key to continue ...   "
   SETCOLOR(cnorm)
   SET CURSOR(.F.)
   INKEY(10)
   SET CURSOR(.T.)
   RESTORE SCREEN
   RETURN
*
CASE TYPE(mvar) == "L"
   SAVE SCREEN
   CLS()
   M_HELP()
   SETCOLOR(cline)
      @ 06,24 TO 08,56 DOUBLE
   SETCOLOR(chelp)
      @ 07,25 SAY " Press [Y] for Yes, [N] for No "
   SETCOLOR(cnorm)
   SET CURSOR(.F.)
   response = INKEY(0)
   KEYBOARD(CHR(response)+CHR(13))
   SET CURSOR(.T.)
   RESTORE SCREEN
   RETURN
*
CASE mvar == "MEXPNAMNT"
   SAVE SCREEN
   CLS()
   M_HELP()
   SETCOLOR(cline)
      @ 06,23 TO 11,57 DOUBLE
   SETCOLOR(chelp)
      @ 07,24 SAY " Enter the total charge for this "
      @ 08,24 SAY " expense.                        "
      @ 09,24 SAY "                                 "
      @ 10,24 SAY " Press any key to continue ...   "
   SETCOLOR(cnorm)
   SET CURSOR(.F.)
   INKEY(10)
   SET CURSOR(.T.)
   RESTORE SCREEN
   RETURN
*
CASE mvar == "MRCPTAMNT"
   SAVE SCREEN
   CLS()
   M_HELP()
   SETCOLOR(cline)
      @ 06,23 TO 11,57 DOUBLE
   SETCOLOR(chelp)
```

```
  @ 07,24 SAY " Enter the total amount received "
  @ 08,24 SAY " for this receipt.               "
  @ 09,24 SAY "                                 "
  @ 10,24 SAY " Press any key to continue ...   "
  SETCOLOR(cnorm)
  SET CURSOR(.F.)
  INKEY(10)
  SET CURSOR(.T.)
  RESTORE SCREEN
  RETURN
*
CASE SUBSTR(mvar,6) == "DESC"
  SAVE SCREEN
  CLS()
  M_HELP()
  SETCOLOR(cline)
    @ 06,23 TO 11,57 DOUBLE
  SETCOLOR(chelp)
    @ 07,24 SAY " Enter a brief description of   "
    @ 08,24 SAY " expense or receipt.            "
    @ 09,24 SAY "                                "
    @ 10,24 SAY " Press any key to continue ...  "
  SETCOLOR(cnorm)
  SET CURSOR(.F.)
  INKEY(10)
  SET CURSOR(.T.)
  RESTORE SCREEN
  RETURN
*
CASE mvar == "MCHEKNUMB"
  SAVE SCREEN
  CLS()
  M_HELP()
  SETCOLOR(cline)
    @ 06,23 TO 10,57 DOUBLE
  SETCOLOR(chelp)
    @ 07,24 SAY " Enter a check number if known. "
    @ 08,24 SAY "                                "
    @ 09,24 SAY " Press any key to continue ...  "
  SETCOLOR(cnorm)
  SET CURSOR(.F.)
  INKEY(10)
  SET CURSOR(.T.)
  RESTORE SCREEN
  RETURN
*
CASE mvar == "MINVCNUMB"
  SAVE SCREEN
  CLS()
  M_HELP()
```

```
   SETCOLOR(cline)
     @ 06,23 TO 10,57 DOUBLE
   SETCOLOR(chelp)
     @ 07,24 SAY " Enter the invoice number.        "
     @ 08,24 SAY "                                   "
     @ 09,24 SAY " Press any key to continue ...     "
   SETCOLOR(cnorm)
   SET CURSOR(.F.)
   INKEY(10)
   SET CURSOR(.T.)
   RESTORE SCREEN
   RETURN
*
ENDCASE
RETURN
```

```
* Program Name .......... l_expn.prg
* Revised Date .......... 07/01/88
*
PARAMETERS s_expn
*
DO CASE
  CASE s_expn = 1
    header = "All Expenses"
  CASE s_expn = 2
    header = "Expenses Sorted by Expense Type"
  CASE s_expn = 3
    header = "Expenses per Selected Expense Type"
  CASE s_expn = 4
    header = "Expenses Sorted by Supplier"
  CASE s_expn = 5
    header = "Expenses per Selected Supplier"
ENDCASE
*
SAYHEADER("List/Print "+header)
HELPKEY()
DO CASE
  CASE s_expn = 1
    USE expenses INDEX expenses
  CASE s_expn = 2
    M_WAIT()
    USE expenses
    INDEX ON typecode TO tempfile
  CASE s_expn = 3
    STORE SPACE(03) TO mtypecode
      @ 07,20 SAY "Type Code ........."
      @ 08,20 SAY "Description ......."
      @ 07,40 GET mtypecode PICTURE "@!" VALID vl_expn1(mtypecode)
    READ
    IF LASTKEY() = 27
```

```
      RETURN
    ENDIF
    M_WAIT()
    USE expenses INDEX expenses
    COPY TO tempfile FOR typecode == mtypecode
    CLOSE DATABASES
    IF FILE("TEMPFILE.DBF")
      USE tempfile
    ELSE
      RETURN
    ENDIF
  CASE s_expn = 4
    USE expenses
    M_WAIT()
    INDEX ON suppcode TO tempfile
  CASE s_expn = 5
    STORE SPACE(03) TO msuppcode
      @ 07,20 SAY "Supplier Code ....."
      @ 08,20 SAY "Description ......."
      @ 07,40 GET msuppcode PICTURE "@!" VALID vl_expn2(msuppcode)
    READ
    IF LASTKEY() = 27
      RETURN
    ENDIF
    M_WAIT()
    USE expenses INDEX expenses
    COPY TO tempfile FOR suppcode == msuppcode
    CLOSE DATABASES
    IF FILE("TEMPFILE.DBF")
      USE tempfile
    ELSE
      RETURN
    ENDIF
ENDCASE
M_CLEAR()
*
IF RECCOUNT() = 0
  CLOSE DATABASES
  ERASE tempfile.dbf
  ERASE tempfile.ntx
  RETURN
ENDIF
*
SELECT 3
USE suppcode INDEX suppcode
SELECT 2
USE typecode INDEX typecode
SELECT 1
SET RELATION TO typecode INTO b, TO suppcode INTO c
GO TOP
```

```
*
CLS()
SETCOLOR(cline)
  @ 05,01 SAY "Exp#    Date    Expense Description  Type "+;
             "Supp   Amount    Invoice #    Check #  "
  @ 06,01 SAY "————  —————————  ———————————————————  ————  "+;
             "————  —————————  ————————————  —————————"
SETCOLOR(cnorm)
ESCKEY()
DO WHILE .T.
  SCROLL(07,00,22,79,00)
  @ 07,00
  DISPLAY OFF NEXT 10 SPACE(00)+expnnumb,expndate,expndesc,;
    typecode+" ",suppcode+" ",TRAN(expnamnt,"##,###.##"),;
    invcnumb,cheknumb
  mchoice = IIF(EOF(),3,1)
    @ 22,23 PROMPT "Forward"  MESSAGE ;
      "  List the next 10 entries"
    @ 22,31 PROMPT "Backward" MESSAGE ;
      "  List the last (previous) 10 entries"
    @ 22,40 PROMPT "Top"      MESSAGE ;
      "  List at the top of the file"
    @ 22,44 PROMPT "End"      MESSAGE ;
      "  List at the end of the file"
    @ 22,48 PROMPT "Print"    MESSAGE ;
      "  Print the listing"
    @ 22,54 PROMPT "Quit"     MESSAGE ;
      "  Quit and abort"
  CLEAR TYPEAHEAD
  MENU TO mchoice
  M_CLEAR()
  DO CASE
    CASE mchoice = 1
      SKIP 1
      IF EOF()
        FILETONE()
      ENDIF
      SKIP -1
    CASE mchoice = 2
      SKIP -18
      IF BOF()
        FILETONE()
      ENDIF
    CASE mchoice = 3
      SKIP -18
      IF BOF()
        FILETONE()
      ENDIF
      GO TOP
    CASE mchoice = 4
```

```
      SKIP 1
      IF EOF()
        FILETONE()
      ENDIF
      GO BOTTOM
    CASE mchoice = 5 .OR. mchoice = 6 .OR. LASTKEY() = 27
      EXIT
  ENDCASE
ENDDO
*
IF mchoice = 5
  IF ! M_PRTR()
    CLOSE DATABASES
    ERASE tempfile.dbf
    ERASE tempfile.ntx
    RETURN
  ENDIF
  M_PRINT()
  STORE 50 TO mline
  STORE  0 TO mpage
  SET CONSOLE OFF
  SET PRINT ON
  GO TOP
  SUM expnamnt TO mtotal
  GO TOP
  ?? CHR(pcprs)
  DO WHILE ! EOF() .AND. INKEY() <> 27
    IF mline > 40
      IF mpage > 0
        ? CHR(pfeed)
      ENDIF
      STORE 1 TO mline
      STORE mpage+1 TO mpage
      ?   SPACE(122)+"Page "+STR(mpage,2)
      ?   SPACE(122)+DTOC(DATE())
      ?
      ?   CHR(pexpa)+H_CNTR(TRIM(bname),66)
      ?? CHR(prele)
      ??, CHR(pcprs)
      ?
      ?
      ?   H_CNTR(header,132)
      ?
      ?
      ?   SPACE(07)+"Exp#    Date    Expense Description  "+;
          "   Expense Type         Supplier Name       Amount   "+;
          "Invoice #   Check #     Paid  "
      ?   SPACE(07)+"==== ======== ==================== "+;
          "==================== ==================== ========= "+;
          "========== ========== ======="
```

```
      ENDIF
      ? SPACE(07)+expnnumb,expndate,expndesc,typecode->typename,;
        suppcode->suppname,tran(expnamnt,"##,###.##"),invcnumb,;
        cheknumb,paiddate
      STORE mline+1 TO mline
      SKIP
    ENDDO
    ?   SPACE(84)+"---------"
    ?   SPACE(84)+tran(mtotal,"##,###.##")
    ?? CHR(prelc)
    ?   CHR(pfeed)
    SET PRINT OFF
    SET CONSOLE ON
ENDIF
CLOSE DATABASES
ERASE tempfile.dbf
ERASE tempfile.ntx
RETURN
*
FUNCTION vl_expn1
PARAMETERS mtypecode
USE typecode INDEX typecode
SEEK mtypecode
IF FOUND()
   ok = .T.
   SETCOLOR(cinve)
     @ 08,40 SAY typename
   SETCOLOR(cnorm)
ELSE
   ok = .F.
   M_ERROR()
ENDIF
CLOSE DATABASES
RETURN(ok)
*
FUNCTION vl_expn2
PARAMETERS msuppcode
USE suppcode INDEX suppcode
SEEK msuppcode
IF FOUND()
   ok = .T.
   SETCOLOR(cinve)
     @ 08,40 SAY suppname
   SETCOLOR(cnorm)
ELSE
   ok = .F.
   M_ERROR()
ENDIF
CLOSE DATABASES
RETURN(ok)
```

```
* Program Name ......... l_mnte.prg
* Revised Date .......... 07/01/88
*
PARAMETERS m_main
*
DO CASE
  CASE m_main = 4
    header  = "Client Codes"
    dbfvar1 = "CLNTCODE"
    dbfvar2 = "CLNTNAME"
    dbfname = "CLNTCODE"
    ntxname = "CLNTCODE"
  CASE m_main = 5
    header  = "Supplier Codes"
    dbfvar1 = "SUPPCODE"
    dbfvar2 = "SUPPNAME"
    dbfname = "SUPPCODE"
    ntxname = "SUPPCODE"
  CASE m_main = 6
    header  = "Expense Type Codes"
    dbfvar1 = "TYPECODE"
    dbfvar2 = "TYPENAME"
    dbfname = "TYPECODE"
    ntxname = "TYPECODE"
ENDCASE
*
SAYHEADER("List/Print "+header)
*
USE (dbfname) INDEX (ntxname)
IF RECCOUNT() = 0
  CLOSE DATABASES
  RETURN
ENDIF
*
SETCOLOR(cline)
  @ 05,27 SAY "Code              Name            "
  @ 06,27 SAY "————  ————————————————————"
SETCOLOR(cnorm)
DO WHILE .T.
  SCROLL(07,27,18,53,00)
  @ 07,00
  DISPLAY OFF NEXT 10 SPACE(26)+&dbfvar1+"   "+&dbfvar2
    @ 22,23 PROMPT "Forward"  MESSAGE ;
      " List the next 10 codes"
    @ 22,31 PROMPT "Backward" MESSAGE ;
      " List the last (previous) 10 codes"
    @ 22,40 PROMPT "Top"      MESSAGE ;
      " List at the top of the file"
    @ 22,44 PROMPT "End"      MESSAGE ;
      " List at the end of the file"
```

```
      @ 22,48 PROMPT "Print"      MESSAGE ;
         "  Print the listing"
      @ 22,54 PROMPT "Quit"       MESSAGE ;
         "  Quit and abort"
   CLEAR TYPEAHEAD
   MENU TO mchoice
   M_CLEAR()
   DO CASE
     CASE mchoice = 1
       SKIP 1
       IF EOF()
         FILETONE()
       ENDIF
       SKIP -1
     CASE mchoice = 2
       SKIP -18
       IF BOF()
         FILETONE()
       ENDIF
     CASE mchoice = 3
       SKIP -18
       IF BOF()
         FILETONE()
       ENDIF
       GO TOP
     CASE mchoice = 4
       SKIP 1
       IF EOF()
         FILETONE()
       ENDIF
       GO BOTTOM
     CASE mchoice = 5 .OR. mchoice = 6 .OR. LASTKEY() = 27
       EXIT
   ENDCASE
ENDDO
*
IF mchoice = 5
  IF ! M_PRTR()
    CLOSE DATABASES
    RETURN
  ENDIF
  M_PRINT()
  STORE 50 TO mline
  STORE  0 TO mpage
  SET CONSOLE OFF
  SET PRINT ON
  GO TOP
  ?? CHR(pcprs)
  DO WHILE ! EOF() .AND. INKEY() <> 27
```

```
    IF mline > 40
      IF mpage > 0
        ? CHR(pfeed)
      ENDIF
      STORE 1 TO mline
      STORE mpage+1 TO mpage
      ?  SPACE(122)+"Page "+STR(mpage,2)
      ?  SPACE(122)+DTOC(DATE())
      ?
      ?  CHR(pexpa)+H_CNTR(TRIM(bname),66)
      ?? CHR(prele)
      ?
      ?
      ?  H_CNTR(header,132)
      ?
      ?
      ?  SPACE(53)+"Code          Name         "
      ?  SPACE(53)+"====  ===================="
    ENDIF
    ? SPACE(53)+&dbfvar1+"    "+&dbfvar2
    STORE mline+1 TO mline
    SKIP
  ENDDO
  ?? CHR(prelc)
  ?  CHR(pfeed)
  SET PRINT OFF
  SET CONSOLE ON
ENDIF
CLOSE DATABASES
RETURN
```

```
* Program Name ......... l_rcpt.prg
* Revised Date ......... 07/01/88
*
PARAMETERS s_rcpt
*
DO CASE
  CASE s_rcpt = 1
    header = "All Receipts"
  CASE s_rcpt = 2
    header = "Receipts Sorted by Client"
  CASE s_rcpt = 3
    header = "Receipts per Selcted Client"
ENDCASE
*
SAYHEADER("List "+header)
HELPKEY()
DO CASE
  CASE s_rcpt = 1
    USE receipts INDEX receipts
```

```
   CASE s_rcpt = 2
     m_wait()
     USE receipts
     INDEX ON clntcode TO tempfile
   CASE s_rcpt = 3
     STORE SPACE(3) TO mclntcode
       @ 08,20 SAY "Client Code ......."
       @ 09,20 SAY "Description ......."
       @ 08,40 GET mclntcode PICTURE "@!" VALID vl_rcpt1(mclntcode)
     READ
     IF LASTKEY() = 27
       RETURN
     ENDIF
     M_WAIT()
     USE receipts INDEX receipts
     COPY TO tempfile FOR clntcode == mclntcode
     CLOSE DATABASES
     IF FILE("TEMPFILE.DBF")
       USE tempfile
     ELSE
       RETURN
     ENDIF
ENDCASE
M_CLEAR()
*
IF RECCOUNT() = 0
  CLOSE DATABASES
  ERASE tempfile.dbf
  ERASE tempfile.ntx
  RETURN
ENDIF
*
SELECT 2
USE clntcode INDEX clntcode
SELECT 1
SET RELATION TO clntcode INTO b
GO TOP
*
CLS()
SETCOLOR(cline)
  @ 05,09 SAY "Rct#    Date    Receipt Description  Clnt "+;
              "Amount       Check #   "
  @ 06,09 SAY "____ _____ _____ ____ "+;
              "_____ _____"
SETCOLOR(cnorm)
ESCKEY()
DO WHILE .T.
  SCROLL(07,00,22,79,00)
  @ 07,00
  DISPLAY OFF NEXT 10 SPACE(08)+rcptnumb,rcptdate,rcptdesc,;
    clntcode+" ",TRAN(rcptamnt,"##,###.##"),cheknumb
```

```
    mchoice = IIF(EOF(),3,1)
      @ 22,23 PROMPT "Forward"  MESSAGE ;
        "  List the next 10 receipts"
      @ 22,31 PROMPT "Backward" MESSAGE ;
        "  List the last (previous) 10 receipts"
      @ 22,40 PROMPT "Top"      MESSAGE ;
        "  List at the top of the file"
      @ 22,44 PROMPT "End"      MESSAGE ;
        "  List at the end of the file"
      @ 22,48 PROMPT "Print"    MESSAGE ;
        "  Print the listing"
      @ 22,54 PROMPT "Quit"     MESSAGE ;
        "  Quit and abort"
    CLEAR TYPEAHEAD
    MENU TO mchoice
    M_CLEAR()
    DO CASE
      CASE mchoice = 1
        SKIP 1
        IF EOF()
          FILETONE()
        ENDIF
        SKIP -1
      CASE mchoice = 2
        SKIP -18
        IF BOF()
          FILETONE()
        ENDIF
      CASE mchoice = 3
        SKIP -18
        IF BOF()
          FILETONE()
        ENDIF
        GO TOP
      CASE mchoice = 4
        SKIP 1
        IF EOF()
          FILETONE()
        ENDIF
        GO BOTTOM
      CASE mchoice = 5 .OR. mchoice = 6 .OR. LASTKEY() = 27
        EXIT
    ENDCASE
ENDDO
*
IF mchoice = 5
  IF ! M_PRTR()
    CLOSE DATABASES
    ERASE tempfile.dbf
```

```
        ERASE tempfile.ntx
        RETURN
     ENDIF
     M_PRINT()
     STORE 50 TO mline
     STORE  0 TO mpage
     SET CONSOLE OFF
     SET PRINT ON
     GO TOP
     SUM rcptamnt TO mtotal
     GO TOP
     ?? CHR(pcprs)
     DO WHILE ! EOF() .AND. INKEY() <> 27
       IF mline > 40
         IF mpage > 0
           ? CHR(pfeed)
         ENDIF
         STORE 1 TO mline
         STORE mpage+1 TO mpage
         ?   SPACE(122)+"Page "+STR(mpage,2)
         ?   SPACE(122)+DTOC(DATE())
         ?
         ?   CHR(pexpa)+H_CNTR(TRIM(bname),66)
         ?? CHR(prele)
         ?? CHR(pcprs)
         ?
         ?
         ?   H_CNTR(header,132)
         ?
         ?
         ?   SPACE(28)+"Rct#   Date   Receipt Description  "+;
             "   Client Name        Amount   Check #  "
         ?   SPACE(28)+"==== ======== ==================== "+;
             "==================== ========= =========="
       ENDIF
       ? SPACE(28)+rcptnumb,rcptdate,rcptdesc,b->clntname,;
         TRAN(rcptamnt,"##,###.##"),cheknumb
       STORE mline+1 TO mline
       SKIP
     ENDDO
     ?   SPACE(84)+"---------"
     ?   SPACE(84)+TRAN(mtotal,"##,###.##")
     ?? CHR(prelc)
     ?   CHR(pfeed)
     SET PRINT OFF
     SET CONSOLE ON
   ENDIF
   CLOSE DATABASES
   ERASE tempfile.dbf
   ERASE tempfile.ntx
```

```
RETURN
*
FUNCTION vl_rcpt1
PARAMETERS mclntcode
USE clntcode INDEX clntcode
SEEK mclntcode
IF FOUND()
  ok = .T.
  SETCOLOR(cinve)
    @ 09,40 SAY clntname
  SETCOLOR(cnorm)
ELSE
  ok = .F.
  M_ERROR()
ENDIF
CLOSE DATABASES
RETURN(ok)
```

```
* Program Name .......... m_expn.prg
* Revised Date .......... 07/01/88
*
DO WHILE .T.
  SAYHEADER("Expenses Menu")
  HELPKEY()
  MENUBOX(07,27,13,52)
    @ 08,28 PROMPT "Enter a new expense       "
    @ 09,28 PROMPT "Change/Delete an expense"
    @ 10,28 PROMPT "View/Search expenses      "
    @ 11,28 PROMPT "List/Print expenses       "
    @ 12,28 PROMPT "Text edit expense memos '
  CLEAR TYPEAHEAD
  MENU TO m_expn
  DO CASE
    CASE LASTKEY() = 27
      EXIT
    CASE m_expn = 1
      DO e_expn
    CASE m_expn = 2
      DO c_expn
    CASE m_expn = 3
      DO v_expn
    CASE m_expn = 4
      DO s_expn
    CASE m_expn = 5
      DO e_memo
  ENDCASE
ENDDO
RETURN
```

```
* Program Name ......... m_file.prg
* Revision Date ........ 07/01/88
*
DO WHILE .T.
  SAYHEADER("File Utilities Menu")
  HELPKEY()
  MENUBOX(07,30,12,49)
    @ 08,31 PROMPT "Backup data        "
    @ 09,31 PROMPT "Recall backup data"
    @ 10,31 PROMPT "Index databases    "
    @ 11,31 PROMPT "Summarize data     "
  CLEAR TYPEAHEAD
  MENU TO m_file
  DO CASE
    CASE LASTKEY() = 27
      EXIT
    CASE m_file = 1
      DO d_back
    CASE m_file = 2
      DO d_rcll
    CASE m_file = 3
      DO d_indx
    CASE m_file = 4
      DO d_summ
  ENDCASE
ENDDO
RETURN
```

```
* Program Name ......... m_main.prg
* Revised Date .......... 07/01/88
*
DO WHILE .T.
  SAYHEADER("Main Menu")
  HELPKEY()
  MENUBOX(07,26,16,53)
    @ 08,27 PROMPT "Expenses Menu             "
    @ 09,27 PROMPT "Receipts Menu             "
    @ 10,27 PROMPT "Analysis Reports Menu     "
    @ 11,27 PROMPT "Clients Maintenance Menu   "
    @ 12,27 PROMPT "Suppliers Maintenance Menu"
    @ 13,27 PROMPT "Types Maintenance Menu    "
    @ 14,27 PROMPT "Operations Menu           "
    @ 15,27 PROMPT "File Utilities Menu       "
  CLEAR TYPEAHEAD
  MENU TO main
  DO CASE
    CASE LASTKEY() = 27
      EXIT
    CASE main = 1
      DO m_expn
    CASE main = 2
```

```
      DO m_rcpt
    CASE main = 3
      DO m_rprt
    CASE main = 4
      DO m_mnte WITH main
    CASE main = 5
      DO m_mnte WITH main
    CASE main = 6
      DO m_mnte WITH main
    CASE main = 7
      DO m_oper
    CASE main = 8
      DO m_file
  ENDCASE
ENDDO
RETURN
```

```
* Program Name ......... m_mnte.prg
* Revised Date ......... 07/01/88
*
PARAMETERS m_main
*
DO WHILE .T.
  DO CASE
    CASE m_main = 4
      SAYHEADER("Clients Menu")
      hcode = 4
    CASE m_main = 5
      SAYHEADER("Suppliers Menu")
      hcode = 5
    CASE m_main = 6
      SAYHEADER("Expense Types Menu")
      hcode = 6
  ENDCASE
  HELPKEY()
  MENUBOX(07,29,12,50)
    @ 08,30 PROMPT "Enter a new code      "
    @ 09,30 PROMPT "Change/Delete a code"
    @ 10,30 PROMPT "View/Search codes     "
    @ 11,30 PROMPT "List/Print codes      "
  CLEAR TYPEAHEAD
  MENU TO m_mnte
  DO CASE
    CASE LASTKEY() = 27
      EXIT
    CASE m_mnte = 1
      DO e_mnte WITH m_main
    CASE m_mnte = 2
      DO c_mnte WITH m_main
    CASE m_mnte = 3
```

```
            DO v_mnte WITH m_main
        CASE m_mnte = 4
            DO l_mnte WITH m_main
      ENDCASE
ENDDO
RETURN
```

```
* Program Name ......... m_oper.prg
* Revised Date ......... 07/01/88
*
DO WHILE .T.
  SAYHEADER("Operations Menu")
  HELPKEY()
  MENUBOX(07,29,12,50)
     @ 08,30 PROMPT "Error tones toggle  "
     @ 09,30 PROMPT "Color display change"
     @ 10,30 PROMPT "Printer codes change"
     @ 11,30 PROMPT "Business name change"
  CLEAR TYPEAHEAD
  MENU TO m_oper
  DO CASE
    CASE LASTKEY() = 27
      EXIT
    CASE m_oper = 1
      DO c_tone
    CASE m_oper = 2
      DO c_cols
    CASE m_oper = 3
      DO c_prtr
    CASE m_oper = 4
      DO c_name
  ENDCASE
ENDDO
RETURN
```

```
* Program Name ......... m_rcpt.prg
* Revised Date ......... 07/01/88
*
DO WHILE .T.
  SAYHEADER("Receipts Menu")
  HELPKEY()
  MENUBOX(07,28,12,52)
     @ 08,29 PROMPT "Enter a new receipt    "
     @ 09,29 PROMPT "Change/Delete a receipt"
     @ 10,29 PROMPT "View/Search receipts   "
     @ 11,29 PROMPT "List/Print receipts    "
  CLEAR TYPEAHEAD
  MENU TO m_rcpt
  DO CASE
    CASE LASTKEY() = 27
```

```
      EXIT
    CASE m_rcpt = 1
      DO e_rcpt
    CASE m_rcpt = 2
      DO c_rcpt
    CASE m_rcpt = 3
      DO v_rcpt
    CASE m_rcpt = 4
      DO s_rcpt
  ENDCASE
ENDDO
RETURN
```

```
* Program Name ......... m_rprt.prg
* Revised Date ......... 07/01/88
*
DO WHILE .T.
  SAYHEADER("Analysis Reports Menu")
  HELPKEY()
  MENUBOX(07,25,12,55)
    @ 08,26 PROMPT "Client Analysis Report         "
    @ 09,26 PROMPT "Supplier Analysis Report       "
    @ 10,26 PROMPT "Expense Type Analysis Report "
    @ 11,26 PROMPT "Full Business Analysis Report"
  CLEAR TYPEAHEAD
  MENU TO m_rprt
  DO CASE
    CASE LASTKEY() = 27
      EXIT
    CASE m_rprt = 1
      DO r_clnt
    CASE m_rprt = 2
      DO r_supp
    CASE m_rprt = 3
      DO r_type
    CASE m_rprt = 4
      DO r_full
  ENDCASE
ENDDO
RETURN
```

```
* Program Name ......... r_clnt.prg
* Revised Date ......... 07/01/88
*
SAYHEADER("Client Analysis Report")
*
STORE BEGMONTH(DATE()) TO mdbeg
STORE DATE()           TO mdend
*
HELPKEY()
```

```
    @ 08,26 SAY "Beginning Date ...." ;
           GET mdbeg PICTURE "@D"
    @ 09,26 SAY "Ending Date ......." ;
           GET mdend PICTURE "@D" VALID v_date(mdbeg,mdend)
READ
M_CLEAR()
IF LASTKEY() = 27
   RETURN
ENDIF
*
M_WAIT()
*
mcondx = "RCPTDATE >= mDBEG .and. RCPTDATE <= mDEND"
USE receipts
COPY TO temp1 FOR &mcondx
CLOSE DATABASES
*
IF ! FILE("TEMP1.DBF")
   RETURN
ENDIF
*
USE temp1
INDEX ON clntcode TO temp1
TOTAL ON clntcode FIELDS rcptamnt TO temp2
CLOSE DATABASES
*
USE temp2
SUM rcptamnt TO alltotal
*
SELECT 2
USE clntcode INDEX clntcode
SELECT 1
SET RELATION TO clntcode INTO b
GO TOP
*
CLS()
SETCOLOR(cline)
   @ 05,21 SAY "Code        Client Name         Amount   "
   @ 06,21 SAY "————  ——————————————————————  ——————————"
SETCOLOR(cnorm)
ESCKEY()
DO WHILE .T.
   SCROLL(07,00,20,79,00)
   @ 07,00
   DISPLAY OFF NEXT 10 SPACE(20)+clntcode+"   "+;
     clntcode->clntname+"  "+TRAN(rcptamnt,"###,###.##")
   @ 22,23 PROMPT "Forward"  MESSAGE ;
     "  List the next 10 clients"
   @ 22,31 PROMPT "Backward" MESSAGE ;
     "  List the last (previous) 10 clients"
```

```
@ 22,40 PROMPT "Top"        MESSAGE ;
   "  List at the top of the file"
@ 22,44 PROMPT "End"        MESSAGE ;
   "  List at the end of the file"
@ 22,48 PROMPT "Print"      MESSAGE ;
   "  Print the report"
@ 22,54 PROMPT "Quit"       MESSAGE ;
   "  Quit and abort"
CLEAR TYPEAHEAD
MENU TO mchoice
M_CLEAR()
DO CASE
   CASE mchoice = 1
     SKIP 1
     IF EOF()
       FILETONE()
     ENDIF
     SKIP -1
   CASE mchoice = 2
     SKIP -18
     IF BOF()
       FILETONE()
     ENDIF
   CASE mchoice = 3
     SKIP -18
     IF BOF()
       FILETONE()
     ENDIF
     GO TOP
   CASE mchoice = 4
     SKIP 1
     IF EOF()
       FILETONE()
     ENDIF
     GO BOTTOM
   CASE mchoice = 5 .OR. mchoice = 6 .OR. LASTKEY() = 27
     EXIT
   ENDCASE
ENDDO
*
IF mchoice = 5
  IF ! M_PRTR()
    CLOSE DATABASES
    ERASE temp1.dbf
    ERASE temp2.dbf
    ERASE temp1.ntx
    RETURN
  ENDIF
  M_PRINT()
  STORE 50 TO mline
```

```
      STORE   0 TO mpage
      SET CONSOLE OFF
      SET PRINT ON
      GO TOP
      DO WHILE ! EOF() .AND. INKEY() <> 27
        IF mline > 40
          IF mpage > 0
            ? CHR(pfeed)
          ENDIF
          STORE 1 TO mline
          STORE mpage+1 TO mpage
          ?? CHR(pcprs)
          ?   SPACE(122)+"Page "+STR(mpage,2)
          ?   SPACE(122)+DTOC(DATE())
          ?
          ?   CHR(pexpa)+H_CNTR(TRIM(bname),66)
          ?? CHR(prele)
          ?? CHR(prelc)
          ?
          ?
          ?   H_CNTR("Client Analysis Report from "+DTOC(mdbeg)+;
                  " to "+DTOC(mdend),80)
          ?
          ?
          ?   SPACE(21)+"Code       Client Name          Amount  "
          ?   SPACE(21)+"====  ====================  =========="
        ENDIF
        ? SPACE(21)+clntcode+"    "+clntcode->clntname+"  "+;
        TRAN(rcptamnt,"###,###.##")
        STORE mline+1 TO mline
        SKIP
      ENDDO
      ? SPACE(49)+"----------"
      ? SPACE(49)+TRANSFORM(alltotal,"###,###.##")
      ? CHR(pfeed)
      SET PRINT OFF
      SET CONSOLE ON
   ENDIF
   CLOSE DATABASES
   ERASE temp1.dbf
   ERASE temp2.dbf
   ERASE temp1.ntx
   RETURN
```

```
* Program Name ......... r_full.prg
* Revised Date ......... 07/01/88
*
SAYHEADER("Full Business Analysis Report")
*
STORE BEGMONTH(DATE()) TO mdbeg
```

```
STORE DATE()              TO mdend
*
HELPKEY()
  @ 08,26 SAY "Beginning Date ...." ;
          GET mdbeg PICTURE "@D"
  @ 09,26 SAY "Ending Date ......." ;
          GET mdend PICTURE "@D" VALID v_date(mdbeg,mdend)
READ
M_CLEAR()
IF LASTKEY() = 27
  RETURN
ENDIF
*
M_WAIT()
*
mcondx1 = "EXPNDATE >= mDBEG .and. EXPNDATE <= mDEND"
mcondx2 = "RCPTDATE >= mDBEG .and. RCPTDATE <= mDEND"
*
CREATE dummy
STORE "DATE      D8  "  TO field1
STORE "EXPNAMNT  N8 2"  TO field2
STORE "EXPNDATE  D8  "  TO field3
STORE "RCPTAMNT  N8 2"  TO field4
STORE "RCPTDATE  D8  "  TO field5
FOR F = 1 TO 5
  fnumber = IIF(F<10,STR(F,1),STR(F,2))
  APPEND BLANK
  STORE "field" + fnumber TO fn
  REPLACE field_name WITH SUBSTR(&fn,1,10);
          field_type WITH SUBSTR(&fn,11,1);
          field_len  WITH VAL(SUBSTR(&fn,12,2));
          field_dec  WITH VAL(SUBSTR(&fn,14,1))
NEXT
CREATE temp1 FROM dummy
CLOSE DATABASES
ERASE dummy.DBF
*
USE temp1
APPEND FROM expenses FOR &mcondx1
APPEND FROM receipts FOR &mcondx2
REPLACE ALL DATE WITH expndate FOR ! EMPTY(expndate)
REPLACE ALL DATE WITH rcptdate FOR ! EMPTY(rcptdate)
INDEX ON DATE TO temp1
TOTAL ON DATE TO temp2 FIELDS expnamnt, rcptamnt
CLOSE DATABASES
*
USE temp2
SUM rcptamnt TO mreceipts
SUM expnamnt TO mexpenses
GO TOP
```

```
*
CLS()
SETCOLOR(cline)
  @ 05,18 SAY "  Date       Expenses     Receipts      Profit   "
  @ 06,18 SAY "_____    _____   _____   _____"
SETCOLOR(cnorm)
ESCKEY()
DO WHILE .T.
  SCROLL(07,00,20,79,00)
  @ 07,00
  DISPLAY OFF NEXT 10 SPACE(17)+DTOC(DATE)+"   "+;
    TRANSFORM(expnamnt,"###,###.##")+"   "+;
    TRANSFORM(rcptamnt,"###,###.##")+"   "+;
    TRANSFORM(rcptamnt-expnamnt,"###,###.##")
  @ 22,23 PROMPT "Forward"  MESSAGE ;
    "  List the next 10 dates"
  @ 22,31 PROMPT "Backward" MESSAGE ;
    "  List the last (previous) 10 dates"
  @ 22,40 PROMPT "Top"      MESSAGE ;
    "  List at the top of the file"
  @ 22,44 PROMPT "End"      MESSAGE ;
    "  List at the end of the file"
  @ 22,48 PROMPT "Print"    MESSAGE ;
    "  Print the report"
  @ 22,54 PROMPT "Quit"     MESSAGE ;
    "  Quit and abort"
  CLEAR TYPEAHEAD
  MENU TO mchoice
  M_CLEAR()
  DO CASE
    CASE mchoice = 1
      SKIP 1
      IF EOF()
        FILETONE()
      ENDIF
      SKIP -1
    CASE mchoice = 2
      SKIP -18
      IF BOF()
        FILETONE()
      ENDIF
    CASE mchoice = 3
      SKIP -18
      IF BOF()
        FILETONE()
      ENDIF
      GO TOP
    CASE mchoice = 4
      SKIP 1
      IF EOF()
```

```
        FILETONE()
      ENDIF
      GO BOTTOM
    CASE mchoice = 5 .OR. mchoice = 6 .OR. LASTKEY() = 27
      EXIT
  ENDCASE
ENDDO
*
IF mchoice = 5
  IF ! M_PRTR()
    CLOSE DATABASES
    ERASE temp1.dbf
    ERASE temp1.ntx
    ERASE temp2.dbf
    RETURN
  ENDIF
  M_PRINT()
  STORE 50 TO mline
  STORE  0 TO mpage
  SET CONSOLE OFF
  SET PRINT ON
  GO TOP
  DO WHILE ! EOF() .AND. INKEY() <> 27
    IF mline > 40
      IF mpage > 0
        ? CHR(pfeed)
      ENDIF
      STORE 1 TO mline
      STORE mpage+1 TO mpage
      ?? CHR(pcprs)
      ?  SPACE(122)+"Page "+STR(mpage,2)
      ?  SPACE(122)+DTOC(DATE())
      ?
      ?  CHR(pexpa)+H_CNTR(TRIM(bname),66)
      ?? CHR(prele)
      ?? CHR(prelc)
      ?
      ?
      ?  H_CNTR("Full Business Analysis Report from "+DTOC(mdbeg)+;
              " to "+DTOC(mdend),80)
      ?
      ?
      ?  SPACE(18)+" Date      Expenses    Receipts     Profit  "
      ?  SPACE(18)+"======= ========== ========== =========="
    ENDIF
    ? SPACE(18)+DTOC(DATE)+"  "+;
      TRANSFORM(expnamnt,"###,###.##")+"  "+;
      TRANSFORM(rcptamnt,"###,###.##")+"  "+;
      TRANSFORM(rcptamnt-expnamnt,"###,###.##")
    STORE mline+1 TO mline
```

```
      SKIP
   ENDDO
   ? SPACE(28)+"----------  ----------  ----------"
   ? SPACE(28)+TRANSFORM(mexpenses,"###,###.##")+"   "+;
     TRANSFORM(mreceipts,"###,###.##")+"   "+;
     TRANSFORM(mreceipts-mexpenses,"###,###.##")
   ? CHR(pfeed)
   SET PRINT OFF
   SET CONSOLE ON
ENDIF
CLOSE DATABASES
ERASE temp1.dbf
ERASE temp1.ntx
ERASE temp2.dbf
RETURN
```

```
* Program Name ......... r_supp.prg
* Revised Date ......... 07/01/88
*
SAYHEADER("Supplier Analysis Report")
*
STORE BEGMONTH(DATE()) TO mdbeg
STORE DATE()           TO mdend
*
HELPKEY()
   @ 08,26 SAY "Beginning Date ...." ;
           GET mdbeg PICTURE "@D"
   @ 09,26 SAY "Ending Date ......." ;
           GET mdend PICTURE "@D" VALID v_date(mdbeg,mdend)
READ
M_CLEAR()
IF LASTKEY() = 27
   RETURN
ENDIF
*
M_WAIT()
*
mcondx = "EXPNDATE >= mDBEG .and. EXPNDATE <= mDEND"
USE expenses
COPY TO temp1 FOR &mcondx
CLOSE DATABASES
*
IF ! FILE("TEMP1.DBF")
   RETURN
ENDIF
*
USE temp1
INDEX ON suppcode TO temp1
TOTAL ON suppcode FIELDS expnamnt TO temp2
CLOSE DATABASES
```

```
*
USE temp2
SUM expnamnt TO alltotal
*
SELECT 2
USE suppcode INDEX suppcode
SELECT 1
SET RELATION TO suppcode INTO b
GO TOP
*
CLS()
SETCOLOR(cline)
   @ 05,21 SAY "Code      Supplier Name            Amount   "
   @ 06,21 SAY "——    ——————————————    —————————"
SETCOLOR(cnorm)
ESCKEY()
DO WHILE .T.
   SCROLL(07,00,20,79,00)
   @ 07,00
   DISPLAY OFF NEXT 10 SPACE(20)+suppcode+"    "+;
     suppcode->suppname+"  "+TRAN(expnamnt,"###,###.##")
   @ 22,23 PROMPT "Forward"  MESSAGE ;
      " List the next 10 suppliers"
   @ 22,31 PROMPT "Backward" MESSAGE ;
      " List the last (previous) 10 suppliers"
   @ 22,40 PROMPT "Top"      MESSAGE ;
      " List at the top of the file"
   @ 22,44 PROMPT "End"      MESSAGE ;
      " List at the end of the file"
   @ 22,48 PROMPT "Print"    MESSAGE ;
      " Print the report"
   @ 22,54 PROMPT "Quit"     MESSAGE ;
      " Quit and abort"
   CLEAR TYPEAHEAD
   MENU TO mchoice
   M_CLEAR()
   DO CASE
     CASE mchoice = 1
       SKIP 1
       IF EOF()
         FILETONE()
       ENDIF
       SKIP -1
     CASE mchoice = 2
       SKIP -18
       IF BOF()
         FILETONE()
       ENDIF
     CASE mchoice = 3
       SKIP -18
```

```
        IF  BOF()
           FILETONE()
        ENDIF
        GO  TOP
      CASE mchoice = 4
        SKIP  1
        IF  EOF()
           FILETONE()
        ENDIF
        GO  BOTTOM
      CASE mchoice = 5 .OR. mchoice = 6 .OR. LASTKEY() = 27
        EXIT
    ENDCASE
ENDDO
*
IF mchoice = 5
  IF ! M_PRTR()
     CLOSE DATABASES
     ERASE temp1.dbf
     ERASE temp2.dbf
     ERASE temp1.ntx
     RETURN
  ENDIF
  M_PRINT()
  STORE 50 TO mline
  STORE  0 TO mpage
  SET CONSOLE OFF
  SET PRINT ON
  GO TOP
  DO WHILE ! EOF() .AND. INKEY() <> 27
    IF mline > 40
      IF mpage > 0
        ? CHR(pfeed)
      ENDIF
      STORE 1 TO mline
      STORE mpage+1 TO mpage
      ?? CHR(pcprs)
      ?  SPACE(122)+"Page "+STR(mpage,2)
      ?  SPACE(122)+DTOC(DATE())
      ?
      ?  CHR(pexpa)+H_CNTR(TRIM(bname),66)
      ?? CHR(prele)
      ?? CHR(prelc)
      ?
      ?
      ?  H_CNTR("Supplier Analysis Report from "+DTOC(mdbeg)+;
              " to "+DTOC(mdend),80)
      ?
      ?
      ?  SPACE(21)+"Code     Supplier Name         Amount  "
      ?  SPACE(21)+"====  ====================  ========="
```

```
      ENDIF
      ? SPACE(21)+suppcode+"    "+suppcode->suppname+"   "+;
        TRAN(expnamnt,"###,###.##")
      STORE mline+1 TO mline
      SKIP
    ENDDO
    ? SPACE(49)+"----------"
    ? SPACE(49)+TRANSFORM(alltotal,"###,###.##")
    ? CHR(pfeed)
    SET PRINT OFF
    SET CONSOLE ON
ENDIF
CLOSE DATABASES
ERASE temp1.dbf
ERASE temp2.dbf
ERASE temp1.ntx
RETURN
```

```
* Program Name .......... r_type.prg
* Revised Date .......... 07/01/88
*
SAYHEADER("Expense Type Analysis Report")
*
STORE BEGMONTH(DATE()) TO mdbeg
STORE DATE()           TO mdend
*
HELPKEY()
   @ 08,26 SAY "Beginning Date ...." ;
           GET mdbeg PICTURE "@D"
   @ 09,26 SAY "Ending Date ......." ;
           GET mdend PICTURE "@D" VALID v_date(mdbeg,mdend)
READ
M_CLEAR()
IF LASTKEY() = 27
   RETURN
ENDIF
*
M_WAIT()
*
mcondx = "EXPNDATE >= mDBEG .and. EXPNDATE <= mDEND"
USE expenses
COPY TO temp1 FOR &mcondx
CLOSE DATABASES
*
IF ! FILE("TEMP1.DBF")
   RETURN
ENDIF
*
USE temp1
```

```
INDEX ON typecode TO temp1
TOTAL ON typecode FIELDS expnamnt TO temp2
CLOSE DATABASES
*
USE temp2
SUM expnamnt TO alltotal
*
SELECT 2
USE typecode INDEX typecode
SELECT 1
SET RELATION TO typecode INTO b
GO TOP
*
CLS()
SETCOLOR(cline)
  @ 05,21 SAY "Code     Expense Type Name      Amount   "
  @ 06,21 SAY "——— ——————————————— —————————"
SETCOLOR(cnorm)
ESCKEY()
DO WHILE .T.
  SCROLL(07,00,20,79,00)
  @ 07,00
  DISPLAY OFF NEXT 10 SPACE(20)+typecode+"    "+;
    typecode->typename+"  "+TRAN(expnamnt,"###,###.##")
  @ 22,23 PROMPT "Forward"  MESSAGE ;
    "  List the next 10 expense types"
  @ 22,31 PROMPT "Backward" MESSAGE ;
    "  List the last (previous) 10 expense types"
  @ 22,40 PROMPT "Top"      MESSAGE ;
    "  List at the top of the file"
  @ 22,44 PROMPT "End"      MESSAGE ;
    "  List at the end of the file"
  @ 22,48 PROMPT "Print"    MESSAGE ;
    "  Print the report"
  @ 22,54 PROMPT "Quit"     MESSAGE ;
    "  Quit and abort"
  CLEAR TYPEAHEAD
  MENU TO mchoice
  M_CLEAR()
  DO CASE
    CASE mchoice = 1
      SKIP 1
      IF EOF()
        FILETONE()
      ENDIF
      SKIP -1
    CASE mchoice = 2
      SKIP -18
      IF BOF()
        FILETONE()
```

```
      ENDIF
   CASE mchoice = 3
     SKIP -18
     IF BOF()
        FILETONE()
     ENDIF
     GO TOP
   CASE mchoice = 4
     SKIP 1
     IF EOF()
        FILETONE()
     ENDIF
     GO BOTTOM
   CASE mchoice = 5 .OR. mchoice = 6 .OR. LASTKEY() = 27
     EXIT
  ENDCASE
ENDDO
*
IF mchoice = 5
  IF ! m_prtr()
    CLOSE DATABASES
    ERASE temp1.dbf
    ERASE temp2.dbf
    ERASE temp1.ntx
    RETURN
  ENDIF
  M_PRINT()
  STORE 50 TO mline
  STORE  0 TO mpage
  SET CONSOLE OFF
  SET PRINT ON
  GO TOP
  DO WHILE ! EOF() .AND. INKEY() <> 27
    IF mline > 40
      IF mpage > 0
        ? CHR(pfeed)
      ENDIF
      STORE 1 TO mline
      STORE mpage+1 TO mpage
      ?? CHR(pcprs)
      ?  SPACE(122)+"Page "+STR(mpage,2)
      ?  SPACE(122)+DTOC(DATE())
      ?
      ?  CHR(pexpa)+H_CNTR(TRIM(bname),66)
      ?? CHR(prele)
      ?? CHR(prelc)
      ?
      ?
      ?  H_CNTR("Expense Type Analysis Report from "+DTOC(mdbeg)+;
              " to "+DTOC(mdend),80)
```

```
        ?
        ?
        ?    SPACE(21)+"Code    Expense Type Name       Amount    "
        ?    SPACE(21)+"====    ====================    =========="
     ENDIF
     ?  SPACE(21)+typecode+"    "+typecode->typename+"   "+;
        TRAN(expnamnt,"###,###.##")
     STORE mline+1 TO mline
     SKIP
  ENDDO
  ? SPACE(49)+"----------"
  ? SPACE(49)+TRANSFORM(alltotal,"###,###.##")
  ? CHR(pfeed)
  SET PRINT OFF
  SET CONSOLE ON
ENDIF
CLOSE DATABASES
ERASE temp1.dbf
ERASE temp2.dbf
ERASE temp1.ntx
RETURN
```

```
* Program Name ......... s_expn.prg
* Revised Date ......... 07/01/88
*
DO WHILE .T.
  SAYHEADER("List Expenses Sub-Menu")
  HELPKEY()
  MENUBOX(07,19,13,61)
    @ 08,20 PROMPT "1 List all expenses                      "
    @ 09,20 PROMPT "2 List expenses sorted by expense type   "
    @ 10,20 PROMPT "3 List expenses per selected expense type"
    @ 11,20 PROMPT "4 List expenses sorted by supplier       "
    @ 12,20 PROMPT "5 List expenses per selected supplier    "
  CLEAR TYPEAHEAD
  MENU TO expn2
  IF LASTKEY() = 27
    EXIT
  ELSE
    DO l_expn WITH expn2
  ENDIF
ENDDO
RETURN
```

```
* Program Name ......... s_rcpt.prg
* Revised Date ......... 07/01/88
*
DO WHILE .T.
  SAYHEADER("List Receipts Sub-Menu")
  HELPKEY()
```

```
  MENUBOX(07,22,11,58)
    @ 08,23 PROMPT "1 List all receipts               "
    @ 09,23 PROMPT "2 List receipts sorted by client    "
    @ 10,23 PROMPT "3 List receipts per selected client"
  CLEAR TYPEAHEAD
  MENU TO s_rcpt
  IF LASTKEY() = 27
    EXIT
  ELSE
    DO l_rcpt WITH s_rcpt
  ENDIF
ENDDO
RETURN
```

```
* Program Name .......... v_expn.prg
* Revised Date .......... 07/01/88
*
SAYHEADER("View/Search Expenses")
  @ 07,00 SAY "Expense Number ...."
  @ 07,40 SAY "Expense Date ......"
  @ 08,00 SAY "Expense Amount ...."
  @ 08,40 SAY "Description ......."
  @ 10,00 SAY "Type Code ........."
  @ 10,40 SAY "Description ......."
  @ 11,00 SAY "Supplier Code ....."
  @ 11,40 SAY "Description ......."
  @ 13,00 SAY "Invoice Number ...."
  @ 14,00 SAY "Check Number ......"
  @ 14,40 SAY "Date Paid ........."
  @ 16,00 SAY "Comment (y/n) ....."
SETCOLOR(cline)
  @ 09,00 SAY REPL("-",80)
  @ 12,00 SAY REPL("-",80)
  @ 15,00 SAY REPL("-",80)
SETCOLOR(cnorm)
*
DO WHILE .T.
  M_BLANK()
  HELPKEY()
  STORE 0 TO mexpnnr
    @ 07,20 GET mexpnnr PICTURE "####" VALID vv_expn1(mexpnnr)
  READ
  M_CLEAR()
  IF LASTKEY() = 27
    EXIT
  ENDIF
  STORE STR(mexpnnr,4) TO mexpnnumb
  SELECT 3
  USE suppcode INDEX suppcode
  SELECT 2
```

```
USE typecode INDEX typecode
SELECT 1
USE expenses INDEX expenses
SET RELATION TO suppcode INTO c, TO typecode INTO b
SET SOFTSEEK(.T.)
SEEK mexpnnumb
SET SOFTSEEK(.F.)
DO WHILE .T.
  SETCOLOR(cinve)
    @ 07,20 SAY expnnumb
    @ 07,60 SAY expndate
    @ 08,20 SAY TRAN(expnamnt,"##,###.##")
    @ 08,60 SAY expndesc
    @ 10,20 SAY typecode
    @ 10,60 SAY typecode->typename
    @ 11,20 SAY suppcode
    @ 11,60 SAY suppcode->suppname
    @ 13,20 SAY invcnumb
    @ 14,20 SAY cheknumb
    @ 14,60 SAY paiddate
    @ 16,20 SAY IIF(expnmemo,"Y","N")
  SETCOLOR(cnorm)
    @ 22,15 PROMPT "Next"     MESSAGE ;
            " View the next entry"
    @ 22,20 PROMPT "Last"     MESSAGE ;
            " View the last (previous) entry"
    @ 22,25 PROMPT "Forward"  MESSAGE ;
            " Skip forward 20 entries and view"
    @ 22,33 PROMPT "Backward" MESSAGE ;
            " Skip backward 20 entries and view"
    @ 22,42 PROMPT "Top"      MESSAGE ;
            " View at the beginning of the file"
    @ 22,46 PROMPT "End"      MESSAGE ;
            " View at the end of the file"
    @ 22,50 PROMPT "Search"   MESSAGE ;
            " Enter an expense number to search for"
    @ 22,57 PROMPT "Memo"     MESSAGE ;
            " View the expense memo"
    @ 22,62 PROMPT "Quit"     MESSAGE ;
            " Quit and abort"
  CLEAR TYPEAHEAD
  MENU TO mchoice
  M_CLEAR()
  DO CASE
    CASE mchoice = 1
      SKIP 1
      IF EOF()
        SKIP -1
        FILETONE()
      ENDIF
```

```
  CASE mchoice = 2
    SKIP -1
    IF BOF()
      FILETONE()
    ENDIF
  CASE mchoice = 3
    SKIP
    IF EOF()
      SKIP -1
      FILETONE()
    ELSE
      SKIP 20
    ENDIF
  CASE mchoice = 4
    SKIP -1
    IF BOF()
      FILETONE()
    ELSE
      SKIP -20
    ENDIF
  CASE mchoice = 5
    SKIP -1
    IF BOF()
      FILETONE()
    ELSE
      GO TOP
    ENDIF
  CASE mchoice = 6
    SKIP
    IF EOF()
      SKIP -1
      FILETONE()
    ELSE
      GO BOTTOM
    ENDIF
  CASE mchoice = 7
    EXIT
  CASE mchoice = 8
    STORE "CM"+LTRIM(expnnumb)+".TXT" TO mfilename
    IF FILE(mfilename)
      SAVE SCREEN
      MEMOBOX2()
      MEMOEDIT(MEMOREAD(mfilename),05,04,18,75,.F.,"dbm")
      SETCOLOR(cnorm)
      RESTORE SCREEN
    ENDIF
  CASE mchoice = 9 .OR. LASTKEY() = 27
    CLOSE DATABASES
    RETURN
ENDCASE
```

```
          ENDDO
          CLOSE DATABASES
            @ 07,20 SAY SPACE(04)
            @ 07,60 SAY SPACE(08)
            @ 08,20 SAY SPACE(10)
            @ 08,60 SAY SPACE(20)
            @ 10,20 SAY SPACE(03)
            @ 10,60 SAY SPACE(20)
            @ 11,20 SAY SPACE(03)
            @ 11,60 SAY SPACE(20)
            @ 13,20 SAY SPACE(10)
            @ 14,20 SAY SPACE(10)
            @ 14,60 SAY SPACE(08)
            @ 16,20 SAY SPACE(01)
        LOOP
    ENDDO
    ENDDO
    RETURN
    *
    FUNCTION vv_expnl
    PARAMETERS mexpnnr
    STORE STR(mexpnnr,4) TO mexpnnumb
    USE expenses INDEX expenses
    SET SOFTSEEK(.T.)
    SEEK mexpnnumb
    SET SOFTSEEK(.F.)
    IF FOUND()
      ok = .T.
    ELSE
      IF ! EOF()
        ok = .T.
      ELSE
        ok = .F.
        M_ERROR()
      ENDIF
    ENDIF
    CLOSE DATABASES
    RETURN(ok)
    _____
    * Program Name ......... v_mnte.prg
    * Revised Date ......... 07/01/88
    *
    PARAMETERS m_main
    *
    DO CASE
      CASE m_main = 4
        SAYHEADER("View/Search Client Codes")
        prompt1 = "Client Code ......."
        prompt2 = "Client Name ......."
        memvar1 = "mCLNTCODE"
        memvar2 = "mCLNTNAME"
```

```
   dbfvar1 = "CLNTCODE"
   dbfvar2 = "CLNTNAME"
   dbfname = "CLNTCODE"
   ntxname = "CLNTCODE"
 CASE m_main = 5
   SAYHEADER("View/Search Supplier Codes")
   prompt1 = "Supplier Code ....."
   prompt2 = "Supplier Name......"
   memvar1 = "mSUPPCODE"
   memvar2 = "mSUPPNAME"
   dbfvar1 = "SUPPCODE"
   dbfvar2 = "SUPPNAME"
   dbfname = "SUPPCODE"
   ntxname = "SUPPCODE"
 CASE m_main = 6
   SAYHEADER("View/Search Expense Type Codes")
   prompt1 = "Type Code ........."
   prompt2 = "Type Name ........."
   memvar1 = "mTYPECODE"
   memvar2 = "mTYPENAME"
   dbfvar1 = "TYPECODE"
   dbfvar2 = "TYPENAME"
   dbfname = "TYPECODE"
   ntxname = "TYPECODE"
ENDCASE
*
DO WHILE .T.
  M_BLANK()
  HELPKEY()
  STORE SPACE(03) TO memvar1
    @ 07,20 SAY prompt1 GET memvar1 PICTURE "@!" ;
            VALID vv_mnte(memvar1,dbfname,ntxname)
    @ 08,20 SAY prompt2
  READ
  M_CLEAR()
  IF LASTKEY() = 27
    EXIT
  ENDIF
  USE (dbfname) INDEX (ntxname)
  SET SOFTSEEK(.T.)
  SEEK memvar1
  SET SOFTSEEK(.F.)
  DO WHILE .T.
    SET CURSOR(.F.)
    SETCOLOR(cinve)
      @ 07,40 SAY &dbfvar1
      @ 08,40 SAY &dbfvar2
    SETCOLOR(cnorm)
      @ 22,17 PROMPT "Next"     MESSAGE ;
              " View the next code"
```

```
      @ 22,22 PROMPT "Last"      MESSAGE ;
               "  View the last (previous) code"
      @ 22,27 PROMPT "Forward"   MESSAGE ;
               "  Skip forward 20 codes and view"
      @ 22,35 PROMPT "Backward"  MESSAGE ;
               "  Skip backward 20 codes and view"
      @ 22,44 PROMPT "Top"       MESSAGE ;
               "  View at the beginning of the file"
      @ 22,48 PROMPT "End"       MESSAGE ;
               "  View at the end of the file"
      @ 22,52 PROMPT "Search"    MESSAGE ;
               "  Enter a code to search for"
      @ 22,59 PROMPT "Quit"      MESSAGE ;
               "  Quit and abort"
   CLEAR TYPEAHEAD
   MENU TO mchoice
   M_CLEAR()
   DO CASE
      CASE mchoice = 1
         SKIP 1
         IF EOF()
            SKIP -1
            FILETONE()
         ENDIF
      CASE mchoice = 2
         SKIP -1
         IF BOF()
            FILETONE()
         ENDIF
      CASE mchoice = 3
         SKIP
         IF EOF()
            SKIP -1
            FILETONE()
         ELSE
            SKIP 20
         ENDIF
      CASE mchoice = 4
         SKIP -1
         IF BOF()
            FILETONE()
         ELSE
            SKIP -20
         ENDIF
      CASE mchoice = 5
         SKIP -1
         IF BOF()
            FILETONE()
         ELSE
            GO TOP
```

```
          ENDIF
      CASE mchoice = 6
        SKIP
        IF EOF()
          SKIP -1
          FILETONE()
        ELSE
          GO BOTTOM
        ENDIF
      CASE mchoice = 7
        EXIT
      CASE mchoice = 8 .OR. LASTKEY() = 27
        CLOSE DATABASES
        RETURN
    ENDCASE
  ENDDO
  CLOSE DATABASES
    @ 07,40 SAY SPACE(03)
    @ 08,40 SAY SPACE(20)
  LOOP
ENDDO
RETURN
*
FUNCTION vv_mnte
PARAMETERS memvar1,dbfname,ntxname
USE (dbfname) INDEX (ntxname)
SET SOFTSEEK(.T.)
SEEK memvar1
SET SOFTSEEK(.F.)
IF FOUND()
  ok = .T.
ELSE
  IF ! EOF()
    ok = .T.
  ELSE
    ok = .F.
    M_ERROR()
  ENDIF
ENDIF
CLOSE DATABASES
RETURN(ok)
```

```
* Program Name ......... v_rcpt.prg
* Revised Date ......... 07/01/88
*
SAYHEADER("View/Search Receipts")
  @ 07,00 SAY "Receipt Number ...."
  @ 07,40 SAY "Receipt Date ......"
  @ 08,00 SAY "Receipt Amount ...."
  @ 08,40 SAY "Description ......."
```

```
    @ 10,00 SAY "Client Code ......."
    @ 10,40 SAY "Description ......."
    @ 12,00 SAY "Check Number ......"
SETCOLOR(cline)
    @ 09,00 SAY repl("—",80)
    @ 11,00 SAY repl("—",80)
SETCOLOR(cnorm)
*
DO WHILE .T.
  M_BLANK()
  HELPKEY()
  STORE 0 TO mrcptnr
    @ 07,20 GET mrcptnr PICTURE "####" VALID vv_rcpt(mrcptnr)
  READ
  M_CLEAR()
  IF LASTKEY() = 27
    EXIT
  ENDIF
  STORE STR(mrcptnr,4) TO mrcptnumb
  SELECT 2
  USE clntcode INDEX clntcode
  SELECT 1
  USE receipts INDEX receipts
  SET RELATION TO clntcode INTO b
  SET SOFTSEEK(.T.)
  SEEK mrcptnumb
  SET SOFTSEEK(.F.)
  DO WHILE .T.
    SETCOLOR(cinve)
      @ 07,20 SAY rcptnumb
      @ 07,60 SAY rcptdate
      @ 08,20 SAY TRAN(rcptamnt,"##,###.##")
      @ 08,60 SAY rcptdesc
      @ 10,20 SAY clntcode
      @ 10,60 SAY clntcode->clntname
      @ 12,20 SAY cheknumb
    SETCOLOR(cnorm)
      @ 22,17 PROMPT "Next"     MESSAGE ;
              "      View the next receipt       "
      @ 22,22 PROMPT "Last"     MESSAGE ;
              "  View the last (previous) receipt "
      @ 22,27 PROMPT "Forward"  MESSAGE ;
              "  Skip forward 20 receipts and view"
      @ 22,35 PROMPT "Backward" MESSAGE ;
              "  Skip backward 20 receipts and view"
      @ 22,44 PROMPT "Top"      MESSAGE ;
              "  View at the beginning of the file "
      @ 22,48 PROMPT "End"      MESSAGE ;
              "      View at the end of the file       "
      @ 22,52 PROMPT "Search"   MESSAGE ;
              "   Enter a receipt number to search for   "
```

```
  @ 22,59 PROMPT "Quit"       MESSAGE ;
          "    Quit and abort"
CLEAR TYPEAHEAD
MENU TO mchoice
M_CLEAR()
DO CASE
  CASE mchoice = 1
    SKIP 1
    IF EOF()
      SKIP -1
      FILETONE()
    ENDIF
  CASE mchoice = 2
    SKIP -1
    IF BOF()
      FILETONE()
    ENDIF
  CASE MCHOICE = 3
    SKIP
    IF EOF()
      SKIP -1
      FILETONE()
    ELSE
      SKIP 20
    ENDIF
  CASE MCHOICE = 4
    SKIP -1
    IF BOF()
      FILETONE()
    ELSE
      SKIP -20
    ENDIF
  CASE MCHOICE = 5
    SKIP -1
    IF BOF()
      FILETONE()
    ELSE
      GO TOP
    ENDIF
  CASE MCHOICE = 6
    SKIP
    IF EOF()
      SKIP -1
      FILETONE()
    ELSE
      GO BOTTOM
    ENDIF
  CASE MCHOICE = 7
    EXIT
```

```
        CASE MCHOICE = 8 .OR. LASTKEY() = 27
           CLOSE DATABASES
           RETURN
     ENDCASE
  ENDDO
  CLOSE DATABASES
     @ 07,20 SAY SPACE(04)
     @ 07,60 SAY SPACE(08)
     @ 08,20 SAY SPACE(10)
     @ 08,60 SAY SPACE(20)
     @ 10,20 SAY SPACE(03)
     @ 10,60 SAY SPACE(20)
     @ 12,20 SAY SPACE(10)
  LOOP
ENDDO
RETURN
*
FUNCTION vv_rcpt
PARAMETERS mrcptnr
STORE STR(mrcptnr,4) TO mrcptnumb
USE receipts INDEX receipts
SET SOFTSEEK(.T.)
SEEK mrcptnumb
SET SOFTSEEK(.F.)
IF FOUND()
  ok = .T.
ELSE
  IF ! EOF()
    ok = .T.
  ELSE
    ok = .F.
    M_ERROR()
  ENDIF
ENDIF
CLOSE DATABASES
RETURN(ok)
```

Appendix **B**

Summary of All Clipper Commands

?	Display or print an expression
??	Display or print an expression (no CR)
@ <r,c>	Display or print an expression at r,c
@ <r,c> CLEAR	Clear the screen from r,c
@ <r,c> PROMPT	Define and display menu prompt at r,c
@ <t,l,b,r> BOX	Display box from t,l to b,r
@ <t,l> TO <b,r>	Display box from t,l to b,r
ACCEPT	Store a char string from keyboard to memvar
APPEND BLANK	Add blank record to current database file
APPEND FROM	Add records from file to current database
AVERAGE	Average series of numeric values to memvar
BEGIN SEQUENCE..END	Establish exception handling sequence
CALL	Execute separately compiled routine
CANCEL	Terminate program execution
CLEAR	Clear the screen and all pending GETs
CLEAR ALL	Close all open and related files
CLEAR GETS	Release pending GETs
CLEAR MEMORY	Release PUBLIC and PRIVATE memvars
CLEAR SCREEN	Clear the screen
CLEAR TYPEAHEAD	Clear the keyboard buffer
CLOSE	Close the current database
COMMIT	Perform solid disk write for all work areas
CONTINUE	Resume pending LOCATE
COPY FILE	Duplicate a file
COPY STRUCTURE	Copy current DBF structure to a new file
COPY TO	Copy current database file to a new file
COUNT	Tally number of records in current file
CREATE	Create an empty structure-extended file
CREATE FROM	Create DBF from a structure-extended file
DECLARE	Create a PRIVATE memvar array
DELETE	Mark current database record for deletion
DIR	Display files in specified directory

DISPLAY	Display database records
DO	Execute a specific procedure
DO CASE..ENDCASE	Specify path for program execution
DO WHILE..ENDDO	Execute looping structure
EJECT	Printer form feed
ERASE	Delete a file
EXTERNAL	Declare an external linker symbol
FIND	Position pointer to record meeting condition
FOR..[STEP]..NEXT	Execute a loop
FUNCTION	Define a Clipper User-Defined Function
GO/GOTO	Position pointer to a specific record
IF..[ELSE]..ENDIF	Specify conditional execution of commands
INDEX ON	Create an index file
INPUT TO	Enter an expression into memvar
JOIN WITH	Create new database from merged databases
KEYBOARD	Stuff keyboard buffer with specified string
LABEL FORM	Display labels from a LBL file
LIST	Display database records
LOCATE	Position pointer to record meeting condition
MENU TO	Execute a light-bar menu from menu PROMPTs
NOTE	Comment
PACK	Remove database records marked for deletion
PARAMETERS	Specify memvars to receive passed values
PRIVATE	Declare memvar or array for local procedure
PROCEDURE	Identify the beginning of a procedure
PUBLIC	Declare memvar or array for global use
QUIT	Terminate program execution
READ	Enter full-screen editing of current GETs
RECALL	Recall a record marked for deletion
REINDEX	Rebuild all open index files
RELEASE	Erase memvars
RENAME	Rename a file
REPLACE	Change DBF field contents
REPORT FORM	Display reports from a FRM file
RESTORE FROM	Retrieve stored memvars
RESTORE SCREEN	Redisplay a screen stored in memory
RETURN	Terminate procedure and return to previous
RUN	Execute a DOS program
SAVE SCREEN	Write the current screen to memory
SAVE TO	Save memvars
SEEK	Search an indexed file for keyfield match
SELECT	Change work area
SET ALTERNATE TO	Create a file for capturing command output
SET ALTERNATE on/OFF	Toggle capture of command output
SET BELL on/OFF	Toggle computer bell
SET CENTURY on/OFF	Toggle date century display
SET COLOR TO	Set display color
SET CONFIRM on/OFF	Toggle Return key action

SET CONSOLE ON/off	Toggle display output
SET CURSOR ON/off	Toggle cursor display
SET DATE	Set date format
SET DECIMALS TO	Set number of numeric decimal places
SET DEFAULT TO	Set default drive
SET DELETED on/OFF	Toggle inclusion of deleted records
SET DELIMITERS TO	Set GET delimiters display
SET DELIMITERS on/OFF	Toggle GET delimiters display
SET DEVICE TO	Toggle @..SAY outputs to screen or printer
SET ESCAPE ON/off	Toggle escape key status
SET EXACT on/OFF	Toggle exact match comparisons
SET EXCLUSIVE ON/off	Toggle database to shared or exclusive use
SET FILTER TO	Set database to records meeting a condition
SET FIXED on/OFF	Toggle SET DECIMALS TO decimal places
SET FORMAT TO	Set picture format for READ
SET FUNCTION	Set procedure for function key
SET INDEX TO	Open a specified index file
SET INTENSITY ON/off	Toggle GET display
SET KEY	Set procedure for keypress from wait state
SET MARGIN TO	Set printer and screen left margin
SET MESSAGE TO	Set line number for menu messages
SET ORDER TO	Set controlling index
SET PATH TO	Set path for file access
SET PRINT on/OFF	Toggle printer
SET PRINTER TO	Set destination for printed output
SET PROCEDURE TO	Set a named procedure to be opened
SET RELATION TO	Set a relation between work area files
SET SCOREBOARD ON/off	Toggle Clipper error/warning messages
SET SOFTSEEK on/OFF	Toggle relative SEEKs
SET TYPEAHEAD TO	Set typeahead buffer size
SET UNIQUE on/OFF	Toggle unique index keys
SET WRAP on/OFF	Toggle menu wrapping
SKIP	Move the record pointer
SORT	Copy records to another file in sorted order
STORE	Place an expression into memvar
SUM	Sum numeric values
TEXT	Display a block of text
TOTAL ON	Total numeric values to another file
TYPE	Display file contents
UNLOCK	Release all file and record locks
UPDATE ON	Update one file from another file
USE	Open a database file
WAIT	Suspend program execution
ZAP	Remove deleted records from database file

Appendix C

Summary of All Clipper Functions

ABS( )	Returns absolute value
ACHOICE( )	Executes a pop-up menu of array choices
ACOPY( )	Copies elements of one array to another
ADEL( )	Deletes an array element
ADEL( )	Deletes an array element
ADIR( )	Fills an array with file directory information
AFIELDS( )	Fills an array with database field information
AFILL( )	Fills an array with one value
AINS( )	Inserts a new position into an array
ALIAS( )	Returns the alias of a work area
ALLTRIM( )	Removes leading and trailing blanks
ALTD( )	Invoke/enable/disable Clipper debugger
ASC( )	Returns ASCII code value of left-most character
ASCAN( )	Searches for a specific array value
ASORT( )	Sorts an array in ascending order
AT( )	Returns start position of a string within a string
BOF( )	Indicates beginning of file
BROWSE( )	Browse a database
CDOW( )	Returns the day of the week
CHR( )	Returns a character for the specified ASCII code
CMONTH( )	Returns the name of the month
COL( )	Returns the current cursor column position
CTOD( )	Converts a character string to date
DATE( )	Return the system date
DAY( )	Returns the numeric day of the week
DBEDIT( )	Displays and edits records in browse format
DBFILTER( )	Returns the SET FILTER condition
DBRELATION( )	Returns the SET RELATION TO condition
DBRSELECT( )	Returns the SET RELATION TO target file
DELETED( )	Returns the record deleted status
DESCEND( )	Creates descending order indexes
DISKSPACE( )	Returns number of bytes of available disk space
DOSERROR( )	Returns the last DOS error
DOW( )	Returns numerics day of week
DTOC( )	Converts a date to character

DTOS( )	Converts a date to character for INDEX ON
EMPTY( )	Indicates blank
EOF( )	Indicates end of file
ERRORLEVEL( )	Returns current DOS error level setting
EXP( )	Returns logarithmic value
FCLOSE( )	Closes a DOS file opened with FOPEN( )
FCOUNT( )	Returns number of fields in current database
FCREATE( )	Creates a DOS file
FERROR( )	Returns the DOS error number
FIELDNAME( )	Returns the name of a specified field
FILE( )	Indicates if a file exists
FLOCK( )	Locks a database file in shared environment
FOPEN( )	Opens a DOS file
FOUND( )	Indicates if SEEK, FIND, or LOCATE was successful
FREAD( )	Reads characters from a DOS file into memvar
FREADSTR( )	Reads characters from a DOS file
FSEEK( )	Moves the record pointer in a DOS file
FWRITE( )	Writes a variable to a DOS file
GETE( )	Returns contents of DOS environment setting
HARDCR( )	Replaces all soft CRs with hard CRs
HEADER( )	Returns a file header length in bytes
IF/IIF( )	Provides for conditional processing
INDEXEXT( )	Returns index type (NTX or NDX)
INDEXKEY( )	Returns index key expression
INDEXORD( )	Returns controlling index
INKEY( )	Returns numeric ASCII key value
INT( )	Converts a number to integer
ISALPHA( )	Indicates if first character is alpha
ISCOLOR( )	Indicates if video display card is color
ISLOWER( )	Indicates if first character is lowercase
ISPRINTER( )	Indicates if printer is connected and on-line
ISUPPER( )	Indicates if first character is uppercase
LASTKEY( )	Returns numeric ASCII key value of last keypress
LASTREC( )	Returns number of records in current database
LEFT( )	Returns specified left portion of string
LEN( )	Returns numeric length of character string
LOG( )	Returns natural logarithm
LOWER( )	Converts uppercase to lowercase
LTRIM( )	Removes leading spaces from a character expression
LUPDATE( )	Returns last date a database was updated
MAX( )	Returns the greater of two number/date expressions
MEMOEDIT( )	Displays and edits memo fields
MEMOLINE( )	Returns formatted line from character expression
MEMOREAD( )	Returns text file as a character string
MEMORY( )	Returns available free pool memory
MEMOTRAN( )	Replaces text file carriage returns
MEMOWRIT( )	Writes character string to a text file
MIN( )	Returns lesser of two numbers or dates

MLCOUNT( )	Returns number of lines in a character expression
MOD( )	Returns modulus of two numbers
MONTH( )	Returns numeric month
NETERR( )	Indicates a network file error
NETNAME( )	Returns computer name text
NEXTKEY( )	Reads next keystroke
PCOL( )	Returns current printer column position
PCOUNT( )	Returns number of actual passed parameters
PROCLINE( )	Returns source code line number
PROCNAME( )	Returns source code procedure name
PROW( )	Returns current printer row position
RAT( )	Returns starting position of string search
READEXIT( )	Toggles cursor up-down keys as READ exit keys
READINSERT( )	Indicates insert key status
READVAR( )	Returns current GET/MENU variable
RECNO( )	Returns current record number
RECSIZE( )	Returns record size in bytes
REPLICATE( )	Repeats character expression
RESTSCREEN( )	Restores portion of screen saved with SAVESCREEN( )
RIGHT( )	Returns specified right portion of string
RLOCK/LOCK( )	Attempts to lock the current record
ROUND( )	Returns rounded-off numbers
ROW( )	Returns current cursor row position
SAVESCREEN( )	Saves a portion of screen
SCROLL( )	Scroll a designated window
SECONDS( )	Returns system time in seconds
SELECT( )	Returns number of current work area
SETCANCEL( )	Toggle Alt-c capability
SETCOLOR( )	Sets/resets color configuration
SETPRC( )	Sets internal PROW( ) and PCOL( ) coordinates
SOUNDEX( )	Converts character string to phonetic complement
SPACE( )	Creates character string of specified spaces
SQRT( )	Returns square root of number
STR( )	Converts numeric expression to character
STRTRAN( )	Search and replace within a character string
STUFF( )	Replaces characters in string
SUBSTR( )	Returns specified string portion
TIME( )	Returns system time
TONE( )	Sounds a speaker tone
TRANSFORM( )	Returns character string in specified format
TRIM( )	Removes trailing blanks
TYPE( )	Returns memory variable data type
UPDATED( )	Indicates if last READ changed data GETs
UPPER( )	Converts lowercase to uppercase
USED( )	Indicates if file is in use
VAL( )	Converts character string to numeric value
WORD( )	Converts CALL arguments
YEAR( )	Returns numeric year value

Index

SilverWare Discount Coupon

SAVE 10%

This coupon is valid on
your next purchase of Silverware Products.
Call our Order Desk at (214) 902-0227
for fast delivery.

Photomechanical
reproduction of this
coupon is acceptable.

P.O. Box 781143
Dallas, TX 75234
(214) 902-0227

Clipper:
A Programmer's Guide

If you are intrigued with the possibilities of the programs included in *Clipper: A Programmer's Guide* (TAB BOOK No. 3207), you should definitely consider having the ready-to-compile disk containing the software applications. This software is guaranteed free of manufacturer's defects. (If you have any problems, return the disk within 30 days, and we'll send you a new one.) Not only do you save the time and effort of typing the programs, but also the disk eliminates the possibility of errors that can prevent the programs from functioning.

Available on disk for the IBM PC or PS/2 at $24.95 for each disk plus $1.50 shipping and handling.